AFTER
THE FALL

ALSO BY WALTER LAQUEUR

AFTER THE FALL

THE END OF THE EUROPEAN DREAM
AND THE DECLINE OF A CONTINENT

WALTER LAQUEUR

THOMAS DUNNE BOOKS
St. Martin's Press
New York

THOMAS DUNNE BOOKS.
An imprint of St. Martin's Press.

www.thomasdunnebooks.com
www.stmartins.com

Library of Congress Cataloging-in-Publication Data

Laqueur, Walter, 1921–
    After the fall : the end of the European dream and the decline
of a continent / Walter Laqueur. — 1st ed.
        p. cm.
    ISBN 978-1-250-00008-8 (hardcover)
    ISBN 978-1-4299-5256-9 (e-book)
    1. Europe—Economic conditions—21st century.   2. Europe—
Social conditions—21st century.   3. Europe—Foreign relations—
21st century.   4. Europe—Politics and government—21st century.
5. Europe—History—21st century.   I. Title.
    D2020.L37 2012
    940.56—dc23

                                                        2011033140

First Edition: January 2012

10   9   8   7   6   5   4   3   2   1

For Isaac Peters and Shoshana Semler

CONTENTS

PREFACE

THIS IS NOT THE SAFEST of times to write about the state of Europe, what with so many crises confronting it and the uncertain future of this and other continents. Will it still exist five years from now in its present form? I have learned long ago that a crisis is usually the period between two other crises, but the present one seems to be considerably deeper than those Europe passed through after the Second World War. My memories of Europe go back to a childhood and school in Weimar Germany and the Nazi Third Reich. I left Europe less than a year before the outbreak of the war, and I had known by that time only a small part of the continent.

When I returned for short and long visits soon after the end of the war, it was a different Europe—and I had no reason to disbelieve what I was told. Since then I have been to most European countries, and Europe has been my field of study for much of the time. My children went to school on both sides of the Atlantic; my work has been on both sides too. European culture has been the formative influence of my life, admittedly more of the past than the present. I have had the good fortune in my life to benefit from a variety of global perspectives. When I look out of our window in Washington, D.C., I can see the raccoons and the squirrels on the trees of Rock Creek Park. When I look out of the window in Highgate, London, I can see the squirrels in Waterlow Park and (well, almost) the grave of Karl Marx.

Having seen Europe and the Europeans in good times and bad, the time has come for a summing up. I tried to do so five years ago in a book entitled *The Last Days of Europe*. The reception was skeptical in part. The views I expressed were unfashionable, and the book certainly came too early. Five years can be no more than a minute in history, but it can also be a long, long time. When the book first came out, it was widely believed that all things considered, Europe, and especially the European Union, was not doing too badly. The EU had progressed to a common currency, after all. The reviewer in *The Economist*, my bible among the weeklies, blamed my book for its "unduly apocalyptic conclusions." Now I see that a recent editorial about the future of Europe in the very same journal is entitled "Staring into the Abyss."

I had not been staring into the abyss at the time, and I am not now; I was merely predicting that one of the possible fates of Europe was to turn into a museum or cultural theme park for well-to-do tourists from East Asia—not a heroic or deeply tragic future but not my idea of an abyss or of the apocalypse. True, at the time, dealing with the various problems, I put greater emphasis on the long-term challenges such as the demographic trends, whereas more recently, as the result of the global recession and especially the European debt crisis, the immediate dangers have been in the foreground. This is only natural, for the collapse of banks, rising unemployment, and austerity budgets are clear and present dangers immediately affecting everyone, whereas long-term threats can usually be pushed aside—there is always a chance that they may not happen.

The disbelief that accompanied my book five years ago on the part of some puzzled me. The indications for the decline of

Europe were so obvious even then—how could they be doubted and ignored? They had been noted by many before. There are various explanations for ignoring the obvious but they are now of historical interest only. We face more pressing issues: the decline of Europe seems obvious as far as the foreseeable future is concerned, but it need not be a collapse. What can be done to ensure a soft landing and perhaps even a recovery at some future date? In this context, the problems confronting the European Union have become of central importance rather than the somewhat more distant demographic issues facing Europe. Will Europe opt for a United States of Europe rather than the present halfway house? Or are there only dim prospects for an effective union, and each country may as well face the coming time of troubles on its own? How much power will this new, more centralized and strengthened union have? Will this transfer of sovereignty from the nation-states to the EU extend to foreign policy and defense? Assuming that there will be a United States of Europe rather than the Brussels EU, how important will it be in world affairs?

These are, in my view, the issues that must be addressed, and I have tried to do this, however imperfectly, in these pages. Given all these uncertainties, predictions are impossible. The euro and the Eurozone may be saved in the years to come, but this would not necessarily bring stability, for the next crisis or the one after could cause their downfall. But this, resulting in a European split, would not necessarily mean the end of a united Europe, for a new initiative would probably be made after a decent interval. The same seems likely if the Eurozone should dissolve earlier rather than later. If the financial markets should play a negative role in these coming developments, their survival in the present form is doubtful.

There is an almost unlimited number of possibilities, but it would appear that the decisive issues are not the technical decisions that will be made concerning the economy and the finances of the continent but the deeper political and psychological factors—nationalism or postnationalism, whether dynamism or exhaustion will prove stronger in Europe. There are trends that can be predicted with a certain degree of probability, but there are also the *imponderables* that cannot be measured or weighted let alone predicted because they can be subject to sudden change. And it seems that the imponderables will be more decisive.

The Europe I have known, I wrote five years ago, is in the process of disappearing. What will take its place? The importance of Europe in the world has been shrinking, but it probably still has a future, albeit apparently a modest one, something in between a regional power and indeed a valuable museum. For the time being I tend to agree, despite everything, with Alfred, Lord Tennyson, who wrote in "Locksley Hall," "Better fifty years of Europe than a cycle of Cathay."

There is much that is admirable in Europe's past and even in its present weakened state. But I am no longer certain to what extent Tennyson's sentiments are shared by a majority of Europeans, to what degree there still is firm belief in a European identity, a European model, and European values—and above all the will to defend them. Instead, there is the comforting thought that other parts of the world seem to be in decline too. The present crisis is not primarily a crisis of financial debt but a crisis of lack of will, inertia, tiredness, and self-doubt, and, however often "European values" are invoked, a crisis of lack of self-confidence, a weak ego in psychoanalytic terms.

Europe's status in the world was predominant for a few centuries just as that of other powers earlier on; this has come to an end. All recorded history is the story of rise and decline. Unlike university professors, superpowers have no tenure.

The causes of collective exhaustion are manifold and can be discussed at great length. Rise and decline too have been studied and commented on since ancient times. At the dawn of the modern age, Giambattista Vico, in his famous and influential *Scienza Nuova*, argued that history moves in recurrent cycles— the divine, the heroic, and the human (an imperfect translation of "l'età degli uomini"). That Europe is postheroic goes without saying, but who could say with conviction what stage Europe has reached and what the next will be?

Perhaps Robert Cooper is right. He has been advising EU foreign policy on and off for a long time. In his view Europe is postmodern, believing in peaceful interdependence and modern cooperation, whereas the policy of others is rooted (at best) in ideas of traditional zones of influence and balance of power. But how will the postmodern survive in a premodern or modern world in which all too often chaos prevails, not the laws of the International Criminal Court, but the laws of the jungle? The postmoderns will have to act according to two sets of rules, the one while dealing with each other, the other ("the rougher methods of an earlier era") when dealing with the ruffians who have not yet reached the advanced stage of postmodernism. This sounds sensible, but how practical is it? *Liberal imperialism* is an unnecessarily provocative term, and it's not a realistic policy, for sending a few thousand people for a limited time to a far away country with the order not to shoot, whatever happens, does not really amount to imperialism.

Cooper's theses, not surprisingly, have irritated those willing to forgive clerical fascism, dictatorship, even genocide, provided they happen outside Europe and the United States. But the real weakness of this policy is elsewhere: playing according to two sets of rules and sets of standard demands is not only discrimination but also a determination that seems to be absent in Europe these days. Europe as a forceful player would be most welcome, but how does one become a forceful player? Does Europe in its apathy want this role? As Schopenhauer put it: to wish is easy, but to wish to wish ("wollen wollen"), next to impossible. The pharmacologists have produced several useful drugs for invigorating people and against individual depression; perhaps they will one day discover a treatment for the depression of nations and generations and for generating political will. But this day has not arrived yet, and depression is only part of the European malaise.

Part One of the present book deals with the unfolding of the European crisis in recent years and its likely consequences; two chapters of the second part that cover the road to the crisis, while updated and not identical with *The Last Days of Europe,* are based in part on it. For a more detailed discussion of immigration into Europe and the attempts to integrate it, I refer the reader to this earlier book.

—WALTER LAQUEUR
Washington, D.C., and London, 2011

PART ONE

CRISIS

THE EUROPEAN DREAM:
"THE DAY WILL COME . . ."

ON A DEPRESSING MORNING WITH the only news in the media about Ireland on the brink of the abyss, America diminished and paralyzed, Britain facing years of austerity, Greece in despair, Portugal beyond despair, Italy and Spain in grave danger, "chronically weak demand," "debilitating cycle," "collision course in Europe," "killing the euro," "pernicious consequences," "towards the precipice," perhaps the only comfort was offered by looking back six or seven years to the inspiring literature on the European dream, a postnationalist model of peace, prosperity, social justice, and ecological virtue. It is certainly encouraging to know that the homicide rate in Europe is one quarter that of the United States, that the literacy rate is higher as well as the life span and the amount of humanitarian aid dispensed. A revolution had taken place in Europe during the last sixty years, which most Americans had simply not noticed. It had achieved a new balance between individual property rights and the common good, between government regulation and the free market, between liberty and equality—which America with its naive belief in the all-curative power of the free market had never achieved. The excesses of consumer capitalism had been tempered. Then one would proceed to another book predicting in convincing detail that the future belonged to the European model, that it would be emulated all over the world, a shining beacon to all mankind. It had pioneered a new approach to a humanitarian foreign policy. At long last it had come to live in peace with itself and the rest of the world. Europe was healthy and sustainable; it was stress-free in contrast to feverish, unbalanced America. The future belonged to it.

There are still a few voices maintaining that Europe is a rising superpower in a bipolar world, and it is probably welcome to have such uplifting messages in a time of doom and gloom. Europe's influence in the world (it is announced) is rising for a variety of reasons, among them the fact that the material and ideological conflicts between Europe and the other powers are decreasing. The European continent has been pacified. Elsewhere all major governments want to adapt European societal norms, moving toward democracy and cooperative international relations. Great are the powers of human self-deception. One apocryphal story stands out, that of the senior member of the British foreign office, who, complaining about the constant warnings of his junior colleagues on the danger of a war, declared that he had been in office for forty years from 1910 to 1950, and it had been a calm period but for two relatively short unpleasant interruptions—in 1914 and in 1939.

It is easy, far too easy, to ridicule now the illusions of yesteryear. The postwar generation of European elites aimed to create more-democratic societies. They wanted to reduce the extremes of wealth and poverty and provide essential social services in a way that prewar government had not. They wanted to do all this not just because they believed that it was morally right but because they saw social equity as a way to temper the anger and frustrations that had led to war. They had quite enough of unrest and war. For several decades, many European societies more or less achieved these aims, and they had every reason to be proud of this fact. Europe was quiet and civilized, no sounds of war, no threat of civil war either. The welfare-state concept was admirable. Its political economy was based on the assumption of permanent substantial economic growth, a Ponzi scheme of sorts but not an unreasonable or dishonorable one.

On what was Europe's success based? Partly on recent painful historical experience, the horrors of two world wars, on the lessons of dictatorship, on fascism and communism that should never happen again. But above all it was based on a feeling of European identity and common values. What was this identity and how to define the common values? Or was it simply a community of material interests? It began after all as an iron, steel, and coal union. True, Jean Monnet, the father of the European Union, later said that he would put the emphasis on culture rather than the economy if he had to start all over again. But he did begin with the economy, and this approach was probably not without reason.

Among the European values and fundamental rights most often mentioned were the respect for human dignity, the rule of law, peace, respect for the environment, perhaps, above all, tolerance—the great diversity of European culture and the willingness to accept it. But were these values specifically European? Sixty-seven percent of Europeans thought they were specifically European in comparison with other continents. But such an answer was possibly misleading—more than half of Europeans doubted whether there was a shared European culture.

Why was European integration so difficult? It had to overcome what some called the artificial concept of nation statehood.

But nation statehood had developed over the centuries; perhaps the world and Europe would have been better without it, but it was certainly not artificial. On the contrary, it could be argued that a community of communities was artificial. All investigations have shown that 90 percent of Europeans feel an attachment to the place and the country in which they were born, but much less so to a wider institution involving a different way of life and a different language. According to a 1996 Eurobarometer survey, only 51 percent of Europeans "felt European," and this seems not to have increased since. Various attempts have been made since to strengthen the feeling of a common cultural heritage, including a European anthem and a European flag, but they have not had a great impact so far. Some common cultural events have been slightly more successful, including the Eurovision Song Contests (which also generated a considerable amount of ill will as the result of political maneuvering) or the Vienna New Year's Day Johann Strauss concert, although this was also listened to by many millions in China and Japan.

Lessons of the past gradually fade away. True, the lesson that there should be no wars in Europe had sunk in, for the price that had been paid had been too high, and, in any case, Europe was now too weak to wage war. It had been at long last realized in this postheroic age that Europe, and a fortiori a shrinking Europe, had all the lebensraum it needed.

But these were negative lessons, teaching Europe what not to do. The feeling of European solidarity and of common values had not made great progress, after some uncertain beginnings—if it made progress at all. There was not even agreement about the borders of Europe. Was the United Kingdom closer to the United States or to Bulgaria or Turkey? Nor was it realistic to expect such progress—how could it compete with national feelings, which had developed over many centuries?

If common values were few or weak, what of common interests and common threats as a glue? These certainly existed, and not only in the economic field, but such a union resembled a financial company with limited responsibility; people might feel solidarity with their compatriots and be willing to make sacrifices for their homeland, but why do so for a community of economic interests? There were common political interests but also conflicts of interest; differences of opinion existed between countries and within countries.

When was it first realized that all was not well as far as the European Union was concerned? There had been a European crisis in the 1970s and the feeling that Europe was running out of steam after a promising beginning. There had been major crises elsewhere—in Russia in the 1990s and also in Asia (1997–98), Latin America (1999–2002), and even in the United States, and the countries affected had all recovered. As for global prospects in the 1980s there were wide divergences of opinion. The Cassandras (not many at the time) saw mostly doom and gloom, and it is of course true that sooner or later disasters do happen somewhere. But the majority view as expressed at the time in the leading works of political scientists on the rise and fall of great powers was that America was overextended and therefore bound to fall; stagnating Russia was also not in good shape, though hardly anyone foresaw how close the collapse was. China and India were more or less ignored, which is understandable because the great jump forward was just about to begin.

If there was mild optimism among the prophets, it concerned Japan and Europe. These powers were not overextended but made steady, gradual progress—in the case of Europe, accepting new members and moving toward a common currency. Some enthusiasts went further, describing how the European way was the best hope in an insecure world and how the

European dream was quietly replacing the American dream, the term *quietly* being very often used in this context.

These were wrong assumptions and predictions, but they seemed not that far-fetched at the time. The Soviet Union disappeared, and the United States for a while became the only superpower, much to the chagrin of some who predicted further overextension and consequently even greater decline. Others took a more sanguine view. In the meantime, Europe was also expanding. By now, its population was greater than that of the United States and its GNP was also greater. But its growth was very much slowing down, and individual countries faced major problems. In 2005 the CIA published a report in which it predicted that, by 2020, the EU (and NATO) would disappear unless they carried out the most far-reaching reforms.

The reasons given were interesting but not wholly convincing: the European welfare state had become too expensive, virtually unaffordable, and made it impossible for Europe to compete on the world markets. This was quite correct— people lived longer, and medical treatment became more and more expensive. But the American authors of these reports seem to have ignored that the same applied to the United States, which had no welfare state (or merely a very limited one) but spent on health twice as much per capita as the Europeans. In the meantime some European countries, notably Sweden but also Germany, had proved that abuses of the welfare state could be put right and a great deal of money saved. Some of these cuts were painful, but many of the essentials of the welfare state were preserved.

In the 2005 forecast, yet another main reason was given for the coming collapse of the EU—the fact that Germany's sluggish growth was negatively affecting the European economic performance, Germany being the strongest economic power. This was the perspective of 2005, but five years later the European situation looked very different indeed, with Germany as the undisputed leader and everybody compelled to dance to its tune. This showed again the pitfalls and difficulties of prediction. Some of the factors were a priori unpredictable, others were mainly psychological or had to do with the efficacy of government confronting a crisis. It was clear, for example, that if major banks engaged in foolish and imprudent activities, a price would have to be paid sooner or later. But it still depended on how the authorities and the public coped with such a situation. A collapse could be prevented, unless the foolishness and the damage had been monumental. Or there could be a panic, a mass run on the banks with equally foolish countermeasures taken, in which case the consequences could be far reaching and disastrous.

American global overextension with insufficient resources may indeed have been very damaging, and the European welfare state may have become a very heavy burden. But these were not the main factors that caused the great crisis of 2008. Mainly responsible were the enormous debts incurred by both America and Europe and the lack of financial oversight that led to the great instability on the markets caused by banks, governments, and individual debtors.

But the causes were not only economic in character— perhaps not even mainly so. As far as Europe is concerned it was the mistaken idea that there could be an economic union without a political union. There was little enthusiasm on the part of the richer European countries to help get the weaker economies out of trouble, especially if these weaker ones had behaved irresponsibly, or even fraudulently. Why should Germans retire at sixty-seven so that Greeks could retire at fifty-three? In other words, with all the talk about European identity and common values, there was little solidarity. Perhaps there could not be.

This should not have come as a great surprise. Looking at world history of the last hundred years, there are few cases of countries uniting and more of splitting. The Soviet Union split into a dozen constituent parts, Yugoslavia into nearly half a dozen, and Czechs and Slovaks reached the conclusion that they would be better off if they parted ways. Even in countries that had been united for a long time, separatist tendencies ran strong. When the United Nations was founded, it had 51 members; today there are 193.

The European dream had not come suddenly. In 1849 a peace congress took place in Paris. The opening address was given by Victor Hugo, in which he said,

> A day will come when you France, you Russia, you Italy, you England, you Germany, you all nations of the continent without losing your distinct qualities and your glorious individuality will be merged closely within a superior unit and you will form the European Brotherhood. . . . A day will come when the bullets and the bombs will be replaced, by votes by the universal suffrage by the peoples, by the venerable arbitration of a great sovereign senate which will be to Europe what the parliament is to England, what this diet is to Germany what this legislative assembly is to France.

Victor Hugo went on for a long time. It was a stirring speech, but the day, alas, has not come yet.

THE RECESSION

ONLY A FEW YEARS AGO, the "European model" was widely praised, and Americans admonished to emulate it. Far from disparaging and belittling the European model, I admired many of its aspects and thought it worthy of serious study rather than ill-informed denunciations dismissing it as a socialist horror story. But could Europe afford it, or had far-reaching changes become overdue? Was it not true that the ethnic composition of Europe was undergoing (in part, had already undergone) important changes and that people lived much longer, which was bound to have political and economic consequences? There was until recently a great temptation to dismiss such concerns. Such skepticism could have been generated only by ignoring the great progress achieved in Brussels and by Brussels and by grossly overrating the impact of the immigration of a relatively small number of Muslim immigrants. Above all, if Europe was facing serious problems, wasn't it true that the United States, the empire in decline, was confronting even greater threats? True enough, but my subject in *The Last Days of Europe* was Europe, not America, and I failed to understand in what way the miseries of America would benefit Europe, let alone help Europe, except perhaps psychologically by way of *schadenfreude*.

The recovery of Europe after the Second World War had been spectacular and in many ways promising, but there had not been much progress after the first three decades. Storm clouds were gathering on the horizon. The European economies showed signs of weakness, the welfare state seemed to rest on an insufficiently strong economic base, and there was growing indebtedness as in the United States. The new European political structures that had emerged left much to criticism; there had been little progress toward concerted action in the fields of foreign and defense policy as well as energy supplies. The influx of millions of immigrants, above all from Muslim countries, had generated serious problems; neither the multicultural approach nor integration seemed to work.

In brief, there was not one European crisis in the offing but multiple crises. Above all, there was a strong tendency to ignore these negative developments and the threats ahead. There was a false optimism, difficult to understand even now with the benefit of hindsight.

In 2008, the global economic crisis broke, and the optimism about the future of Europe of yesteryear gave way to pessimism, even panic. Why? Because the other threats facing Europe, however serious, were not clear and present dangers, whereas economic crises have an immediate impact. Not just the future of the euro suddenly became a matter of speculation, more often than not pessimistic. The future of the European Union, after years of expansion, seemed no longer certain.

When writing about Europe more than five years ago, I did not deal with the economic situation in any detail, and I do not intend to do so now. Others, more qualified, are dealing with this subject. But the repercussions of a recession worse than any that had occurred since the 1930s were not only economic in character, and any discussion of the present state of Europe and its prospects, however cursory, has to take this crisis as its point of departure.

It began in Iceland in 2007, even though few realized at the time that events in a very small and apparently wholly unimportant country could be an indication of the shape of things to come. The three leading Icelandic banks had reached the conclusion that, money being so cheap and easily attainable, a great amount of money could be made by extending their activities abroad, mainly through lending operations. At the end their total assets abroad were fourteen times as large as Iceland's GNP. But when the global lending market froze, they were no longer able to fulfill their obligations and faced bankruptcy. This could have been prevented if the banks had not been reckless and if there had been oversight and regulation. Having realized that it could not bail out the banks, the government of Iceland eventually decided (in 2011) to let them collapse and make the creditors take the losses.

Events in Iceland were followed by the collapse of Bear Stearns and Lehman Brothers in the United States for, broadly speaking, similar reasons, which caused nervousness on the international markets.

To what extent was America responsible for the European crisis that followed? The subprime crisis and the Lehman Brothers disaster no doubt caused instability in the world markets, and some of the major European banks were affected. The U.S. commission investigating the causes of the crisis concluded: the financial crisis was avoidable, it was a dramatic failure of corporate governance and risk management, a combination of excessive borrowing, risky investment, and lack of transparency, and the government was ill prepared for the crisis.

But what had happened in America would not have affected the situation in Europe to such an extent but for the fact that the European economy was far weaker and more vulnerable than commonly assumed. Credit expansion had gone much too far. Interest had been too low, which led (among other things) to a housing crisis and eventually to a banking crisis. Heavy debts had accumulated in most countries. "Bubbles" had been in existence not only in the United States but in Europe as well. Not much attention was paid in the beginning in Europe to the American crisis. "Europe is not America," announced the *Frankfurter Allgemeine Zeitung*. Other media maintained that American conditions were unthinkable in Europe. But it did not take long until these facts and the implications of the debt crisis shook Europe.

Iceland seemed to be an isolated case. Some, however, were already arguing that the difference between Iceland and Ireland was one letter and six months. After Iceland there was the Greek crisis, in which the country was found to have borrowed and spent too much for years. It had nearly a million state employees getting substantial salaries as well as high pensions at an early age. Retirement age was lower (at fifty-three on the average) than in most other European countries, and there had been other social services the country simply could not afford. Furthermore, it had not been truthful in reporting its financial situation to the EU's other members and central institutions. All this was no secret, but no attention was paid, for reasons that will no doubt be explored in detail by future historians.

When the facts became fully known (or, to be precise, sank in), there was the urgent necessity to bail out Greece; not doing so would not merely have caused the bankruptcy of this country, it would have had incalculable consequences on the capital markets and might have spelled disaster for the euro. But there was considerable reluctance to take such a course of action, mainly on the part of Germany (which would have had to bear the main burden), as well as other countries. Germany stressed that, unless there was far more effective oversight, such crises would recur with fatal consequences for the European Union.

Eventually a compromise was reached after Greece promised to mend its ways, slash its budget, and introduce a system of austerity (which led to mass strikes). In the end, only Slovakia refused to participate in the salvage operation, arguing that it was unjust that a small country, poorer than Greece, should be made responsible for the stupidity and short-sightedness of a bigger and more prosperous one. The EU decision making progress in this, as in other cases, was agonizingly slow. America was watching Europe's inability to act with increasing incredulity and anxiety. Washington had perhaps realized by that time that it should have stepped in earlier to deal with the Lehman Brothers situation. It took several phone calls by President Obama to persuade European leaders to speed up their action. But it soon appeared that the first Greece rescue package was not big enough, and there was great resistance against a second bailout. It eventually emerged that the Greek debt burden was too big to be paid out and in the meantime even more dangerous emergencies appeared in other European countries.

There followed the Irish crisis, but there were also danger signals from Portugal, Spain, and Italy. The GNP of Italy fell by 6 percent during the crisis, and recovery was exceedingly slow. No European country seemed safe. Ireland, for a long time one of the most backward European countries, had been the great success story of the previous twenty years. By 2007 its per capita income was higher than that of Britain. By the summer of 2010, the *Irish Star* published a cartoon on its front page showing a gravestone with the inscription "Ireland R.I.P." How was it possible that a country with a population of 4.6 million had incurred banking debts of more than 100 billion euros—with no one paying attention? There had been a bubble (in housing, for one) as in the other countries, bad debts, and lack of caution by the banks.

There was an inclination (not only in Ireland) to put all the blame on the euro; but while the existence of the euro made a cure more difficult, it was not really the main cause of the disaster. The Irish economic base was far sounder than the Greek, but the three leading Irish banks had acted without elementary prudence. According to some experts the managers of the banks had been operating on the basis of "false mathematics," but it is doubtful whether this could have been the principal explanation. There was, as in other such cases, the temptation to attract foreign money into a country with low income tax (a 12 percent corporate tax!) and to make great riches.

The situation in Spain, another success story of the last decades, was yet again different inasmuch as its debts were low, much lower than in many other European countries, and Spain even registered budget surpluses. But there had been a huge housing boom financed mainly from abroad. Furthermore, Spanish prosperity had led to a considerable rise in inflation and increase in prices of goods and services—which made Spain less competitive on the world markets. The result was a major bank crisis and steep, increasing unemployment. According to the experts, the Spanish government should have carried out pension and labor reforms but failed to do so. This kept the trade unions happy and prevented mass strikes, but it also made the unemployment rate rise to almost 20 percent, and, in the words of *The Economist,* condemned a third of the working force to unstable, unprotected, temporary jobs.

Italy too was in deep trouble, even though in this case the deeper problems go much further back than the global crisis of 2008. The country had not been harder hit by the crisis than others in Europe. No bank went bankrupt, but its economy was stagnating, its productivity declining, and it had greater debts than any other member state of the EU. Italian industry found it increasingly difficult to compete on the world markets. The situation was not helped by the shenanigans of its longtime prime minister, one of the richest men in the country. Libya, once an Italian colony, became one of the most important trade partners, buying up banks, oil companies, and a significant share in Juventus Turin, a leading football club. When Muammar Khaddafi visited Italy in 2010, he was received as an honored guest. During this visit Khaddafi tried to convert to Islam a largish group of young women who had been mobilized by a local agency. Khaddafi was never in great awe of Europe, which, as he said in a number of speeches and articles, would be a Muslim continent with Turkey acting as a fifth column. When his son Hannibal was briefly arrested in a Swiss hotel, having been accused of severely beating his servants, the father declared a jihad against Switzerland. Earlier on he had threatened Britain with serious retaliation if the Libyan official convicted of the Lockerbie murder was not released from prison. And he got his way—the Libyan prisoner was released. The holy war did not take place, but two Swiss businessmen who happened to be in Libya were arrested and, despite the intervention of the president of Switzerland, who flew to the Libyan capital, held there for almost two years.

The case of the EU relationship with Khaddafi ought to be recalled at least in passing: it blatantly exposed (as the *Financial Times* put it) the ineptitude of EU foreign policy. Following a summit in Tripoli in 2010 the EU expressed its "gratitude to

the leader of the revolution and the people of the Great Socialist
Libyan Jamahirya for the care, hospitality and attention extended to the participants of the summit." This was just a few
weeks before Khaddafi began to massacre his own people. Some
said he was a psychopath, but, if so, his mental state had not
significantly changed over the forty-two years he had been in
power. However, given Europe's inability to reduce its dependence on Middle Eastern and Russian oil and gas supplies, such
demeaning declarations may well have been inevitable.

The United Kingdom (like the United States) had engaged
for years in profligate spending; personal indebtedness was
higher than in other major countries. It amounted to one trillion dollars even back in 1995. In 2010 the sovereign UK debt
was 63 percent of the gross national product, even higher than
the American. The British were particularly indebted to credit
card companies; it was estimated that in a few years the debt
per family would amount to 80,000 pound sterling. Personal
debts in Britain in 2010 totaled about two trillion dollars. The
new Tory government decided to cut state spending in 2010 to
an extent that was thought politically impossible in Washington. There was a tendency in Britain to make the government
in power wholly responsible for the country's woes. Tony Blair
and Gordon Brown were made the chief culprits, and their
Labor party suffered a resounding defeat in the election of 2010.
But within a few months, public opinion polls were showing
that Labor had again overtaken the Tories, who had been compelled to adapt very unpopular austerity measures. Students
were smashing the windows of the Tory party office. There
was no acceptance among the wider public that there was to
be some connection between slow growth, overspending, and
living for years beyond their means.

To deal with this situation, drastic measures became imperative, more drastic than any introduced since the Second World War. They included dismissal of many employees from jobs in government, (500,000 jobs were to go in the public sector in the UK, to mention just one example); the cutting of child benefits as well as pensions and many other services; heavy cuts in allocations to defense, education, culture, and just about everything else. Such stringent measures resulted in mass strikes in France and other European countries. But the strikes were bound to fail if governments lacked the funds that were demanded, there was no room for compromise. Second, even if they had been willing to do so, under the Lisbon treaty of 2007 the budgets were increasingly controlled by outside forces, be it the European Union or the World Bank or the International Monetary Fund. Thus resentment was bound to be directed not only against one's own government but against Brussels and Strasbourg, as well as the countries that were the donors, not the recipients of EU funds. This state of affairs was inevitably going to lead to hostility against the expanding Brussels bureaucracy, whose members' salaries and other benefits were often higher than those of government officials at home and whose functions were deemed superfluous. At a time when Brussels demanded severe cutbacks all around, the leadership of the European Union insisted on enlarging its own budget by 5 to 6 percent; the timing was not good, and the fact that the Brussels leadership was unpopular and less than inspiring did not help either.

The order of the day was cutting back and belt tightening. But it was also clear to most that a responsible policy, that is, an emphasis on saving, while necessary, would eventually reduce the sovereign debt but would do nothing as far as economic growth was concerned—on the contrary, it would hamper it. Nor was there a golden middle way, finding the right

balance, applicable to every country. Ireland came under attack in view of its 12 percent corporate tax, which in earlier
years had attracted many leading international corporations.
But if Ireland gave in to German and French pressure complaining about unfair competition, it would mean that growth
in Ireland would be even slower and would consequently hin-
der its recovery and ability to liquidate its debt in the foreseeable future.

Most European countries suffered from the downturn of
the economy. Forecasts ranged from a fairly rapid recovery in
Slovakia (which for a while had the highest growth rate in all
of Europe) to a collapse of the Romanian economy in 2011—a
decline of 15 percent or even more of Romania's GNP. The
Romanian debt amounted to almost 100 billion euros, the Bul-
garian debt to about 37 million. Recovery in both countries was
hampered by inflation. Trends in these countries were bound
to have a certain impact on the markets, but much less so than
developments in western and southern Europe; the debts involved were not of the same magnitude, nor had they as yet
adopted the euro. A rapid decline in the value of their currency,
or even a collapse of their currency, would not therefore directly affect the Eurozone.

A yet different situation prevailed in Hungary. Hungarian
spokesmen announced in May 2010 that their country faced
a "very grave situation." The external debt amounted to 150
billion euros, the GNP had declined by 6.6 percent the year
before, and the population of the country was shrinking. But a
strongly nationalist party had come to power in Hungary that
year in collaboration with an even more radical semifascist
party, and, being proud Hungarians, they declared that they
would not accept help from international financial institutions
but recover through self-help. In a dramatic gesture they broke

off negotiations with the IMF in July 2010, but soon after renewed them, and three months later obtained a loan of $25 billion. While Hungary's international credit ranking declined, the IMF saw some encouraging signs in 2010 as slight growth was reported in the country.

The economic future of the countries of the Balkans and Eastern Europe very much depended on the health of the major EU countries with whom they traded. According to plan, Bulgaria was to join the Eurozone in 2013, Hungary in 2014, and Romania in 2015. But in view of the condition within the Eurozone and Eastern Europe, it seemed far from certain whether this timetable would be kept. The consequences of the great recession will be felt for a long time to come, and it will take even longer to gain a full and realistic picture as far as its causes are concerned and the efficacy of the measures taken to confront it. At the present time, even an interim balance is risky. It was the end (as Philip Stevens wrote in the *Financial Times*) of Britain's (and France's and Europe's) post imperial reach, the end also of self-confident globalism and liberal internationalism.

It seemed that the euro had been saved; in fact, by the end of 2010 it had appreciated so much against the dollar and the yen that the European ability to compete on the world markets had been endangered. But why had it risen so much? The same economic problems, such as the Greek and the Irish crises that had caused its downfall, still persisted. The debt crisis continues, an end is not in sight, the only certainty being that Europe will be poorer as long as one can see ahead.

The European Union had not been very successful combating unemployment. In countries such as France and Spain, unemployment had been high even before the crisis, and even after the crisis was officially declared over, it remained over 10

percent. Why was a country such as Poland less affected? Why
did the countries in Eastern Europe (with one or two exceptions) suffer less grievously than those in western Europe, and
why did recovery come quicker in the former? Why was there
greater readiness in Eastern Europe to accept cutbacks than in
the West? Why was European decision making so lamentably
slow and cumbersome, and what could be done to change this?
To what extent were the causes of the crisis psychological—
aggravated by a panic?

On one rainy Tuesday, November 16, 2010, Herman van
Rompuy, the president of the European Union, announced:
"We are in a survival crisis," adding that if the euro did not survive, neither would the European Union. But three days later,
realizing that his declaration did not have a good effect, he back-
pedaled. His words had been misinterpreted, the euro was in
safe hands, and economic growth in the Eurozone was much
stronger than expected (1.8 rather than 1 percent). He criticized
the doomsayers who were underestimating the political determination of the leaders and the countries. But would 1.8 percent
be sufficient?

In May 2010 the EU established the ESM (European Stabili-
sation Mechanism), a permanent rescue funding of 700 billion
euros to help solve the immediate crisis by providing direct
loans to members in need of liquidities. But was this enough,
and did it come in time? The macro problems that had caused
the debt crisis had not been solved. Did it not mean that taxpayers would have to recompensate the big banks all over
Europe who had acted so foolishly and irresponsibly? Such
measures generated much resistance in those European countries obligated to provide these funds. Almost everywhere, the
ruling pro-EU parties suffered setbacks in elections.

Definite answers to these and other questions will not be
forthcoming soon.

THE POLITICAL IMPACT

THE CRISES, JEAN MONNET ONCE said, are the great federators. The great recession could have given a fresh and powerful impetus to the movement toward a united Europe. But it did not do so, at least not in the short run. It had a political impact, but not a positive one. It led to dejection, which I will discuss later on. It had often been said that while Europe was an economic giant, it was a political dwarf. After the recession it appeared that the giant economy was not as strong and stable either.

There had been, in the 1990s and even in the years after, tremendous optimism about Europe's future as a model to all humankind. Europe was a shining beacon showing the way to humanity and a higher, more civilized way of life. It would dominate the twenty-first century not through its power but by sheer force of example—all the world would try to be like Europe. In countless books, speeches, and conferences, these sanguine voices were heard admittedly with declining conviction after about 2005 or 2006. At the time of the great recession, only a very few intrepid souls were left preaching this gospel. A few Americans were traveling through Europe and explaining to the bemused Europeans that their model was the best and they had little to worry about.

What was the deeper motivation beneath this fervent belief among some Americans in the European model? One day sociologists and psychologists may find it a fascinating topic for their investigations. Ideological considerations did of course play a role; the Europe Firsters (the term I coined for those who put European concerns above all others) thought of themselves as liberals, belonging to the progressive left, whereas the skeptics were right-wing reactionaries. There was probably an element of American europhilia involved, a tradition that precedes Henry James and T. S. Eliot, neither great stalwarts of the left. But it could also be true that it was simply a matter of insufficient knowledge; most of these Americans came to Europe as tourists, for longer or shorter periods, whereas the negative, shadowy aspects were not on their agendas. Even if they were familiar with the language and the historical and cultural background of the countries they visited, they lacked the instinctive, intuitive understanding of the natives, which led to misjudgments.

It is easy, in view of what did happen, to ridicule the naïveté of the singers of the paeans of the European model. But their naïveté would be less than the whole story, for it was accompanied on the other side by the primitive belief quite frequently found in the United States that the market would solve all, or almost all, problems. The European model, after all, had positive lessons to teach. The countries of Europe had been living in peace since the end of the Second World War (to ignore for a moment certain events in the Balkans, the backyard of Europe). There had been more cooperation between the countries of Europe than ever before. The extremes of poverty had been eradicated. A system of social services and a social safety net had been established, which made it possible for hundreds of millions of people to live and die in dignity. Even the less-developed European countries had attained a certain level of prosperity.

Contrast this with the United States, which managed to spend twice as much as Europe (almost 17 percent) on health services that covered a smaller section of the population, which lacked other social services to be found in Europe, and which witnessed a steadily growing inequality in wealth and income. Much of the American disdain toward "socialized medicine" was ridiculously ill informed; true, the health care system worked better in some European countries than in others, and Europeans lived slightly longer than Americans. Some American extremist political figures even argued that the health care system was in violation of the Ten Commandments.

The richest 1 percent of the population in the United States owns more than one quarter of the national wealth, an unhealthy state of affairs both as far as the economy and the political situation is concerned. This development toward a plutocracy has largely taken place during the last thirty years. The material situation of most Americans, the poor and the middle class, has hardly improved during this period. America has become in recent decades the largest debtor country in the world, and, as a very senior official asked, how long could the biggest debtor play the role of a superpower? The answer was given in 2008 and in the years that followed.

Capitalism, or at any rate casino capitalism and the banking system, had suffered a deadly blow, or so it seemed. In a country traditionally not hostile to Wall Street, a majority voiced the opinion (2010) that it was wrong if those who had been responsible through greed and incompetence for the disaster that had occurred were lavishly remunerated and permitted to pay lower taxes. But socialism and the left did not really benefit from the crisis of capitalism; there was no conviction that socialism had an answer to such a crisis, and communist experience had been negative. China had succeeded, but there had been a transition from Maoist communism to something between state capitalism and private cutthroat capitalism. Left-wing ideologues tried to explain why Chinese capitalism, more exploitative than others, was more progressive—because it was not democratic. Not an easy task.

There is much that America can learn from the European experience, both positive and negative. The problem with the European welfare state is not that it was wrong or decadent or conducive to idleness but that it became over the years more and more costly. The same problem faced America. When social security was introduced after the Second World War, people did not live as long as they do in 2011, and medicine was infinitely cheaper what with the sophisticated machinery and drugs introduced in later years. (Citizens of France, Germany, and many other European countries lived twelve to fifteen years longer in 2010 than they did sixty years earlier.) There was full or almost full employment in Europe after World War II. The welfare state functioned reasonably well in Europe, and even the most conservative governments would not have dreamed to introduce drastic cuts. But it was based on the assumption that the economic situation was stable and there would be constant growth—growth to the same extent that social expenses were growing. But what if these assumptions were no longer true, what if the continent was aging, with rising costs and smaller state revenue?

Paradoxically, European social democracy suffered a steep decline just at a time when it should have prospered—during the first decade of the twenty-first century. At the turn of the century, Social Democrats were in power or constituted part of a government coalition in twelve out of fifteen EU countries, but in the years that followed they lost their leading position in country after country, even in Scandinavia, where these parties had been in power for many decades, until there remained only Spain of all the major countries. How could this have happened after years of growing income inequality and often unpopular privatization and, above all, the painful economic recession?

Who benefited from this decline? The center and right-of-center parties profited only to a very limited degree. In Germany, the Linken, the heirs of the East German communists, made some headway but not as much as the Greens, who were anything but a socialist party and whose socioeconomic appeal rested to a considerable extent on a program of extreme vagueness. Elsewhere in Europe, the extreme right had some very modest successes and the anti-immigration movements made some greater headway. But all this did not explain the failure of the democratic left to gather momentum.

Some put the responsibility on the excessive eagerness of Social Democratic parties when they had been in power—such as Labor in Britain—to partake in deregulation and privatization. But since deregulation and privatization had also been the policy of most other parties, it was not a satisfactory explanation. Was it perhaps the fact that social democracy had carried out more or less successfully its traditional program in the decades after the Second World War—the establishment of a welfare state—and had thus exhausted its historical mission?

Or was it because the working class, the traditional base of social democracy in Europe, had numerically shrunk over the years with the deindustrialization in Britain and other countries and that it had furthermore changed its character as the result of the influx of so many immigrant workers? The trade unions had always been the great ally of social democracy, but they too had greatly lost in numbers and influence. Some suggested that these radical Socialist parties no longer had the courage of their convictions. Most of them were pacifist, but none had dared to abolish their armed forces and to redirect the defense budgets to education and other daring and promising economic projects. But this was more than a little utopian in a world in which swords had not yet been beaten into ploughshares and in which the defense budgets had shrank so much that their reinvestment elsewhere would have made little difference. Would much higher taxation of the wealthy have been effective? But taxation was already high in most European countries. Privatization was often unpopular, but nationalization even more so.

Seen in historical perspective, the decline of European social democracy had a variety of causes. Few, even among its critics, doubted that such a party was needed. But at present it is no more than a group of well-meaning people eager to fight for freedom and social justice, in search of a great political task to sponsor in order to become the harbingers of a new world. The old unofficial hymn of German social democracy was the song, originally imported from Russia, "Mit uns zieht die neue Zeit," or "With Us the New Age." But so far Social Democrats have not grasped what exactly the new age is and what it needs.

Was the decline a matter of (missing) leadership? Probably to some extent, and this could refer also to Europe in general. "The Internationale" had told the nineteenth-century working class that salvation would come not from god, emperor, or popular leader. But the early hymn of the German socialists, written by Georg Herwegh, carried another message: "Give us the standard bearer of the new age and we shall carry freedom to all of Europe." And so the European left was waiting for leaders as well as banners and messages. The failures of the free market and the trend toward plutocracy will sooner or later create political resistance. But the reaction has as yet failed to provide clear political alternatives.

A period of great and growing unhappiness generated manifestations, sometimes violent, of students protesting steep increases of university fees. It led to demonstrations by other groups of society particularly hard hit by the crisis and the ensuing policies of cuts and austerity. But it did not produce any signpost to the future. Instead, two French pamphlets received much attention. The first, *Indignez vous*, was written by a former French diplomat who called on his compatriots to be more aware of the inequities of contemporary society and to do something about it, to return to the ideals of the French resistance, to treat illegal immigrants better, and to condemn Israel more severely. The second, by the quasi-anarchist *comité invisible*, was originally published in 2007; while aparently ultra left in intent, it drew much of its inspiration from non- or antidemocratic German thinkers of the far right such as Carl Schmitt and Ernst Juenger. It was antimodern, opposing, for instance, life in big cities. Well-wishers could perhaps detect a certain romanticism in its pages. But there was no indication what kind of society was desired by the authors or on what economic and political foundations it should rest. In brief, the vision of the future was as invisible as the identity of the authors. Such publications and the fact that they were taken seriously reflected the helplessness and confusion that prevailed in circles from which alternative policies were expected.

As I shall try to show later on, if the social contract on which European politics is based at present should break up, if the welfare state disintegrates, a peaceful development seems unlikely even in the presence of left-wing ideological confusion and the absence of leadership. Such a development would lead to radical political change that could be accompanied by violence. It could bring the downfall of the present political institutions and not just of the financial institutions that generated the crisis. Whether the old or the new left would benefit from it is not certain. Once upon a time, the working class was believed to be the main agent of social reform, even revolution. But the working class has shrunk and its ethnic composition has largely changed. It now consists to a considerable extent of immigrants or their descendants, and their political orientation is not that of the left. The middle class, whose living standard and income has declined even before the crisis set in, and in particular the young generation, above all students, will be in the forefront of the struggle against the present system.

A NEW WORLD ORDER

EUROPEAN VIEWS CONCERNING A NEW world order (and Europe's place in that order) have changed dramatically and quite frequently in recent decades. As the cold war ended and the Soviet empire collapsed, it was generally assumed that the United States had emerged as the sole superpower. This was the period of new slogans such as "global hegemony," "world government," "liberal imperialism," "neoliberalism," "neoconservatives," "end of history," "globalism and antiglobalism," "triumphalism," "unipolar," and so on. Underlying was the belief that a new constellation had emerged and that, since America was the only country economically and militarily capable of projecting its power to any part of the globe, it would dominate world affairs in the foreseeable future. This prospect did not provoke great enthusiasm on the European left or on the (nationalist) right, but neither did it generate great panic, except among the antiglobalists.

There was fear that America, lacking international experience, would engage in unwanted and even dangerous adventures that would involve the rest of the world. But on the whole, there was the conviction that the countries of Europe would be freer to engage in their domestic affairs and reduce defense spending, which had risen during the cold war, since there were no more outside dangers. Some major trends in world politics were more or less ignored. During the cold war, with all its negative aspects and threats, a certain order had been imposed by the leading powers. As the cold war ended, there was a marked growth of disorder, nationalist and religious extremism in various parts of the world found much greater freedom of maneuver—and of mischief.

For the same reason—the absence of any serious threat or even competition—one would have expected a movement away from NATO, which had come into being because of a specific danger that no longer existed. The American military presence in Europe was gradually reduced to 65,000 soldiers, but a variety of bases was still maintained. But in principle, there was no strong opposition in Europe against the alliance (occasional protest against the "militarization of the continent" apart), because of inertia or because it was, from the European point of view, an inexpensive insurance. In America too there were growing voices asking against whom Europe needed to be defended and, if it did, why could it not do so by its own forces?

The other development that was overlooked for a long time was the rapid growth of the economy of some of the developing countries, above all China and India. True, as far as scientific and technological development was concerned, these economies were hardly rivals of the EU, but in many other respects, as customers and as suppliers, they were of course of great importance. Nor was great attention paid to the increasing dependence of Europe on oil and gas supplies from Russia and the Middle East. Such was the fixation on the United States that events in other parts of the world, if not overlooked, were not attributed great importance. It would perhaps be exaggerated to call it blindness, because there were voices claiming that the world had not become a safer place with the end of the cold war. But there was little willingness to listen. This was the period of the "European dream."

Why? The explanation is probably mainly psychological. Having lived for decades in a period of tension and conflict, many Europeans felt that at long last they could breathe freely and look with confidence to the future. The cold war had imposed constraints, such as a dependence on America, which could now be discontinued. The list of resentments vis-à-vis America on the part of the European elites was long and need not be reiterated. It was partly cultural in character and goes back a long time. There were political complaints: American military involvements in Iraq and Afghanistan, which were thought by many in Europe to be unnecessary, costly, dangerous, and in any case ineffective in execution; America's uncritical support for Israel, thought to be responsible for many (if not all) major problems in world politics; the economic crisis of 2008 and 2009, considered largely America's fault in view of the huge debt the United States had incurred over the years and the irresponsible if not fraudulent behavior of major American banks (and the reluctance of Washington to impose strict controls over them).

In brief, there was a widespread feeling in Europe that the old continent would be better off if it were to put greater distance between European policies and those of the United States. In any case, the American moment in world history seemed to be over; the unipolar world was being replaced by a multipolar one. At the very height of the economic crisis, European media were giving much space and greater attention to stories about the "Weakling America," the suffering of the average American, Washington's enormous indebtedness, the high rate of unemployment, and other disasters. Usually ignored was that during the last decade the United States had increased its GNP and its population had also grown. Compared with Europe, America had in fact grown stronger. In 2000 the U.S. population was 59 percent as large as that of the fifteen members of the EU. Ten years later it was 78 percent.

While not essentially wrong, the European media failed to notice (or to bring to the public's attention) that the situation in many European countries was at least as bad and that the very survival of the European Union was no longer certain. This was true, for instance, with regard to the debt incurred on both sides of the ocean and the plutocracy that had emerged in the United States—but also in Europe. It was a childish reaction with a dose of *schadenfreude*, but psychologically understandable: "We may be in trouble, but the Americans are not better off"; sorrow shared is sorrow halved—"chagrin partagé," "el dolor compartio," "geteiltes Leid ist halbes Leid." Every European language has words of comfort, but they do not help much.

Back to the European perspective in the precrisis period. True, there were some minor dark clouds on the horizon such as global terrorism. But these dangers, it was widely believed, could be contained, perhaps as the result of negotiations and minor concessions; or perhaps they would gradually fade away. What happened in New York and Washington in September 2001 came as a shock and evoked sympathy in Europe. But its impact faded away after a short time. There was no second attack on such a scale. As for Russia, it seemed in the 1990s that it had been weakened so much that it could not possibly constitute a danger to Europe. When Russia again became stronger and more assertive after the turn of the millennium, there was the hope of a strategic partnership and normal and friendly relations on the basis of common interests.

The eastern European countries did not share such optimism, but their misgivings were not taken very seriously. It was thought in the West that their attitude toward Russia had been greatly shaped by negative historical experience and that they did not realize that a new Russia had come into being. Many Europeans and some Americans sincerely believed in the dawn of a new historical epoch in which European values and the European way of life (different in important aspects from the American) were the wave of the future, that it was a shining beacon to the rest of the world inasmuch as human rights were concerned, that, in brief, the rest of the world was eager to become like Europe and that it was only a question of time until it would become like Europe. In short, having lived for decades through a period of fear, or at any rate of little hope, it was perhaps only human wanting to replace this period with an era of wishful thinking. A new world had come into being, a world without enemies, perhaps even without serious rivals.

But even in a world without threats and enemies, Europe needed a foreign policy and a strategic concept. In yet another conference (Lisbon, December 2009) the so-called EU external active service (EEAS) was established, something akin to a foreign ministry and a diplomatic corps. This seemed the answer to Henry Kissinger's famous complaint (its authenticity has been disputed) many years earlier that if he wanted to contact Europe, there was no one he could call. Now at long last there was such a person to answer the phone. But what could he (or she) say in reply? Within a few weeks, a secretary general and two deputies and six director generals were appointed. Since pay was generous and applicants for the other posts did not expect to be overworked (up to fifteen weeks of annual holidays were offered), more than a thousand EU diplomats

were hired within a short time with more appointments to
follow and a diplomatic academy to be established as well.

Interpretations of what had been resolved in Lisbon were
contradictory. Some maintained that the member states had
more or less surrendered the right to make decisions regarding foreign and defense policy as their sovereign right based
on their national interest. Others, on the contrary, said that in
this respect nothing had been surrendered or signed away.
Secretary of State Hillary Clinton declared in a common press
conference with the EU foreign minister Lady Ashton, "I expect that in decades to come we will look back on the Lisbon
treaty and the maturation of the EU that it represents as a major milestone in world history." Such a view may prevail one
day, but, at the time, it seemed a gross misreading of what had
actually happened; neither France nor Germany, and certainly
not the UK or any other country, had given up the right to take
major foreign policy and defense decisions as they thought fit.
What did happen was that to the many EU institutions, which
were often doing the same thing, another one had been added.

Under the Lisbon treaty, member states were required to
coordinate their actions and frame a common defense policy.
Each member state was obliged to consult the others before
taking action on the international scene that might contravene
EU interests. In the past, unanimous voting had been manda-
tory. Now, majority voting was introduced for twelve different areas of foreign policy. But what did it mean in practice?
Commentators said that "procedure has again trumped policy" and that the EU had "equated the expansion of its bureaucracy with an expansion of its capacity to take on a greater
share of global responsibilities." In brief, as another commentator remarked: "All talk and no action."

Was such criticism unfair? The two most important foreign policy and defense events during the years after Lisbon were the meeting between Angela Merkel, Nicolas Sarkozy, and Dmitri Medvedev, and the British-French decision to closely coordinate defense efforts. Germany wanted to make serious progress on the road toward nuclear disarmament, but France had not the slightest wish to do so, and even Britain would not follow the German lead. Even the German desire was more a wish than a well-thought-out strategy. Neither initiative had been discussed (let alone agreed upon) with the EU.

Nor were policy and trade relations with China coordinated or any other issue of importance. On some occasions the situation became exceedingly confused; when President Sarkozy called for sanctions against Iran after that country had announced that it was now a nuclear state, the foreign minister Lady Ashton declared that she on the contrary agreed with the Chinese foreign minister, who had declared such discussion about sanctions premature and hasty. Whatever her personal opinions, Lady Ashton was employed as the spokeswoman of the EU, not of China.

If there was no European strategy and active foreign policy, what were European views facing a new constellation in world politics? No American president had been popular in Europe in recent decades; Carter had been too weak, Reagan too strong. Reagan's "empire of evil" speech was not forgiven; it was thought most undiplomatic, if not warmongerish. The fact that under Reagan the cold war came to an end was only reluctantly admitted. Bush Junior was particularly unpopular; only Obama was truly welcome, before he became president. When he appeared in Berlin before the elections, he attracted an enthusiastic audience of hundreds of thousands.

Obama's sweeping victory was hailed by José Manuel Barroso, the European Commission president, as a turning point.

It would help to overcome the financial crisis, fight climate change, engage in a new multilateralism, end the mistrust toward the United Nations, bring peace to the Middle East and the rest of the world, and do many other excellent things. A BBC poll showed that in 17 of 22 nations tested it was believed that Obama's win would improve America's relations with the rest of the world. But even at that time, only 33 percent of Europeans thought that strong American leadership in world affairs was desirable. A quarter in Europe thought an assertive United States highly undesirable. Only a very small majority thought that America and the EU had close enough values to make diplomatic cooperation possible and face international crisis together.

It did not take very long to realize, as *Le Monde* put it, that Bush had not really been the problem and Obama was not the solution. Less than two years later, the president of the European Commission told the White House that European frustrations with Washington were great and growing, that there were fundamental disagreements, countless missed opportunities, and culminating in a fundamental clash of ideas at the G20 meeting in Seoul.

What had Obama done wrong? To begin with he had not paid much attention to Europe and had concentrated on other parts of the world instead. He had tried to solve the economic problems by spending America out of the crisis, whereas Europe had limited its spending and adopted a policy of austerity. He had not brought a new era of international cooperation; there was no new "new deal" covering financial stability and global prosperity. The war in Afghanistan still continued, and even Guantánamo had not been liquidated. True, many Guantánamo inmates had been released, but European countries had been most reluctant to accept any of them and there had been loud protest against returning them to their home countries, where they would be rearrested. Some terrorists had reappeared fighting the West from new bases in Yemen and elsewhere. It was not an easy problem to solve.

America had made mistakes; some European solutions had been dubious or illusory. Did responsible European statesmen really believe that if White House attitudes toward the United Nations and other international institutions became less abrasive (which they did), the UN would become an important factor in world affairs making decisive contributions to solving world crises? European expectations were, to put it cautiously, unrealistic, based on the expectation that America would retreat from a unilateral policy practiced by the Bush administration but that European policies would not change, so there was no need to give greater support to American foreign political initiatives.

Foreign political issues such as the Iranian bomb were not really problems to be tackled by Europe except through diplomacy. And if diplomacy did not work, the issue had to be dropped from the European agenda, more or less elegantly. An unknown seventeenth-century Hapsburg statesman had advised his country not to engage in war but to increase its power and well-being by profitable marriages with other royal houses. In a similar vein, the EU was advised in recent years by its wise men not to engage in risky foreign policy but to produce and trade. But this was not easily done.

There was an inclination in Germany (and also in France, less in Britain) to establish a special relationship with Russia (Germany's traditional trading partner) and also with China and other countries. After all, Washington was also engaging in a reset of relations with Russia. But it did not take long to realize that no special relationship would give the EU (or

Germany or France) great benefits that others might not get. Individual corporations might derive considerable profits but seldom if ever the economy of a country as a whole. Russian oil and gas would not become any cheaper and European access to the Chinese market not less complicated. In fact, European access to certain important raw materials and especially rare minerals was bound to become more difficult and expensive, as China had been buying up many promising sources of such materials, especially in Africa and Latin America. Furthermore, the human rights records of China and Russia had certainly greatly improved since Soviet and Maoist days. But it was still far from ideal—and what the EU was preaching to the rest of the world. There was a school of thought in Europe believing that Russia would join NATO if only NATO would be more forthcoming. The fact that most of the political class in Russia, as well as public opinion, still regarded NATO as its main enemy and that for this reason there was no chance for such a rapprochement, was not known, or, if known, was suppressed.

On occasion, it was suggested by some advisers that the EU establish closer relations with fundamentalist (but not terrorist) Islamic movements. But this was not very popular as far as European public opinion was concerned, nor was there great enthusiasm for such an approach in the Middle East. Great expectations (soon to be disappointed) were attached to the "Arab spring" of 2011, which was thought to open a new era of democracy, human rights, stability, and peace in the Middle East and well beyond.

Some European politicians and political commentators persuaded themselves that the Israeli-Palestinian conflict was the most important and dangerous problem in the world and that, if it were solved as the result of stronger pressure on Israel, this policy would bring about a far-reaching improvement with the Muslim world: terrorist attacks would decrease in number and intensity, Muslims living in Europe would be more willing to integrate, and, who knows?, even the price of oil and gas might go down a little. These, needless to say, were mere fantasies. The policy of successive Israeli governments was stupid, was shortsighted, and, if further pursued, would turn their country into a nondemocratic state, since Jews would lose their demographic majority. It would lead Israel to a one-state, binational solution away from a Jewish state and would not lead to peace in the Middle East. All this is true, but the idea that a solution to the conflict would somehow bring about important changes in world politics and ease Europe's standing in the world was mere wishful thinking.

Nevertheless, such EU initiatives were likely to continue as the Democrats' setback in the midterm elections of 2010 presaged a political stalemate as far as the next two years were concerned. America's position in world affairs was clearly weakened and would remain weakened, in all probability, at least for some years to come. This gave the EU some more freedom of maneuver, but freedom to do what? Was it a good time to dissociate from Washington, or, on the contrary, should it establish closer relations?, for the EU also went through a crisis of survival as the result of its sovereign debt and the danger of impending bankruptcy in a number of countries.

Both sides needed allies more than before. As Barroso said in 2010, "The transatlantic relationship is not living up to its potential. I think we should do much more together. . . . It would be a pity if we missed the opportunity." But such exclamations left as many issues open as they raised—what potential and what common action and where? If Obama would see himself an Atlantic rather than a Pacific president, if he would be a little less naive concerning China's and Russia's potential and goodwill as pillars of a new world order, as guarantors not only of stability but the good of all mankind, he would still be faced with a disunited Europe sharing many illusions or rationalizing European weakness. Both sides were in great need of a fresh impetus for a new beginning. Such sudden turning points have happened in history, but not very frequently, and in 2011 one was looking in vain for signs presaging such a near miracle.

THE FOUL MOOD OF EUROPE

DURING THE EARLY YEARS OF the twenty-first century, the mood in Europe toward the EU deteriorated markedly. It was only natural that the erstwhile European enthusiasm (*Europe ma patrie!*) did not last forever; a major historical process such as European unification was bound to suffer setbacks. There was the tradition of a thousand years of nation-states and consequently the reluctance to give up sovereign rights, which had been taken for granted since time immemorial, and to pass them on to a largely anonymous institution whose supreme loyalty was not to a nation-state but to a community of nations.

In these circumstances, it was only natural that critical and hostile attitudes would emerge and become stronger. There was wide agreement that economic cooperation should be strengthened but much hostility toward centralization and attempts to make the union politically stronger. Such attitudes were present even while the economy was doing well, and certain countries like Spain, Ireland, and some of the eastern European countries made spectacular headway. It was inevitable that as the economic situation worsened, attitudes would become more hostile.

According to polls taken in the summer of 2010, the percentage of those who thought that membership in the EU was a good thing had decreased by 10 percent in one year; only every other German still favored EU membership. There was a similar decline in support in virtually all European countries, and the percentage of those European citizens who associated the EU with democracy fell below 20 percent.

When the crisis reached its height and the distinct danger appeared that the Eurozone would collapse, a report prepared by Felipe González, the Spanish prime minister for the EU, stated, "The choice for the EU is clear: reform or decline." But what did reform mean? Stronger governance by the center, no doubt. But what guarantee was there that stronger governance would be more effective? And in whose interests would it be exercised? Around the same time, the EU launched the EU 2020 strategy, a project aimed at preparing the union for the challenges of the next decade, stimulating growth, creating more and better jobs, and making the economy greener and more innovative. But these sentiments had been heard often before. The belief that the EU was the preferred actor to deal with the economic crisis was down to 26 percent, higher in some countries such as Belgium (which during a whole year was without a government) and Poland, lower in others.

What were the main concerns of Europeans during the crisis? They were worried above all about the economic situation and unemployment. Other concerns referred to the euro. In some leading countries the belief had gained ground that the old national currency had been preferable, and even in Greece it was believed that using the drachma would have made it easier to cope with the crisis. Other complaints widely voiced concerned the waste of money by the euro bureaucracy.

Even in Eastern Europe, which had substantially benefited

from membership in the EU, skepticism increased. The new government that convened in July of 2010 in Prague, headed by Petr Nečas, was defined by informed observers as "mildly euroskeptic," whereas Vaclav Klaus, the president of the Czech Republic, was very outspoken on the subject. During the Czech presidency over the EU, he refused to fly the European flag at his seat on the Hradcin. In one of his speeches, he compared the European Union to the Soviet Union, which was a puzzling statement because his attitude toward Russia was by no means hostile.

The crisis, in briefest summary, revealed the weakness of the EU. In theory it should have been entitled (indeed obliged) to enforce its rules, particularly the deficit limits of countries. But the big countries that broke rules (Germany and France) were not punished, and neither were the smaller ones. But wouldn't the crisis give a strong impetus for far stricter control in the future? The Germans and a few others insisted on it (meaning more or less automatic punishment for transgressors), but there was great resistance against it. It was pointed out that it involved changes in the existing treaties. Such changes could be introduced, but there were other problems as well. There was great resistance against cuts in the social budgets, such as cutting child benefits or raising the pension age. The distance between the euro elite and the individual countries of Europe had by no means shrunk. On the contrary, the popularity of Brussels was at a low point. Somehow, the Eurocrats had not managed to become more popular, or, at the very least, to instill a feeling of trust and elementary loyalty among those they had been chosen to represent.

Political Europe was changing during the first decade of the new century. In the UK, Germany, and France, left-wing governments had been replaced by conservative-liberal ones, but they too lost support within a short time. The Scandinavian countries and the Netherlands were ruled by centrist coalitions, and in Italy, Berlusconi seemed to hold on to power forever, until, in 2010, his alliance gave clear signs of brittleness. Only in Spain did the Socialists stay in power, but even their hold seemed to be weakened. However, it was also clear that there would be a swing against the parties in power at a time of economic crisis when unpopular measures had to be introduced. In some countries, notably in Hungary, a sharp swing to the right and even the extreme right took place.

Our main interest has to be focused on the major countries— Germany, France, and the UK. At the height of the crisis, when the very future of the EU seemed at stake, the opinion was voiced that if there was a breakdown, a new beginning would have to be based on the big three or four and their cooperation. But the leading European powers were preoccupied with domestic affairs, and the relations between them, particularly between Sarkozy and Merkel, were not too close; to a certain extent, it was a matter of temperament. Sarkozy wanted things to be done in a hurry, whereas Merkel, who was presiding over Europe's largest economy, wanted careful consideration, since most of the funds, whatever the project, were bound to come from Germany. Furthermore, both were anxious that their national interests were not harmed. Sarkozy and Merkel stood for European political cooperation but felt no particular urge to make progress quickly toward closer collaboration, whereas the British concept of the future Europe was more that of a loose economic framework.

However, Brussels developed a momentum of its own. According to the Lisbon treaty the EU was to have a president ("President of the European Council") and a foreign minister. It is not certain whether those who had signed these earlier treaties had considered the implications. Be that as it may, in 2009, first steps were taken in this direction, and Herman van Rompuy, a former Belgian prime minister, was elected. He began his duties in January 2010. At the same time Lady Catherine Ashton was elected unanimously High Representative of the Union for Foreign Affairs and Security Policy. During 2010 EU ambassadors and many other appointments were made (a foreign policy staff of 7,000 was envisaged).

These appointments were welcomed by some—Gordon Brown called Rompuy an excellent consensus seeker—but more often criticized. A former German prime minister called the new president of the EU Mr. Nobody, and when Rompuy went from Brussels to Paris in a motor cavalcade rather than choosing a train and security considerations were mentioned in explanation, the general reaction was that no one would have recognized the president of the EU anyway. As for the unfortunate Lady Ashton, the near consensus among European parliamentarians was that she did not have experience or ideas or plans. Her previous political experience had been in British local politics and the CND (the campaign for nuclear disarmament). Some of these criticisms were undoubtedly unfair, but it was clear that those elected were not exactly the strongest and most capable personalities.

However, would more forceful and experienced politicians have been more successful? The ambassadors of the EU in the world's capitals could announce (as they did) that the EU was still alive, but not much beyond this. Their tasks and freedom of action were not defined. They could not possibly explain a European foreign policy if none existed. Were they more than figureheads (plastic garden gnomes), as some unkind commentators noted? What was the division of labor between the new EU president, the president of the European Commission

(José Manuel Barroso, the former Portuguese prime minister and head of the European Commission), and the chairman of the council of prime ministers that changed every six months? There was no indication that the national governments had any intention of giving up their foreign policy interests by surrendering them to a new Brussels bureaucracy.

All along the history of the European Union there were doubts and antagonism with regard to this new organization and euroskepticism, mild and severe, above all in the UK. But it manifested itself as a political force only to a limited extent. This changed during the crisis of 2008 and its aftermath, when anti-EU political parties made considerable headway in many countries. Earlier on such populist parties (on which more later) had been preoccupied with the dangers of uncontrolled immigration, but from the 2008 crisis on, criticism of EU policy became of equal if not greater importance.

EUROPEAN FOREIGN POLICY

THE NARROW LIMITS OF EUROPEAN influence in world affairs are all too obvious by now. Europe contributes more to the United Nations budget than any other group of nations, and the same is true with regard to aid to developing nations. Europe prided itself on having saved in recent years 150 million people from starvation—or worse. One would expect, therefore, that European demands and interests would be given some consideration in the activities of the UN, but this has not been the case. The defense of human rights has been high on the European agenda. It figures on or near the top in countless speeches and official documents. But since Europe on its own has been unable or unwilling to do much in this direction, it has been trying to operate through the UN. However, the results have been lamentable.

The European Union was preaching democracy, more politely to major powers, more bluntly to small countries, but without any effect. Such charades were self-defeating, as Chinese diplomats were commenting. Europe had become weak but the fact had not yet registered. A weak continent could no longer interfere in the affairs of others, and the frequent ineffective admonitions only exposed its impotence and subjected it to ridicule. In the 2009 European Union report on the EU and human rights at the UN, it says:

> The number of states most fiercely opposed to the EU human rights positions at the UN has swollen to 40 this year from 19 last year. Since the late 1990s when the EU enjoyed the support of over 70% of the General Assembly in human rights votes, support for the EU's human rights position has haemorrhaged: the EU has lost the backing of 13 former allies on human rights votes in the last year—117 of the U.N.'s 192 members now typically vote against the EU.

The constitution of the UN Council for Human Rights, until very recently headed by Libya, is an obvious example. It consists in its great majority of nondemocratic countries with a bad or very bad record in human rights and acts almost entirely to secure immunity for those of its members (or the friends and allies of its members) who have been guilty of crimes against humanity. One third of the members of this organization belongs to OIC, the Organization of the Islamic Conference, which insists that the legal system of these countries is faultless, cannot be modified, and should not be controlled. It is true that one country and one country only has been frequently condemned (one needs hardly mention what country). It would be a heavenly state of affairs if crimes against humanity would be limited to one single country, but it hardly needs pointing out that this is an absurdity.

Darfur is an obvious example of the consequences. An order for the arrest of Omar el-Bashir, the Sudanese president, was issued in July 2008 by the International Criminal Court, the only such case. But it was of no consequence, because the League of Arab States and the African Union showed solidarity with el-Bashir. He has since been traveling freely in many countries, including Turkey, and was received as an honored guest. The UN has been impotent in the many cases of genocide in Asia and Africa, including Rwanda, Burundi, the Congo, Bengal (now Bangladesh), and others. Even in the former Yugoslavia, the United Nations and Europe proved incapable to intervene, and only because of an American initiative were measures taken. As the German representative dealing with issues of human rights in the UN noted, the number of countries respecting these rights has been shrinking, and the position of the West has weakened. Politics and feelings of solidarity apart, the UN followed the advice of the old Latin adage—*Parvus pendetur fur, magnus abire videtur*—"the small ones are hanged, the big are not touched." If so, what was the point of perpetuating Europe's participation in these charades?

It could be argued that in view of the general weakness of Europe and perhaps above all its dependence on the import of oil and gas (as well as exports to these and other countries), it could not afford to antagonize those on whose goodwill it depended. But in this case, it would have been more honest to desist from verbal denouncements and condemnations that everyone knew meant nothing.

The issue of Turkey's joining the EU is a complicated one, and a variety of reasons could be adduced for and against. But some background information would have helped to shed light on Cameron's emphatic statement (he strongly favored Turkey's adhesion), which sounded strange, even somewhat ludicrous, to Britain's European partners. The aim of his mission to Ankara in 2010 was to double British exports to Turkey (much if not most of British diplomacy has become preoccupied with selling British goods). Turkey, according to Britain, will be the second largest economy in Europe (after Britain) in

2050—an assumption not shared by many economists. It should also be borne in mind that there are few immigrants from Turkey in the UK, nor are many expected to arrive, which is very much in contrast to other European countries. And lastly, Cameron's vision of a European Union is that of a loose economic alliance rather than a close political federation. In other words, unlike Germany and other countries, Cameron was not worried by the influx of hundreds of thousands of Turks from the less-developed regions of their country.

As for Iran, Europe has recommended negotiations concerning that country's nuclear armament. These endeavors have failed, as have the American attempts to reach an agreement with Tehran. Reluctantly, Europe, with the opposition led by Sweden, has joined Washington in adopting economic sanctions. In fairness, it should be said that these are the most far-reaching measures ever agreed upon by the EU. It blocked also the export of dual-purpose items (which could be used for both civilians and military), and it certainly caused a pained outcry on behalf of certain corporations that had been exporting such goods earlier on. But whether these measures would prevent the construction of Iranian bombs was doubtful, to say the least. Anything going beyond this was unthinkable from a European point of view. Since Washington also showed little inclination to adopt more effective measures, it meant that Europe had accepted the considerable likelihood not only of Iranian bombs but of proliferation, a war in the Middle East (with all the likely consequences for Europe's energy supply), and other highly unpleasant results. All this meant that Europe was taken less and less seriously by the rest of the world. It was no longer a factor to be taken into account in international affairs.

It is not clear whether in recent decades European leaders

and the political establishment still had any visions for the future. The resolutions adopted by EU conferences were insipid generalities, often meaningless and probably not taken very seriously by their authors. To the extent that there was vision, it was based on the assumption that economics would trump politics and that political morale would flow from affluence and social security. It was a noble dream, and there was (and is) great resistance against awakening from this dream.

EUROPEAN DEFENSE:
A FAREWELL TO ARMS

THE HEADQUARTERS OF BOTH NATO and the EU are in Brussels, the former in the eastern part near Zaventem, the latter between Brussels Park and Leopold Park, near the Schuman station. But geographic proximity has not made for very close cooperation, which is not surprising because there has been overlap as both organizations have, to a large extent, dealt with the same issues, and there has been rivalry inasmuch as both organizations have been competing for the same resources. Not all member states of the EU belong to NATO, but all the major ones do.

As the cold war ended, many thought that the age of military conflict was over, and the world was moving toward international cooperation, diplomacy, and soft power. In those circumstances there would be no need to maintain more than symbolic forces. But such optimism did not last very long. Ever since, both organizations have been trying to rethink and define their *raison d'être*, discussing "Atlanticist" and "Europeanist'" agendas, various new strategies, equitable burden sharing, missile defense, and other topics. Relations between NATO and the EU were defined at a conference in Washington and again in Lisbon in 2010. Relations between Russia, the EU, and NATO were debated for years.

Of what importance is the EU in the field of defense—is it a paper tiger or a power of substance? Defense has played a minor role in the history of the European Union, and at times it has been altogether ignored. In the early years after the Second World War, attempts were made to set up a European army, but they led nowhere and NATO came into being instead. In theory, it should have been possible to maintain a European army because the total expenditure on defense of the European countries amounted to 200 billion euros (this was admittedly before the cuts caused by the austerity budgets of 2011 and thereafter). But for a great variety of reasons, it simply was not going to happen.

More recently, all kinds of institutions such as the Common Security and Defense Agency and the European Defence Agency were founded by the European Union, but almost all in a mere advisory capacity. Conferences and seminars took place in which the global order and the European order were discussed, as well as the multipolar world and the unipolar moment, not to mention the "arc of responsibility," the "new security architecture," and the security dialogue. Humanitarian missions were planned under the so-called Petersberg agreement (2001). What it all meant was unclear, but it seemed not very important. A European security strategy was first decided upon in December 2003 and updated in 2009. But it was a strategy without significant military forces. There was infinitely more talk than action, more seminars than military maneuvers. If an American president had once said that the business of America was business, the business of the EU was the common market, the economy. It was to engage in crisis management, but not to be involved in war fighting.

If the EU had a strategic concept, it was, as mentioned earlier, that big wars had become impossible, that with the end of the cold war the world had become a much safer place.

Gradually the rest of the world would become more or less like Europe, reasonable and peaceful. In these circumstances, the establishment of European defense forces seemed hardly necessary. Enormous efforts would have to be invested to overcome the different interests and traditions of the various European countries, a great amount of money would be involved, and the outcome would be uncertain. And, in addition, there was of course NATO, to which most EU countries belonged. In *Project Europe 2020,* the need to fight organized crime and terrorism is briefly mentioned, the necessity to develop close relations with neighbors and to act together "in defense of our interests." But what defense meant was not clarified, nor what interests—did it mean more seminars and more dialogues, or something in addition? This was never made clear.

True, for decades, a rapid-deployment force had been discussed, which should have included 60,000 men, 400 aircraft, and 100 warships. But this remained one of many blueprints. Instead, some 19 mini operations have taken place since 2002, ranging from Bosnia to Congo, Chad, and Somalia. These were in the main training missions for judges and policemen rather than military operations. For example, 2,500 soldiers were dispatched to Bosnia, 1,700 to Chad, and 1,800 to Kosovo. They were permitted to undertake tasks such as combating pirates and to escort food vessels on the seas but not to fight rebels in this postheroic age.

While such peacekeeping missions should not be belittled, it is obvious that the figures involved are quite insufficient to deal with situations in which well-armed and determined local forces were involved—say in Lebanon or Somalia. When in the 1990s the need arose to establish a minimum of order in Europe's backyard, the former Yugoslavia, the European Union was incapable of taking the initiative and had to rely on the United States. For a long time, there was no answer when Greece requested help policing its border with Turkey, through which tens of thousands illegal immigrants arrived.

As the years passed, it became clear that the hopes for a new and safer world order after the cold war did not materialize. On the contrary, new conflicts and tensions appeared. China, which had shown much reticence and caution during the cold war, began to flex its stronger muscles, and on occasion even demonstrated hubris. The number of failed states grew, including some that were of vital interest to Europe as suppliers of important raw materials. The proliferation of weapons of mass destruction continued. NATO became weaker and was not doing well in Iraq and Afghanistan. American interest in Europe declined, and Russian foreign political ambitions were less clear than the West desired. There was the urgent need to establish Mediterranean and antipiracy patrols to bring illegal immigration and smuggling under control. But in the deliberations of the EU, war fighting and the use of force did not figure. Defense had become a synonym for preventive diplomacy, always with the assumption that such interpretation would be shared by all others.

The idea that this approach might not be sufficient in the years and decades ahead gained ground in 2008–10 as the result of a number of developments. One was the growing conviction that Europe could not indefinitely count on the American safety net. Another was the great recession, which led to cuts in defense spending in most European countries. It became more and more obvious that, on their own, European countries could no longer provide the very minimum of security needed. Since it seemed unrealistic to wait for an initiative (let alone full agreement) on the part of all twenty-seven EU members, the initiative was taken by the two countries, Britain and France, that provided half of European military expenditure. Britain and France were the only major European countries (other than Poland) that spent 2 percent of their budget on defense. At the same time, there was greater willingness on the part of the EU to consider certain ideas concerning a European security treaty that had been mooted by Russian leaders.

These new departures were welcomed. Close military cooperation in peacetime between the UK and France had been thought impossible earlier on by most. But they created new problems by undercutting the idea of EU defense, and, of course, the role of NATO. Some media hailed these "sweeping defense pacts." Others called it an "entente frugale," in contradistinction to the pre–First World War "entente cordiale," given the modest means at the disposal of both sides. Deployments of no more than five thousand soldiers were envisaged. Other projects included industrial cooperation, for instance with regard to unmanned combat air systems (such as drones) and also collaboration over British and French nuclear deterrents.

It remained unclear, however, how such collaboration would fit into other plans that had been discussed, such as President Medvedev's proposal of 2008 (repeated subsequently) concerning a new security treaty for Europe that included Russia and the United States ("from Vancouver to Vladivostok"). This was followed by a more specific treaty draft in December 2009 and also a dialogue between NATO and Moscow.

These various initiatives reflected interest and goodwill in the West and the East to cooperate more closely, but it was not at all clear what they would mean in practice. It was highly unlikely that Russia would join NATO, which had been its bugbear for decades, nor was it clear what the assignment of the small British-French deployments could be, except perhaps peacekeeping missions, which could equally be carried out by the United Nations or some other organization. The Baltic countries and those of Eastern Europe, on the other hand, were expecting from a European defense treaty reassurance against pressure by the Russians, which the Merkel-Medvedev plan hardly provided.

In these circumstances, the eastern Europeans were more likely to seek such assurance in a NATO-sponsored security treaty rather than a German-Russian pact. The ideas floated to include Turkey in these schemes rested on the assumption that this not very helpful NATO member would be interested in "strengthening its European identity" (as one of the many position papers put it), an assumption that could, however, by no means be taken for granted.

In brief, the various plans to strengthen European security have not made significant progress. It is not even certain that they will provide a minimum of security if threats should arise. To stress this is not euroskepticism but a realistic evaluation of what has not been achieved. The European Union as an effective defense force does not exist and is not likely to come into being in the next ten or even twenty years. Hervé Morin, a recent French defense minister (whose role models, he says, are de Gaulle and Mendès-France), said in 2010 that Europeans have to decide whether they want to be actors in a play they are not writing.

It would perhaps be more accurate to say that Europeans prefer not to think about the consequences of their actions, hoping like a famous Dickens character that something or someone will turn up in an emergency to protect them. In a similar vein, Uffe Ellemann-Jensen, a former Danish foreign minister, wrote in December 2010 that if Europeans want their ambitions to be taken seriously, they must find ways to deal with the decline in European military power. Political leaders will have to tell their constituents that there are limits to how much military budgets can be cut as the "peace dividend" from the cold war's end was digested long ago. Otherwise, Europe's global political ambitions become untenable. It could well be that these words refer not to a process likely to take place at some future date but to one that has already occurred. Europe's global political ambitions, to the extent that they still exist, are no longer taken very seriously in Asia or even the Middle East, where defense spending is higher than in Europe. If Europe reached the conclusion that it can no longer afford the minimum of defense spending needed, it might be wise to adjust its rhetoric correspondingly in order to prevent embarrassment on future occasions.

AMERICA: PITIED, ENVIED, FEARED

THERE HAVE BEEN TENSIONS BETWEEN Europe and America almost since the days of Christopher Columbus. In the eighteenth century, the French Abbé Raynal, considered a leading expert on America, wrote, "America has poured all the sources of corruption on Europe." Another clergyman, the Abbé Corneille de Pauw, wrote, "Americans, a degenerate species of the human race, cowardly, impotent, without physical strength, without vitality, without elevation of mind." There was, at the time, widespread conviction that the discovery of America had been a mistake. However, there were also famous other voices, such as Goethe's, and, despite the jeremiads of the politicians and the intellectuals, many millions of Europeans migrated to the United States in the hope of finding there a better and freer life. There was Tocqueville, more optimistic about the future of America than his own country—or Europe in general.

Some visitors did not like what they saw, among them Maksim Gorky, Knut Hamsun, and Ferdinand Kürnberger, the Viennese author of the famous nineteenth-century novel *Der Amerikamüde* (a hundred years later the novel was reprinted in East Germany to little political effect). Unlike the hero of this story of disappointment, very few of the immigrants returned to Europe. Most stayed and built America and, in the course of time, showed enough vitality to make her a great and powerful country. At the same time, American views of Europe were by no means admiring. The founding fathers strongly admonished their successors not to get involved in Europe's internal quarrels.

Such tensions between countries were of course by no means uncommon—conflicts between Britain and France, between France and Germany, between Russia and the German-speaking countries dominated the eighteenth and nineteenth century. The fact that America came to Europe's help in the First and Second World Wars and helped rebuild the old continent gave rise to feelings of gratitude but also its opposite; there was fear of American political and cultural domination and of American mass culture (above all Coca-Cola and later also McDonald's). The fact that, after 1945, Europe was weak and America strong generated resentment.

Anti-Americanism was by no means monopolized by one party. It was as strong among the Nazis as among the Communists and also widely accepted by the center. There were big anti-American demonstrations in Paris as early as 1950 at the time of the war in Korea, and these feelings reached their climax during the younger Bush years. Feelings of cultural superiority aside, there was the conviction that American foreign policy was cowboylike, militarist, likely to draw the whole world into a horrible conflict in which weapons of mass destruction would be used. Nor could it be argued that the negative attitude toward certain aspects of American life was unjustified in the age of casino capitalism running wild. As these lines are written in December 2010, Wall Street's thirty-five leading financial companies were handing out $144 billion in bonuses to some of their executives. Most of these institutions had been doing badly for their shareholders.

The conviction gained ground in many circles that, after Bush, there would be a far-reaching change in European attitudes toward America. When Barack Obama visited Europe before he became president, masses of people congregated to express great enthusiasm. But, as some had predicted, these feelings were not going to last. For, while Bush had indeed been unpopular, there had been strong anti-Americanism under Clinton too. Bush served to a large extent as a lightning rod. The underlying phenomenon was far deeper and more complicated. It would probably persist as long as America was a great power (all great powers in history have been unpopular), and it was not even certain that a weak America that had abdicated from world politics would mean an end to anti-Americanism. The United States had been Europe's protector for decades, and if it would no longer fulfill this function, it will probably again be blamed. Yet another reason for anti-Americanism was Washington's support for Israel, which according to polls carried out in Europe, was thought to be the country most dangerous to world peace—ahead of Iran, North Korea, and others.

Why attribute such great importance to relations between Europe and America? It was and is largely a one-sided affair; most Americans were not very well informed about European moods, and, if they had known more, they would not have greatly cared. America's attention has switched to a considerable extent to the Pacific and to a lesser extent to Southeast Asia and the Middle East. It was perhaps symptomatic that President Obama, during his first two years in office, had devoted little if any time to European affairs and even stayed away from important conferences dealing with Europe's future.

But for Europe, the American connection remained of paramount importance, not only because of NATO but also because Europe measured itself by American standards, largely ignoring the changes that were taking place in world politics and even more in the world economy. When the financial crisis occurred and even thereafter there was a considerable amount of *schadenfreude* in Europe. We may have suffered, but America had become even weaker, perhaps it was about to collapse, wrote *Der Spiegel,* the leading German news magazine, in October 2010. True, the American economy was in a mess, but even in its weakened state the American position was stronger than that of Europe. Its growth rate was higher, its unemployment rate slightly lower.

This preoccupation with America, based quite often on a less than full understanding of that country, was bound to lead European observers to dangerous misjudgments. America for most European countries was both example and deterrent, and this led them to forget that if indeed the United States was in steep decline, Europe would in no way benefit but, on the contrary, would suffer politically and economically. Furthermore, with the growth of the Chinese and the Indian economies (and some of the smaller Asian economies), not only new opportunities but also new dangers would open up for Europe. Its dependence on exports was growing, and it was more than likely that the high-quality commodities exported by Europe would gradually be produced in countries with far lower labor costs, with which Europe could not compete.

Anti-Americanism is important, even though its importance as a major political factor in Europe has sometimes been overrated. In creating a European identity, the continent had to distance itself from its longtime partner and ally. As Andrei Markovits has noted, for most of the time anti-Americanism has been an elite phenomenon; only a minority of Europeans had a negative opinion of America. Millions had voted with their feet, as has been pointed out, and emigrated to America despite all the horrors that had been described in countless books and pamphlets. In the twentieth and twenty-first centuries the academic brain drain was virtually all in one direction—few American intellectuals went to Europe except for visits, short and long. During the early years of the twenty-first century there was a significant change in European attitudes toward America. Positive opinions dropped from 62 percent to 41 percent in France, from 78 percent to 45 percent in Germany, and from 50 to 38 percent in Spain. But no one could say with any certainty how deep these feelings were running.

Anti-Americanism became almost a lingua franca of the European elite, culturally perhaps even more than politically. America was (to cite Markovits again) uncouth, arrogant, uncultured, devoid of authenticity, having no respect for human rights, ignorant, inconsiderate, and aggressive. It was not the lingua franca of the general public: An American friend after a long stay in London told me that dozens of neighbors (but also perfect strangers) had told him that New York was wonderful, a much more beautiful city than London; however, my friend had made his home in the East End of London, not in Hampstead or Chelsea.

This exchange of politeness was not wholly one-sided; the European elites were often considered in America decadent and defeatists, the workers lazy, British diplomats and politicians supercilious and weak, their French counterparts duplicitous and untrustworthy. More positive views prevailed among the intelligentsia of the countries of Eastern Europe, which had been exposed to Soviet rule.

But with all this, it seemed doubtful that anti-Americanism, either in a blunt or more subtle form, could serve as the main plank of an emerging European ideology. For if Europeans did not think highly (to put it mildly) of America, they also did not think highly of one another either. Northern Europeans said they had little in common with the Italians (and the northern Italians had similar feelings with regard to those in the south). The Germans were respected but certainly not loved. The French were suspected of pursuing only their own national interests and caring about a united Europe only to the extent that they could dominate it. As for the British, they were believed to be no good Europeans at all, to have only a limited interest in a European Union, and to be trying to keep the Europeans at arm's length as long as possible.

The antagonism toward America was rooted to a large extent in the fear of its power. Strong powers, let alone superpowers, have never been popular in world history. Their very presence has always induced misgiving, to say the least. As Reinhold Niebuhr commented many years ago, "Hatred is compounded by envy and fear, and power breeds both." The fear is justified, because powerful individuals and even nations, when they make benevolent pretensions, are not as generous as their pretensions or even as their intentions.

Like all generalizations, this too does not always apply. When America suffered from states of weakness this did not make it necessarily more popular. If Turkey took its distance from America and even became hostile on various occasions, it was precisely because Turks were no longer afraid of America. They would never have dared to provoke the Soviet Union in the postwar period precisely because they were apprehensive of Soviet and Russian threats.

With the election of Barack Obama, there was hope in Europe and also in some circles of America that a new page had been turned in European attitudes toward America. Madeleine Albright, a former secretary of state, was one of several commentators arguing that the deterioration was all the fault of the second Bush administration, and it is true that the style of Bush and his representatives had been very unwelcome in Europe. Many European politicians had believed that America, traditionally a violent country, had overreacted in the fight against terrorism after 9/11, that the second Iraq war (and possibly also the first) was unnecessary and harmful, that Europe was not defended in Afghanistan, and that, generally speaking, American foreign political initiatives should be closely coordinated with European interest since European experience in the conduct of foreign affairs is vastly superior to American "cowboy" extravaganzas.

While Europeans perceived Obama to be moving in the right direction, he did not proceed fast and far enough. Guantánamo was not closed down within a few weeks, American retreat from Iraq was not fast enough, and, despite certain promises, an end to the war in Afghanistan was too far ahead. When the Democrats suffered heavy losses in the midterm elections of 2010 and with the emergence of the Tea Party, there was a fresh upsurge of anti-Americanism in Europe. The Tea Party militants had received a bad press in Europe; they were wacky, incoherent, perverse, nutty, dim-witted, buffoons, charlatans. "Mad" and "bad" were some of the milder epithets used. Interestingly, some American radical commentators, like Noam Chomsky, took a more nuanced approached toward this new phenomenon and its motives.

To regard such reaction to the Obama administration and its policies as completely wrong would certainly be exaggerated. There were extreme, anarchic, and stupid elements in these reactions. But it was ignored, for instance, that the foreign policy of the Tea Party (to the extent that it had any clear concepts) would be more likely to lead to isolationism and to fortress America than a militant American foreign policy. It was equally ignored that the foreign policy (or its absence) of sections of the Democrats would have the same effect. American imperialism, liberal or otherwise, was not liked, but isolationism was not welcome either. Domestic developments in the United States—also under Reagan and Clinton—did not add to its popularity. America, in brief, found it exceedingly difficult to do right by Europe.

As far as the defense of Europe was concerned, much of the burden had been shouldered all along by the United States through NATO. The defense budgets of the countries of Europe had been only a fraction of the American, and, as a consequence of the economic crisis, they had been further slashed. According to a British white paper in 2010, the main dangers facing the UK were terrorism and hostile computer infiltration. Consequently, 40 percent of the army's tanks and artillery were scrapped. Britain would have only one aircraft carrier, the *Arc Royal,* capable of launching fixed-wing jets. But it seemed doubtful whether there would be planes for aircraft carriers. As prime minister Cameron said, "We have been punching above our weight in the world and we should have no less ambition in [the] future." But punching above one's weight more often than not ends in disaster, and, rhetoric apart, Britain's capacity to intervene in conflicts in distant countries virtually disappeared, even if military cooperation with France, which underwent similar cuts, became much closer.

For some, the drastic reduction of the defense budget was a source of pride as a milestone toward universal disarmament. These cuts indeed made sense on the assumption that in the world of tomorrow there was no need for military power. Unfortunately, it was a mistaken assumption. The cuts meant a decline in British global influence at a time when military power still continued to count. If additional evidence was needed, it was provided by developments in North Africa in early 2011. When the civil war in Libya broke out, Britain and France took an active (but halfhearted) part intervening militarily in protection of the anti-Khaddafi forces. But Germany and Italy refused to intervene, and the British-French intervention limited to air cover did not prove sufficient to bring this civil war to a speedy end.

A MORAL SUPERPOWER?

THE TERM *CIVILIAN POWER* (*MORAL superpower* came somewhat later) was coined in Britain in the early 1970s by several leading public intellectuals such as François Duchêne, Andrew Shonfield, and Alastair Buchan, all of whom headed or were connected with prestigious think tanks such as Chatham House. It rested on the assumption that military conflicts were becoming less and less likely, that economic interdependence was far more important, and that in order to move with the times and not be left behind, the European Union, at that time barely twenty years old, had to base its policy on this insight. This led in subsequent years to discussions of what civilian power really meant. New terms were introduced such as *moral power, ethical power, smart power, soft power*; with all differences as to detail, there was broad agreement on a number of propositions.

One such proposition was that Europe would gradually become a superpower owing to its economic strength, and that its main assignment should be working for economic development all over the world, the strengthening of international law, climate change, improving health services, and other issues beneficial to all humankind.

In the 1990s, the conviction prevailed that Europe had already become a superpower. With the breakdown of the Soviet empire, it seemed obvious that the world had turned a decisive corner—a world without war, at least without major conflicts. Consequently, additional assignments were suggested for the new superpower. These included the enlargement of the EU, more humanitarian assistance for nation building, closer trade relations with those not associated with the EU, more peacekeeping when and where necessary, and, generally speaking, the promotion of democracy and human rights not by exerting force but by being a model.

Such optimistic beliefs were based on the assumption that the world was moving in a desirable, more humanitarian direction; corrupt, authoritarian, and intolerant governments were losing ground and were being replaced by democratic (or at any rate *more* democratic) ones. The new European superpower, to repeat once again, would spread its gospel by being an example, showing the whole world its vision of liberty.

The most recent version of this school of thought, such as was presented by Tim Parks in 2010, was far more subdued if not pessimistic. The vision that Europe needed was to refashion the world rather than fight to keep it as it is: "Our present way of life is unsustainable . . . our present torpor" a "disgrace." There was no "shared vision," no courage, and no enthusiasm. "The notion that life is about . . . the accumulation of goods and [being an] amiable partner in a castle home will have to go." But he asked, "How could such a change of heart be achieved?" The author admitted that he had "no idea and little hope." "Openness, generosity and tolerance seem essential," he wrote, adding "It's not going to happen. To talk about the future of Europe is to risk serious depression."

Richard Youngs, another supporter of this school of thought

and critic of EU inaction on human rights abuses throughout the world, demanded that, despite its enfeebled state, Europe must not stand aside spinelessly but "[get] strategic about ideals and values." It should give up its outdated sphere of thinking and return to the core values, including the energetic promotion of human rights. The EAS (the new foreign ministry of the EU) should report each year in what way it has helped advance human rights in ten countries. At the same time, the author stresses that discretion and respect for other political values and systems are absolutely necessary.

How helpful is such advice? Control mechanisms as to how much has been achieved in the field of human rights may be all to the good, but what progress will the poor EAS be able to show unless it is based on a considerably stronger European Union? (Not to mention the fact that there have been such evaluation studies in the past—without much effect.) And what if the political values and systems of the other countries are incompatible with or even opposed to those of the EU?

It is sad to follow the road from the enthusiastic belief of the 1970s and 1980s to the depression and the lip service of a generation later. It was bound to happen, because this belief was based on unrealistic foundations and a false view of the world and the direction in which it was moving. How had this come about?

A number of reasons come to mind. It was a mistake to believe in the 1970s and even after the breakdown of the Soviet Union that the world would be relatively free of conflicts. If the likelihood of a nuclear war had receded (but even this could not be taken for granted in an age of proliferation), the cold war with all its threats had imposed a certain amount of control on the part of the superpowers, especially the United States and the Soviet Union. With the end of the cold war such brakes no longer existed. Nor was it taken into account that, with the economic rise of China, its political assertion would become stronger and that even seemingly economic conflicts could spill over into the political field, such as access to oil and other raw materials. Nor was it anticipated that new aggressive forces such as jihadism would make their appearance on the international scene. Finally, there was the mistaken belief that Western (European) values would become universally acclaimed and emulated. The human rights situation in China and Russia had of course improved since the days of Stalin and Mao and might improve further in the future. But at present neither the rulers of these countries nor public opinion thought that European-style democracy and liberalism was a fitting way of political life for them. The fact that Europe had not done too well under this system only strengthened their aversion. What they saw in Europe was a strong economy—at least until the recent crisis—but also weakness, lack of purpose and unity in most other respects, and a continent rationalizing its weakness by the frequent evocation of democracy and human rights.

Soft power is important and has often been neglected by major powers, not least the United States. But soft power has its obvious limits. In the 1970s and 1980s, Albania had the strongest broadcasting station by far in the eastern Mediterranean, but it did not do the country any good. (The fact that as a political or economic model Albania was not the most attractive of systems certainly played a role.) An example of the successful application of soft power was the campaign during the last phase of the cold war, which resulted in many tens of thousands of Russian Jews being given the permission to emigrate under the pretext of family reunion. In this instance the wish of the Soviet authorities to get rid of many of them no doubt played a decisive role. It would be difficult to think of an instance in which soft power succeeded where the core interests of a country were concerned.

Given this huge discrepancy between rhetoric and reality, between how Europe saw itself and how others saw it, what could Europe do to promote its ideas and interests? It is, after all, the essence of a power, let alone of a superpower, to have influence and the ability to use it to some effect on the international scene. That *power* was not a synonym for *military power* goes without saying, but it was even more mistaken to assume that, given the realities of the contemporary world, there could be power without military strength. Such delusions were bound to lead Europe down the road to irrelevance.

How did European policy makers and substantial sections of the political class react to such a mistaken assessment of the political situation that was due partly to wishful thinking and partly to ignorance about the world outside Europe? This is yet another fascinating question that demands detailed and dispassionate investigation. A variety of strange theories about the nature of power were developed in our time by some political scientists, but it is doubtful whether the political leadership was influenced by academic theories, was even aware of their existence—they reached their mistaken conclusions independently and instinctively.

The EU, according to its charter (articles 6 and 11) and countless resolutions, is firmly committed to promoting the universal principles of liberty and democracy, respect for the rule of law, human rights, and fundamental freedoms through its presence in international forums. It also says that it "has a wide range of tools to implement the human rights dimension of its [foreign] policy . . . among them more than 30 human rights dialogues with third countries, eight human rights guidelines, regular declarations."

What is one to make of statements of this kind? To take even one of the less important points mentioned ("through its presence in international fora"), in 2010 the European Union was refused membership in the General Assembly of the United Nations. It could rightly be argued that such membership would have made no difference at all inasmuch as the promotion of human rights is concerned, but it certainly reflected the low prestige and international standing the EU enjoys.

Even the most sympathetic outside studies of the EU's record in this respect have noted that, while the EU is high on rhetoric, its achievements are less than modest. Even at the best of times (in the 1990s and up to about 2005), no one expected the EU to work miracles promoting democracy and human rights. If the demands of the EU in this respect—democracy and the rule of law—endanger the hold of the ruling elites of a major country, say China or Russia, they will under no circumstances be ready to accept them or even make compromises. Political survival, needless to say, is more important for them than being in the good books of the European Union. Far from progressing on the road to a more democratic system and respect for the rule of law, developments in Russia and China have gone in the opposite direction during the last decade. Whenever the EU or individual Western countries have offered advice in this field or registered protest, they have been told, in increasingly rude terms, to mind their own business.

But not only superpowers have been impervious to EU admonitions. The same applies to most other countries. Oil-producing countries had to be treated with great caution in view of Europe's dependence on its energy supply, others because they belonged to groups of states that offered mutual protection, such as the UN Human Rights Council, the African

Union, the Arab League, and the Organization of the Islamic Conference. The Organization of Latin American States has refused to take a stand whenever human rights problems arise in Venezuela. An investigation of the efforts by the EU to promote democratic governance in the Arab world reaches the conclusion that the EU has failed either to overcome the resistance of Arab regimes or to consolidate the local forces of reform. It should have been noted, however, that the "forces of reform" more often than not were the Muslim Brotherhood and allied organizations—under a variety of names.

This regrettable outcome stems from three factors: a lack of clarity, a conflict of priorities, and a conflict of interests. Of these three causes, the third is undoubtedly the most important by far—lack of clarity and a conflict of priorities can be overcome, but a conflict of interests might be, and often is, fundamental. What has been said about the Arab countries applies to the rest of the world, perhaps with the exception of some isolated, small, and powerless countries. But if the EU were to concentrate its human rights efforts on these countries at the exclusion of all others, some of which are more powerful and well connected, it would expose itself to obvious criticism—if not ridicule.

What can be done by Europe in its present state to promote what were considered its core values? European promotion of human rights and of democracy, even on the purely rhetorical level, has palpably declined over the years and will decrease more in the future to the extent that Europe will be further enfeebled, economically and in other respects. When France is trying so hard to persuade the Kremlin to buy French assault ships and not those produced by other nations, it is pointless to expect the French government to protest Russian human rights violations. But why single out France? The same applies to all European countries and, of course, to the EU. The UK cannot afford to offend Turkey if it wants to enhance British exports to this country, as Italy could not afford to provoke the anger of Khaddafi, one of the main investors in the country.

True, there have been a few praiseworthy exceptions. Norway, not a member of the EU, decided to give the Nobel Peace Prize to a dissident, just as Sweden, even during the cold war, gave Nobel prizes to Pasternak, Solzhenitsyn, and Sakharov. Norway, an oil and gas exporter, could afford to ignore Chinese threats, and Sweden could always argue that the Nobel Foundation was not a government institution and it therefore could not intervene in its decisions.

Would it be preferable if the European Union were to declare a moratorium on protests against human rights violations, unless and until such protests are more than mere talk? Should it decide that, as a matter of principle, there should be no threats, let alone military intervention, even in blatant cases of massive genocide—that such actions should be left to the United Nations, even if it is clear that this is no more than a meaningless evasion? Such a policy would have the advantage of honesty and the end of make-believe, but it would be a painful admission of failure. Against this, it could be argued that even gross violators of humanitarian norms dislike publicity and that even halfhearted criticism may on occasion help improve a situation.

There is no ideal way out of the dilemma facing the European Union. A continuation of the present policy of paying lip service will reveal European impotence more than necessary and even expose it to ridicule. Europe has been sidelined and ignored on many occasions in the recent past; it is a sad list of humiliation, and why prolong it? But neither can it give up the moral principles on which the union is based unless it decides to become what it was originally—a coal and steel enterprise. Individual European countries are running the danger of being reminded of the cardinal principle of Victorian education, that children should be silent (unless asked for their opinion) in the presence of adults. The issue of how much promotion of democracy and freedom Europe can afford will be one of the most difficult confronting the EU and its individual members in the years to come, always assuming that the European Union will still exist.

Human rights are very important unless they collide with strategic and, above all, business interests. This is not written in the EU constitution but appears in Brecht's famous *Three Penny Opera*. It is and will be the guideline, "Erst kommt das Fressen, dann kommt die Moral." Beggars, as Brecht put it so vulgarly, cannot be moralists.

TOWARD A EUROPEAN NATIONALISM

SHAKEN BY THE AGONIZING SLOWNESS of European unification and shocked by the rejection of the European constitution in 2005, a number of prominent European intellectuals published manifestos during the first decade of the twenty-first century. In earlier ages such initiatives had come from political leaders (including Napoleon and Hitler, when the war Hitler had unleashed began to go badly). In the absence of such statesmen, Jürgen Habermas and Jacques Derrida took the initiative in a manifesto published in May 2003, titled, "February 15, or What Binds Europeans Together: A Plea for a Common European Foreign Policy, Beginning in the Core of Europe."

Why February 15? Because on that day, mass demonstrations had taken place in many European capitals, protesting the launching of the second Iraq war. As Dominique Strauss-Kahn wrote a day later, "On February 15, 2003 a new nation was born—the European nation." However, this anti-American statement did not prevent Strauss-Kahn, in later years, from working closely and amicably with the American authorities as the head of the International Monetary Fund in Washington, D.C.

Such emphasis on the world-historical significance of February 15, 2003, may have been unwise, even apart from the fact that it was wrong. Even if the war in Iraq was misguided and showed that there were basic differences of opinion between Washington and much of Europe, it was not an ideal starting point. If this war had been carried out efficiently and with overwhelming power, if it had resulted in the overthrow of the Saddam Hussein regime in a very short period and also the exodus of American forces from Iraq, the Habermas-Derrida initiative would have appeared quite unconvincing as a call for paving the way toward a common European foreign policy. Their search for a "European identity" was legitimate, as was the thesis that the values and interests of the United States were not necessarily those of Europe and that there could be no Western solidarity ignoring this.

Habermas, who argued all along that the new project should be spearheaded by the core powering Europe, France and Germany, tended to ignore the fact that there was by no means unanimity between these two, and there was even less between them and the other members of the EU, who could, after all, not be ignored. Habermas, Europe's most prestigious public intellectual and the driving force behind the document, admitted that his project was a construct, that its final aim was not to create yet another nationalism but to lead to a Kantian perpetual peace. It rested on a number of dubious assumptions— that a world power could come into existence by resting entirely on soft power and rejecting *a priori* violence, that a feeling of European nationalism (or patriotism) already existed all over the continent and was sufficiently strong to serve as a base for the emergence of a great power. Would it not be necessary to exclude Britain and most of Eastern Europe from such an entity, and would not the inclusion of a country such as Turkey be altogether unthinkable? Should Hungary be included?

A number of leading European intellectuals joined in the debate. Most of them argued that while the search for a European identity was praiseworthy, the self-determination of Europe as un- or even anti-American was doomed; it would not unify Europe but divide it. Umberto Eco adduced another reason for moving toward closer unity: American interests were focusing more and more on other regions of the world—Europe must unite or become irrelevant.

And yet, with all its weaknesses, the Habermas-Derrida manifesto reflected a strong current of thought and mood in Europe. Even those who believed in Western solidarity, at least up to a point, felt that it should not be pressed too far. America was a superpower and its ambitions and policies were not necessarily those of Europe, whose global interests were quite limited. This had been emphatically stated years earlier by Hubert Védrine, the French foreign minister, and the theme was again taken up. Many, probably most, Europeans were not convinced that their interests had to be defended in Iraq and at the Hindu Kush. Europe had no desire to play a global military role in defense of a world order. Europe was preoccupied with its internal problems and the defense of human rights as befitting a civilian superpower.

NATO might have been a vital necessity at the time of Soviet aggression in the 1940s and 1950s, but the cold war was over and there was no Soviet threat. The global constellation that had led to the establishment of NATO and, generally speaking, a close alliance with America had changed, and what had been self-evident thirty years earlier—following the American lead—was no longer true.

The Habermas-Derrida manifesto had no political consequences. However, its underlying idea of a European foreign policy should have been put in place, because potentially there was much sympathy for it. Why did it remain a dead letter? Because the differences between the various components of the EU were too big, because the Habermas-Derrida project would have meant a basic reorientation and transformation and there seems to have been an instinctive objection against major reforms. A European foreign policy would have meant reducing individual countries' sovereignty and freedom of action.

Instead, the individual countries of Europe preferred to conduct their own foreign policy, especially concerning Turkey and Russia. Britain became a strong proponent of Turkey's joining the EU. Some of its advisers argued that Turkey had made enormous economic progress and was likely to make more, that it had become both a European and a regional power, and that under its AKP leadership it had become truly pro-Western. Other countries, especially those with a strong Turkish community, were far less enthusiastic, claiming that, on the contrary, the country had become more anti-Western (and anti-democratic) under the AKP leadership, that it was neither a European nor a regional power, and that it had strengthened its ties with Iran and the radical Arab countries, even hosting Omar al-Bashir, the Sudanese leader who was on the Interpol wanted list. These debates are likely to continue for a long time.

As for Russia, Europe faced a major handicap. Moscow preferred to deal with the individual European countries rather than the EU as a whole. But this meant that the Russians, like the Chinese and others, would try to play one country against another to obtain more favorable conditions. Europe understood that, in principle, it was in its best interests if it coordinated its policy vis-à-vis its eastern neighbor. But commercial rivalries frequently prevented such coordination.

Europe's other strategic handicap is its dependence on import of oil from Russia (82 percent of the total) and gas (57 percent). Ways have been considered since 2005 to reduce this dependence, but without great success so far. This dependence is likely to grow in the case of a Middle Eastern war. It has been argued that Russia was equally dependent on its European consumers, since oil and gas are its most important exports by far. But this is no longer true to the same extent because of China's enormous energy needs and the building of direct pipelines leading from the Siberian oilfields to the east.

Russian relations with the UK remain frosty because London is not willing to close the book on the FSB (the successor of the KGB) activities in the UK, of which the murder of Alexander Litvinenko, a Russian defector who had worked for the KGB, was the most spectacular. Russia refused to hand over Andrei Lugovoi, suspected of the murder, and he became a member of the Russian parliament. Putin seemed to have been annoyed that so much fuss should be made about this minor affair.

RUSSIA AND EUROPE: PARTNER AND RIVAL

RUSSIA FIGURED PROMINENTLY IN EUROPEAN thinking during the early years of the new century. Was it friend or foe or something in between? Did it belong to Europe or to Asia? It was a crucial issue for Europe even after the downfall of the Soviet Union. It took Germany a mere fifteen years after the defeat in the First World War to return to the international scene as a major player. It took Russia even less time after the breakup of the Soviet Union. In what direction was Russia moving? What will it be like ten or twenty years from now?

Speculation on the future of nations rests on both near certainties and on imponderables that defy prognostication. Russia's demographic problems provide some near certainties. More than twenty thousand villages and small towns have ceased to exist. This could be explained as part of the general worldwide process of urbanization. But the Russian birthrate is very low, even though it has climbed a little as of late. Russian men now live a little longer than they did ten or twenty years ago, but this merely means that Russia is graying more quickly. The immigration of central Asian and Chinese workers and traders to Russia continues, and a radical reversal of these trends seems most unlikely. It means that there will be fewer ethnic Russians in the future. More Muslims now reside in Greater Moscow (1.5 million, more according to some estimates) than in any other European city. Will Russia be able to hold onto the Far East and all the territories beyond the Urals?

As for the imponderables, if it had not been for Mikhail Gorbachev it seems quite likely that the Soviet system, though eventually doomed, would have been able to hang on for another decade or two. From 1972 to 2008, the price of crude oil went up from $2 a barrel to $150 (in September 2011 it was $87). In other words, Russia would still be the Soviet Union, and the enormous windfall would not be ascribed to the wise statesmanship of Putin but to Leninism and to the farsighted leadership of Yuri Andropov's successors. To a decisive extent, Russia's prospects will continue to depend on the export of gas and oil.

If the harrowing predictions about global warming come true, Russia may soon have access to considerable quantities of rare and important raw materials now locked under permafrost, although it may not be able to extract them without outside help. Even if plans for economic modernization fail, Russia may not face a dramatic economic deterioration and a corresponding political crisis. But expectations in Russia have risen in recent years, and they will probably not be fulfilled.

Russians traditionally have a strong belief in manifest destiny: the idea of Moscow as a third Rome, world revolution, the building of socialism in one country, and so on. Among the current intellectual-political fashions are the so-called "Russian idea" and neo-Eurasianism, neither very friendly toward Europe and the West. Democracy is not held in high esteem, a feeling that is largely the result of well-placed people under Yeltsin's rule (but also during the years thereafter) who have used their positions to amass great riches. Not all of

Oswald Spengler's predictions were wrong. In a book published in 1933, he wrote that when the Communist regime breaks down, its leading officials will turn into shareholders. Thus, *democracy* became a synonym in the late 1990s for *kleptocracy* and *oligarchy*. For centuries, Russia had a terrible record as far as corruption is concerned. When the nineteenth-century tsar was asked by a relative what was new in his native country after a long absence, he answered, "Nichevo, kradut" ("Nothing, people are stealing"). But the practices of the 1990s were different from the pervasive "normal" corruption; a few people in strategic positions acquired enormous riches in a very short time.

The new Russian self-confidence, generated by the oil windfall, reached its climax in 2006 and 2007 in a number of speeches by the then president Putin. He called his opponents "jackals funded by the West" who wanted a weak and chaotic Russia, much like their sponsors. In a speech in Munich in 2007, he dwelt on the decisive change in the global balance of power and the decline of Europe and the United States. On another occasion, Putin predicted that by 2020 Russia would be not only among the richest and most powerful nations but also among the most progressive and dynamic. One of Putin's advisers declared that the whole world would be grateful to Russia for acting as a counterweight to Western hegemony.

Such speeches sounded more than a little overconfident considering that, despite the great windfall, Russia's GNP was not larger than that of France, namely $2.1 trillion. The mood changed after 2007, and there were several reasons for it. Russia was affected by the global financial crisis—the Russian GNP decreased by 6 percent. The Russian stock market nearly collapsed. The political elite began to realize that the country's near-total dependence on energy exports was dangerous.

Russia had to be able to compete on the world markets, and this could only result from far-reaching structural reforms. Putin's machismo was a shrewd strategy in the short run and added to his popularity, but it would almost certainly backfire in the long run.

Furthermore, it dawned on the Kremlin that the shift in the global balance of power, about which Putin had talked quite often and positively, was by no means all that favorable from the Russian point of view. How would the rise of China and the decline of Europe and the United States benefit Russia? What would happen in Afghanistan after the exodus of NATO? Moscow regards central Asia as its zone of "privileged interest," which also means a zone of political responsibility. Islamist groups would immediately threaten central Asia, and Russia would again be drawn into a conflict it escaped with great difficulty in the 1990s.

Why were these threats not recognized much earlier by the Kremlin? At the bottom of this blindness was the almost single-minded preoccupation and even obsession of the Russian leadership with the West and with NATO. These were the traditional enemies. All other problems seemed to be of little importance. But in the course of time, at least part of the Russian political elite began to recognize these trends. A new détente with the West was needed, and this strategy showed itself in a variety of events—Russia's voting for sanctions against Iran, expressing remorse about the Katyn massacre, inviting a contingent of NATO soldiers for the annual victory parade on Red Square.

It was precisely because of the relative decline of Europe and the United States that a Russian rapprochement with the West became more attractive and perhaps even imperative in Moscow's eyes. Hence the new conciliatory approach that manifested itself in the famous May 2010 document by the Russian Foreign Ministry about the improvement of relations with the outside world and in particular with the West. Hence also the call for economic reform, which implied political dé-tente, for it was unlikely that major Western investments and Western technology would be forthcoming unless they could be reasonably certain that Russian authorities, be it state or-gans or the police, would not interfere with their business, engage in extortion, and make normal operations and transac-tions impossible

The Kremlin was faced with a dilemma. Most accepted the necessity of basic economic reform. But they also understood that a political price had to be paid. It was unthinkable that there would be "concessions" (like in China before the Second World War), with one law for foreigners and another for Rus-sians. But Putin and the majority of the Russian political class, the *siloviki,* did not want the political price to be too high—not too much democracy and freedom, not too quickly. Democ-racy European-style was not in the Russian tradition. The country needed a strong hand and the various public opinion polls seemed to bear this out. The popularity rate of Putin and also of Medvedev, who replaced him as president, even while declining were higher than those of any Western leader. They probably would have been even higher if Russia had a free press, freedom of assembly, free political parties, a free judiciary, and other free institutions—which it does not. The majority of Russians appeared to be deeply conservative (and apathetic), maybe because the country had witnessed too much radical and negative change in its recent history. *Democrats* and *democ-racy* had become terms of opprobrium during the Yeltsin years when they also meant the freedom of some well-placed indi-viduals, the oligarchs, to enrich themselves and when for many *democracy* became a synonym for *kleptocracy.*

The belief in a specific Russian mission still seemed strong, and so did the old Russian propensity to believe in conspiracy theories—the more far-fetched, the more popular. It was still widely accepted that the breakdown of the Soviet empire was the greatest disaster of the twentieth century, that it had been caused largely by the West, and that Russia had no trustworthy friends and allies other than its army and artillery.

Putin and many of his entourage had received their political education in the KGB, where it had been axiomatic that the whole outside world was hostile or potentially hostile. And they also believed that, unless the security organs were strong, hard and omnipresent on the domestic front, Russia's enemies would undermine the country and cause its descent into chaos—or worse. Europe and America's constant harping on human rights abuses and the lack of democracy, even though it has abated somewhat, also annoyed the Russian leadership, who may have regarded it as a greater threat than any other. No such admonitions were likely to come from China or other Asian and African countries. The admonitions were more than annoying; they were potentially undermining the position of Russia's new class. Chinese policy weakened Russia in Asia, Western human rights policy hurt the hold of the Kremlin leadership, and, with all their patriotism, these leaders were apparently more concerned with the dangers to their power than the threats to their country.

But such time-honored anti-Western beliefs collided with new developments inside Russia and abroad. It was difficult to argue at one and the same time that the West was in steep decline but also a mortal threat. So the attitude softened a bit. The Russian foreign minister declared that NATO was no longer a danger, only a threat, although the difference between these two concepts was not immediately obvious. The Russian authorities did want *some* reform but not democratization.

The country was not ripe for it and perhaps never would be. It was to proceed vertically, from the top down, and to be steered by the state. It was argued that modernization had proceeded like this in most countries (except the Anglo Saxon).

Some on the Russian right admired the Chinese model. China had made, after all, tremendous economic progress and not given up the monopoly of power held by the Communist Party. They tended to forget that the Chinese model was hardly of any help to Russia. As one Russian commentator pointed out, the Chinese had been accustomed to work hard for very little money since time immemorial.

The more liberal elements in Moscow who favored deeper modernization did not want radical political change either, but they insisted on certain steps in this direction. They were aware that advanced technology could be bought, borrowed, or stolen from the West, but, according to past experience, more often than not it had been impossible to absorb such technology and make it work. The sort of modernization attempted in Andropov's days, the late Soviet period, was perhaps helpful to combat hooliganism in the streets, but it would not promote the kind of creative thinking needed for a modern information society. And, to repeat once again, reform seemed impossible without some kind of détente or even rapprochement with the West. Western corporations had of course been active in Russia (and even the Soviet Union) well before, but these had been isolated ventures. Something far broader and ambitious was now needed.

Putin assumed that not many political concessions would be needed to attract Western capital and know-how. Western capitalists were more interested in stability in Russia than they were in human rights. Given the economic situation in Western Europe, the temptation would be great to increase activities in Russia. The invasion of Georgia in 2008, the maintenance of Russian military units in Moldova, and the pressure exerted on the Ukraine had all been stumbling blocks on the road to the improvement of relations between western Europe and Russia. But the impression gained ground in Berlin and Paris that Russian ambitions did not go much beyond establishing the former Soviet Union as a sphere of "privileged influence." Russian claims in the Arctic are another potential bone of contention in a long-term perspective, but it has not yet become an acute problem.

Historically, Germany, followed by France, was Russia's main trading partner in the West. But at present, Russia accounts for very little in Germany's foreign trade—far less than the countries of Eastern Europe. Berlusconi also tried hard to ingratiate himself with the Kremlin. Relations between Moscow and London remained somewhat cooler, partly because of reasons already mentioned, such as KGB activities in the UK, but also because Britain felt less sanguine about business prospects in Russia.

The other problem was the EU, meaning the Europe of the twenty-seven. Most of the Eastern European and Baltic countries are traditionally suspicious of Russian designs, even though, outwardly, relations with the eastern neighbor had been normalized. This problem could be circumvented by direct meetings between German and French leaders with the Russians such as the meeting in Deauville, France, in October 2010. It was not universally welcome; *Gazeta Polska,* a Polish newspaper, published the news about the Deauville meeting under the headline, "Troika Carves Up Europe," without even the benefit of a question mark.

What Russia hoped to achieve in these meetings with German and French leaders was a general rapprochement, support for Russia joining the WTO (World Trade Organization), and free travel for Russian citizens in Europe without the need to apply for a visa. On one occasion, in November 2010, Putin mentioned the possibility of a common currency. But there were also constant conflicts of interest mainly concerning oil and gas supplies. Both the Russian agreement with Poland and with Bulgaria were in violation of the EU antimonopoly legislation.

This legislation was a thorn in the eyes of the Kremlin, which attacked it on many occasions. The Russian target was, after all, not only to get a high price for its exports, the mainstay of its economy, but also to have a monopoly position as far as Europe's energy supplies were concerned. But this was a matter of great concern to Brussels and the individual European countries. However desirable a rapprochement with Russia, they did not want to become Russian satellites. Furthermore, an EU-Russia political and security committee, chaired by Lady Ashton for western Europe, was to be established on top of the already-existing NATO-Russia Council, and this new committee was to set ground rules for joint civilian and military crisis management. Such bodies had been in existence for a number of years, and their importance had been questionable. It had not meant much in the past, and whether the "recommendations on various conflicts and crisis situations" would have any political significance in the future remained to be seen.

During the last few years, Moscow has shown great interest in close relations with Europe; suggestions for a Russian-European security pact go back to 2008, if not further. Gorbachev in an address to the Council of Europe in 1989 already had talked about a "common European home." The idea of a pact was repeatedly brought up by Medvedev and Putin in meetings with European leaders. If the Europeans insisted on including the United States, Moscow indicated that it might accept such a scheme on the assumption that NATO has lost its raison d'être, that America could eventually be squeezed out or lose interest, and that Russia, in any case, would have a veto right in such an organization. The probability is taken into account that other powers such as China or some Muslim countries might take a dim view of a European orientation on Russia's part. Moscow could argue that, in a Russian-European axis, the Kremlin would be the stronger partner and that the policy of such a purely defensive pact would be shaped to a large extent by Russia.

There was no great enthusiasm for a scheme of this kind in the European capitals and even less in Washington. It was considered an attempt to extend the Russian sphere-of-influence policy. While everyone favored peace, security, and close relations in all fields, these could be achieved within the framework of existing institutions, without giving the Kremlin a right of veto on virtually all European foreign political and defense initiatives. Would Europe have a similar veto with regard to Russian foreign policy, and could it have persuaded the Kremlin, for instance, not to invade Georgia in 2008? While relations between Europe and Russia had certainly improved, they had not improved to the extent of regarding contemporary Russia a Western-style democracy. The situation had been succinctly summarized by Dmitry Rogozin, the outspoken Russian ambassador to NATO and earlier a well-known right-wing politician, who said, "We are told by the West that they like NATO and the European Union as it is, they suit us fine. Well, they do not suit us. We do not like it."

While the European Union was willing to accept that Russia was not a democratic country by Western standards and under the present leadership was not on the road to democracy, it had no interest, if it could help it, in strengthening Russian political and economic influence in Europe.

MUSLIMS IN EUROPE

BEFORE THE OUTBREAK OF THE economic crisis, the problems of the Muslim minorities in Europe figured prominently on the agenda of the public discourse. There was awareness that integration had not worked well (Merkel had said it, as well as Cameron), and the emergence of "parallel societies" was not welcome by most. There had been the French riots of 2005 and fear of terrorist attacks following similar events in London, Madrid, and elsewhere. But the French riots simmered down, although law and order was never fully restored in the French banlieues, and there were no major attacks in Europe, even though quite a few were planned. Those eager to engage in active jihad went to Pakistan or Afghanistan to fight. Some plans to carry out terrorist attacks in Europe were hedged, but they seem to have been amateurish and were intercepted and prevented by European security forces.

Thus the Muslim problem in Europe, if indeed there was such a problem, seemed to have become a social and demographic issue, that is to say a long-term problem. When the recession came, it no longer figured prominently among the political issues discussed. But not for long. By 2009, it came back with a vengeance. In the traditional, most tolerant European countries such as Sweden and the Netherlands, anti-immigration parties made great electoral progress. In Holland, Norway, and Denmark, they were part of the ruling govern-ment coalitions. In Germany, a book published by Thilo Sar-razin, *Germany Abolishes Itself,* became a runaway, probably unprecedented, nonfiction bestseller and generated a debate that dominated public life for many weeks. This was followed by a speech by Angela Merkel, the chancellor, who was sharply critical of Sarrazin. She had not read his book, but admitted that integration in Germany had been a total failure.

Sarrazin was not a raving neo-Nazi but a Social Democrat, a banker who had been the finance minister of the Berlin local government. In his book, he stressed that the rapidly growing Muslim communities were becoming an intolerable burden on German society inasmuch as only relatively few of them could make a positive contribution to the German economy, social life, and culture because of their low cultural level and their lack of skills. There were some half-baked asides in this book about the genetic roots of Muslim backwardness on which Sarrazin's critics fastened. But these were not the main points he had made in his book, and most of the facts and sta-tistics he adduced were unassailable and were accepted and repeated by others with an intimate knowledge of the state of affairs, such as the Social Democrat mayor of Neukölln, the place with the largest Turkish concentration in Berlin.

Politically, Sarrazin did not fare well. He was dismissed from his post as one of the chief officials of Germany's state bank. In Germany, even more than in other European coun-tries, public opinion and printed opinion are often miles apart. The political class and most intellectuals almost unanimously condemned him, but there was a massive groundswell in his favor among the general public, and the debate that followed only showed how out of touch the elite was with public opinion. Sigmar Gabriel, head of the German Social Democrats, went on record demanding that those immigrants who did not want to integrate should leave the country, which went beyond what Sarrazin had ever suggested.

According to official German statistics, 72 percent of the immigrants between the age of twenty and sixty-four had neither graduated from any school nor had any other professional training. (Young women did, on the whole, better than young men, but most of them were not permitted to work outside their homes.) Other official German statistics showed that in another few years, in many major German cities, more than half of the age cohort under forty will be of Muslim background. This meant that but for a radical change, there would be a rise of a new underclass and "a vicious circle of poverty, violence and any lack of social perspective," in the words of one commentator. It also meant that an aging Germany, at present the main engine of the EU, would no longer be in a position to compete on the world markets.

Some of the Muslim immigrants had made it and been professionally successful. They became physicians, lawyers, businessmen and businesswomen, sometimes against considerable odds. Some of these successful immigrants have been quite critical of their own communities. Ahmed Abu Taleb, the mayor of Rotterdam, holds both Dutch and Moroccan citizenship. But this has not prevented him from advising his countrymen who did not like it in the Netherlands to pack their belongings and return to their home country. Jeff Cohen, the longtime mayor of Amsterdam, would not and could not have offered similar advice. Nyamko Sabuni, the Swedish minister for integration and gender equality demanded an investigation as to how many immigrant girls had been subject to genital mutilation, while she also opposed the veil and forced marriages. This initiative did not succeed, but again, no native Swedish official would have dared to make a similar proposal.

But these critics were a small minority. Furthermore, a significant part of Turkish students graduating from German universities were returning to Turkey because career prospects were better there. Turkish building workers, to give another example, had an excellent reputation all over the Middle East and central Asia, but few if any of them had migrated to Europe. Germany had absorbed immigrants from backward villages of eastern Anatolia. And the same was true, mutatis mutandis, with regard to the Pakistanis in Britain or the North Africans in France and Italy and Spain. Not the most qualified had come, but the uneducated and unskilled.

Professional success was important, but it would be mistaken to regard it as a panacea against radicalization and the spread of violent Islamism. Most of those who had joined the jihadists in Europe were not from the poorest and unemployed but rather from a middle-class background. Turkey has made considerable economic progress during the last decade, emerging as the OECD "tiger." But at the same time the influence of Islamism and anti-Westernism in Turkey has markedly increased.

Why had these problems not been recognized earlier on? Ideological blinkers were part of the explanation. Many migration experts had claimed that the lack or failure of integration was mainly, or even entirely, the fault of the Europeans, as if integration was a one way street. Every immigration wave, even in typical immigration countries such as the United States, had encountered hostility, which the immigrants had to overcome. The difficulty with Muslim immigration to Europe was that many of these Muslims did not want to become part of the host society but instead preferred life in a ghetto and were encouraged to stay there by their spiritual leaders and also by leading Muslim politicians. At the same time, they argued that they were discriminated against, and the young among them seemed to enjoy their victim status. Those who had made it and risen in the social scale more often than not moved out from the ghettos, unlike, for instance, in India, where the Muslim middle class continued to live in the districts inhabited by their coreligionists.

Among those who took a sanguine view of the results and prospects of integration were two French writers, Justin Vaïsse and Jocelyne Cesari, and a Danish American professor, Jytte Klausen. Vaïsse and Cesari claimed, following earlier statements by Oliver Roy, that certain difficulties in the course of integration or even conflicts, like the Paris riots, were essentially social, not religious-political in character, that, in brief, "it was Marx, not Muhammad, stupid." This statement was not entirely wrong. If the immigrants had attained within a few years a standard of living equal to that of Kuwait, there would, in all probability, have been no mass riots. According to Professor Klausen, who had interviewed some five hundred Muslim professionals, men and women in various European countries, all middle- or upper-class—businesspeople, professors, lawyers, and physicians—they were all content with their life and circumstances. They identified with their newly adopted country and were eager to participate in and contribute to its political and cultural life.

Perhaps the most optimistic was Dalia Mogahed, an American of Egyptian origin, head of the Islam project of the Gallup poll, who became President Obama's adviser on Muslim affairs. According to her findings, Muslims in France, Britain, and Germany have no sympathy for terrorist acts, do not want to isolate themselves from the rest of society, and are more loyal to their new country than the rest of the population. They also have greater confidence in the police, the government, the judicial system, the transparency of elections, and other national institutions.

Such findings, if correct, would be excellent news, for it would mean that integration succeeded above all expectations. If this were the true state of affairs, how to explain that the general public gained a very different impression? How to explain the frequent complaints that they feel like strangers in their own country? Was it a case of misplaced fear or hallucinations if most members of the general public have not realized that all had gone well with absorption of the immigrant communities?

Can the findings of the pollsters be trusted? Or could it be that those who answered the survey, being polite people in the first place, provided answers that they believed would please the investigators? Could it be that, if asked about support for terrorism, they might not be wholly truthful when confronted by people whom they do not know and trust and who could be, for all they know, working for the security forces? If there was universal condemnation (and even fear) of terrorism in the Muslim communities, one would expect massive cooperation with the police in order to prevent terrorist attacks. However, according to all information, this has not been the case. Mogahed strongly condemned the obsession with the differences between the communities rather than with the communalities. But Mogahed appears veiled in public, and the veil is not a religious commandment but endeavors to stress the differences between believers and unbelievers.

Investigations of this kind may not necessarily be all wrong, but they cannot be considered reliable either. Mogahed might

have gained a more realistic picture of the true state of affairs
had she watched a soccer game in Paris or Berlin when France
played Algeria or when Germany lined up against Turkey.
With what team did much of the public identify? What national anthem did they sing?

The wider public in Europe did not share the optimistic
views of Cesari. When Thilo Sarrazin's *Germany Abolishes Itself*
appeared in 2010, it sold more than a million copies in a few
months. Sarrazin claimed that the future Germany would be
smaller and more stupid. The Islamic immigrants had a higher
birthrate than the native Germans. They were undereducated
and overly dependent on state help. Their crime rate was higher,
and most women were not allowed to work outside the home.
Most of Sarrazin's facts and figures could not seriously be disputed. Where he opened himself to serious criticism was in
some of his projections into the future.

Given the fact that the Muslim immigrants are undereducated and their offspring more often than not fail to complete
their education in school or professional training, is there not
a chance that their educational level will rise over time? Is it
true, as Sarrazin claims, that intelligence is inherited? If a majority of male young Turks were school dropouts, was it not
also true that of those hailing from Iran, Iraq, and Afghanistan
(usually of middle-class background) a higher percentage graduated than of the native German population?

In brief, Sarrazin's misguided and unnecessary excursions
into the field of genetics opened him to attack. This was a discipline in which he was clearly much less at home than when
dealing with present social conditions. The harsh tone of
Sarrazin's writing could also be criticized. What attracted so
many readers and produced so much assent were his comments on the present situation. Many of his facts were well-

known and had hardly been in dispute, but they had never been openly discussed.

Political correctness had long prevented a frank debate of the state of the immigrants and their communities as well as what was done and what could be done to improve it. Merkel denounced Sarrazin's book as unhelpful, but it is doubtful whether, without its publication and the heated debate following it, she would have admitted that multiculturalism had failed. The German political elite had ignored the failures of integration, and it had been tacitly assumed that all or almost all was well in this respect and that only a few extreme right wingers and Islamophobes would not accept this. It came as a great surprise to the German political elite when it realized that this opinion was by no means shared by the great majority of the public. It took only a small provocation to cause an explosion of indignation. What was true with regard to Germany also applied to virtually all other European countries that had become home to major Muslim communities.

Was Sarrazin's book indeed as unhelpful as Angela Merkel said? She was right inasmuch as he did not offer solutions. He had analyzed and described a major problem facing Germany; the Muslim immigrants would not leave Germany and could not be deported. Many had acquired German citizenship. If so, how to solve the problem or at least defuse it and improve the situation? The key to a solution was education, for those who had not graduated or acquired a trade or profession would have no chance in the labor market. However, at this point the difficulties arose—parents unwilling to send their children to school, especially girls who were more eager to learn than boys, the unruly behavior of Turkish boys, German teachers unwilling to stay in schools in which they were vilified and physically attacked. It was suggested that sanctions, such as fines, should be taken against parents not sending their children to school.

How to deal with children imbued with deep, aggressive anti-intellectualism? How to confront the hostility toward those of their classmates studying eagerly and successfully? Parents of Muslim schoolchildren have complained that their daughters have been exposed in state schools to music lessons, which, according to one hadith, is strictly forbidden. An English teacher in a predominantly Muslim school was fired (and therefore went to court) because she disagreed with a curriculum that included anti-Christian and anti-Jewish propaganda. The children were also taught in some Islamist-controlled schools that the perpetrators of 9/11 in New York and Washington were great heroes.

No wonder that children will be confused if told at home that Christian and Jews are enemies and devils whereas in state schools they will be taught that they themselves were the terrorists. In other schools in the UK, non-Muslim teachers were instructed not to touch Muslim pupils because they considered all unbelievers unclean. Did the school authorities have the right to ignore the beliefs and sensitivities that Muslim students are told at home and through Turkish and Arab television? French educational authorities have, on the whole, taken a much less liberal line than the German and British.

Another issue that became a major bone of contention in Europe was the banning of the burqa. This garment, which was introduced by the Taliban, covers the whole body of a woman, as does the niqab, which leaves a slit open for the eyes. The hijab, on the other hand, is a head scarf. These garments can be bought in every Muslim store in London or other major European cities for as little as a few euros. More elegant versions are available at high fashion stores for hundreds of euros.

These garments, except the hijab, which comes in many versions (including a festive version, with sequined patterns), were virtually unknown in Europe until a few years ago. They were also virtually unknown in most Muslim countries, simply because they interfered with women's work. The hijab was banned until recently in certain Muslim countries, such as Turkey and Tunisia, and at times in Egypt. The burqa is banned in Syrian schools and universities. Town women did away with covering their faces in Afghanistan under King Amanullah in 1927 and in Persia, now Iran, under Reza Shah in 1926. In Malaysia, public servants were forbidden to wear the niqab, and so were doctors and nurses in Egyptian hospitals. The British Department of Health, on the other hand, permitted doctors and nurses to wear long sleeves for "religious reasons" despite the increased risk of transmitting infections. The Koran says, "Draw veils over your bosoms," but the burqa and the niqab do much more than that. The hijab covers the hair but not the bosom.

How did they become fashionable suddenly? It seems to have to do mainly with identity politics, with distancing oneself from nonbelievers to make it absolutely clear that Muslim women have nothing in common with other women. If Western feminists were to suddenly adopt the burqa out of solidarity with their Islamist sisters, this would create a major problem for burqa-wearing Islamist women because they would have to think of some other fashion or garment to stress the fact that they are different.

The appearance of these garments in the streets of Europe, especially the black burqas, created both amusement and annoyance among the local population for a variety of reasons. It is a particularly ugly garment—but not all women's fashions in history have been very beautiful. It symbolized in the eyes of many the inferior status of women in Islam, their repression, and it was interpreted as a deliberate attempt to annoy and provoke the non-Muslims—"we are not like you; we do not want to be like you."

According to public opinion polls, a majority of Europeans, including those in the most tolerant countries, such as Sweden, expressed the opinion that burqas and niqabs do not belong in their countries and were contrary to female dignity. They were considered a political rather than a religious statement. It was also said that many women were wearing the burqa not because of their free will but because pressure, either individual or social, had been exerted on them. They were banned in public places in France, Belgium, and in certain regions of Spain. A ban was considered in Sweden, Switzerland, and the Netherlands. A German minister called it a "full body prison." Elsewhere it was argued that the burqa and the niqab constituted a security risk in the age of terrorism and especially suicide terrorism. According to reports, some male terrorists had used the burqa to stage an attack or to get away after an attack.

The defenders of the burqa, on the other hand, claimed that only a few women were wearing this garment in public in Europe, that no one had compelled them to do so, and that banning it was depriving them of their elementary human rights. Some Western feminists said a ban was antiwoman and anti–Western ethics, because a woman's body was her own and not state property. How to explain the violent reaction on the part of European society? Strange explanations were adduced. Some women, including non-Muslim women liberationists, claimed that a woman could feel truly liberated only under the cover of the burqa. Other ideologues argued that Europeans were angry and fearful because of their colonialist past. This made even less sense, because European colonialism, if anything, had generated massive feelings of guilt, hence the willingness to make almost any concession to those claiming victim status.

Whatever the motive, the burqa caused a great deal of bad blood mainly because it was seen as an attack against integration. Many saw it as an attempt to perpetuate negative Islamist attitudes toward women, denying them elementary human rights such as education that would eventually lead to trying to impose such coercion on Western women. The fact that a few female Islamists seem to have accepted the burqa voluntarily presented an interesting psychological problem but hardly affected the judgment of outsiders.

If Europe faces a long period of economic depression, the continent could be less of an attraction for immigrants, legal and illegal, from Muslim countries. Could there be perhaps even a Muslim exodus from Europe? There will be fewer workplaces at a time of substantial unemployment and fewer allocations for social assistance. But this seems unlikely for a number of reasons. There is, as earlier mentioned, an exodus of Turkish university graduates from Europe because there are more openings at present in Turkey. But this affects no more than a few thousand. Even if the economic situation in Europe is bad in the future, it will be worse in the countries of the Middle East and North and West Africa, from which most of the immigrants are likely to come. They will not turn to rapidly developing countries such as China and India, which do not accept foreign workers, let alone their dependents. Even the Arab Gulf states that needed workers in the past have expelled many of them in recent years.

The only exception has been Russia. Putin announced in 2010 that Russia will absorb ten to twenty million foreign workers in the years to come. But he was presumably referring to skilled workers from central Asia with a knowledge of Russian. Furthermore, it is doubtful that Russia will indeed need that many, and, in view of growing Russian xenophobia, there will be political resistance that may not be easy to overcome. The antiminority riots in Moscow and other Russian cities in December 2010 will make the Russian authorities think twice about how far to open their gates, even if there is a need for foreign workers because of the shrinking number of Russians of working age.

The issue of Islamophobia is discussed elsewhere in these pages. It is largely a propagandistic term employed for reasons that need hardly be discussed. Sometimes it is used fraudulently, at other times in good faith. There have been, needless to say, cases like the Florida pastor who burned the Koran in public or the German Russian madman who stabbed a Muslim woman to death in a courtroom in Saxony. Individual young Pakistanis were attacked in London in the 1970s under the term *Paki bashing*. But these are few cases compared with the violence shown by young Muslim immigrants toward Jews and other nonbelievers even in traditionally tolerant countries such as Sweden and in parts of France, Belgium, and the Netherlands.

On the whole, the attitude of Europeans toward Islam has been one of indifference rather than enmity. A German study sponsored by a Social Democratic research center showed that about 60 percent of all Germans wanted to restrict the practice of Islam in their country. But closer scrutiny shows that such negative feelings referred to cases in which such practices were carried out in an aggressive way and were detrimental to the rest of the population. The same study presented the dubious thesis that such opinions were predominantly sponsored by the political center, which had been increasingly swayed by extreme right-wing and neo-Fascist views. Less politically motivated studies tend to show that to the extent that such aversions exist, they are not predominant in any particular class or political party but are found in all parts of the social and political spectrum, although they are perhaps slightly more pronounced in the native working class because it has been affected more than the rest of the population by the influx of immigrants. Other studies presented by *Le Monde* in December 2010 reported that 42 percent of Frenchmen and 40 percent of Germans regarded the presence of Muslim communities in their midst a menace. Twenty-two percent and 24 percent, on the other hand, regarded their presence as a cultural enrichment.

Clearly, threats exist. There is a danger that Islamophobia could receive a massive uplift if terrorist acts should multiply in Europe and take many more victims. For while there is little Islamophobia, there certainly exists terror-phobia, and jihadists are not very popular. During the first decade of the twenty-first century, there have been relatively few major terrorist attacks in Europe, London and Madrid being the exception rather than the rule. But there have been many more attempts to carry them out, and hundreds of so-called militants went to fight in Iraq, Afghanistan, Yemen, Somalia, and other fields of battle.

It has been correctly pointed out that the overwhelming majority of Muslim immigrants to Europe have no wish to be involved in terrorist activities. But it is also true that between 10 and 20 percent have expressed sympathy for the jihadists and have been radicalized by propaganda emanating from these circles as well as by the failure of integration in Europe. With the return of jihadists from the Middle East and Asia, there may be even more attacks in Europe in the future.

While Muslim leaders and spokesmen in Europe have often

dissociated themselves from terrorist attacks, their collaboration with local authorities in an attempt to prevent such attacks
has apparently not been very helpful. They have been often
reluctant to act as "informers" on radicals in their midst, but,
without such help, the security forces are greatly hampered.
Experience shows that for the preparation of terrorist attacks,
only a small number of "militants" are needed, not political
parties and mass movements. And this seems also to be true if
terrorists at some future date use weapons of mass destruction
in their attacks, nuclear, chemical, biological, or others. Few
of those who have closely followed developments in this field
doubt that such attacks will occur sooner or later. The first attempts may well fail, but eventually they may succeed. If this
should occur, it would widen and deepen the conflict with the
Muslim communities in the countries affected. This, and not
the largely imaginary and sometimes fraudulent invocation
of Islamophobia, appears to be the real danger in the years to
come.

RUSSIAN ISLAM

IN THE DISCUSSIONS ABOUT MUSLIMS in Europe, seldom if ever is mention made of those living in Russia, even though their number is equal to those in the rest of Europe. In fact, Moscow is home to more Muslims than any other European city and has a population of 1.5 million, possibly more. Alexander Malashenko, one of Russia's leading experts, predicted a few years ago that Islam was Russia's fate. This could be an exaggeration, but not by much. The full implications of these facts are not yet clear to the Russian leadership and the wider public. They are seldom openly discussed.

The Russian encounter with Islam dates back many centuries. Russia became home to many Muslims following the capture of Kazan in 1571 by Ivan IV and the later incorporation of the whole middle Volga region. The conquest of the Caucasus brought more Muslims (and more conflicts) into the Russian orbit. But for the average resident of Moscow, the only encounter with Islam was when he met his janitor, who more often than not happened to be a Tatar.

Following the repression of local resistance in the Caucasus in the nineteenth century and later also in central Asia, Islam seemed to be not much of a political problem under Soviet rule. There was in fact considerable cultural and social assimilation, but this was mainly restricted to the leading stratum in local society as it appeared after the breakdown of Soviet rule. This did not prevent conflicts based on an ethnic background. The major Muslim republics seceded when the Soviet Union broke down, but their dependence on Moscow grew; sometimes it became even stronger.

At the same time, the infiltration of Islamism got under way. Saudi Arabia, Libya, and other Arab countries, as well as Iran, helped to build many new mosques and inspired various nationalist-religious organizations. The Moscow authorities tolerated the influx of foreign money and ideas, partly because they were powerless to stop it and partly because they were not fully aware of it and were preoccupied elsewhere. But the reawakening of Islam (and often of radical political Islam) coincided with the rise of nationalist trends among the Russian population, who said, "Russia for the Russians," and of course the rise of the Orthodox Church. The Russian leadership tried hard but not very successfully to prevent such conflicts at a time when the Russian reputation in the Muslim world was already at a low point following the Russian invasion in Afghanistan and the first Chechen war from 1994 to 1996. Russia even joined the Organization of the Islamic Conference as an observer to demonstrate its interest in Muslim affairs.

If anti-Russian sentiments were running high in the northern Caucasus, the situation was much less tense in the central Volga region, which included Tatarstan and Bashkortostan. When Russia withdrew its troops from Afghanistan, it ceased to be a major target of Muslim hostility, yet terrorist attacks on the part of Caucasian militants continued. On the whole, Russian Muslims showed only limited interest in the affairs of their coreligionists in other countries. The number of the participants in the annual hajj, the pilgrimage to Mecca, Saudi Arabia, was small, even though the trip was subsidized, and the appeal in 2009 to contribute money to the Gaza campaign yielded a mere 100,000 rubles.

On the domestic front, Muslims showed greater activity. There was no danger of secession since the Muslim communities are not in a contingent region but instead dispersed over a wide area. Whereas Daghestan and Chechnya are very poor regions, the central Volga concentrations of Muslims are highly industrialized, largely owing to the oil industry and its various branches. But they still have made growing political and economic demands, floating, for instance, the idea that the deputy president of Russia should always be a Muslim. Radical political Islam has not found many adherents in these areas. The population is mixed; there has been a great deal of intermarriage; and, as for the return to the shari'a, the religious law of Islam, a frequent comment has been, "We do not want to return to the Middle Ages." The influence of modernist Islam has been strong and there has been contempt for fundamentalism. Opposition to Moscow is based far more on nationalist than religious grounds. However, in December 2010 Russian security forces discovered Islamist terrorist cells in the Volga region, and there were fatalities in the clashes that ensued. On the whole there is a very long tradition of tolerance in the region and interethnic marriages are frequent. But some Muslim countries have invested money in the building of mosques and similar institutions that preach a radical, aggressive version of Islam and try to propagate militancy.

The other main concentration of Russian Muslims is in Greater Moscow. Whole quarters of the Russian capital, especially suburbs such as Butovo, have been taken over by Muslim newcomers. There are as yet not many mosques, hence the pictures, as in other European capitals, of tens of thousands of the faithful praying in the streets. This has not been, by and large, the result of deliberate discrimination. There were not many churches or synagogues under Soviet rule either. As in other European countries, there has been opposition among Russians against the growing Muslim presence. But, on the whole, the authorities have been helpful. Muslim clubs, hospitals, kindergartens, schools, supermarkets (such as Appelsina) have mushroomed. There are Muslim bookshops selling the works of the ideologues of Islamism by Sayed Qutb and Mawdudi, whose works have been translated into Russian. The immigration of Muslim workers from the central Asian republics has not been stopped and is, in some cases, even encouraged.

The Russian authorities don't seem to feel threatened by the Muslim communities, either in the middle Volga region, in towns such as Kazan, or in the big cities such as Moscow. But there have been, in recent years, clashes in Moscow over ethnic background. There seems to be a good deal of explosive material, and a wider spread of riots is always possible. Looking further ahead and considering the higher birthrate of the Muslim communities, the situation could deteriorate. In another decade or two, every third recruit to the Russian armed forces will be of Muslim background and the Russian contingent may have declined to less than half. Perhaps Russia will have accepted by that time the necessity of a professional army. But this will not be the only major difficulty on Russia's road ahead.

The northern Caucasus is the third and most dangerous Muslim concentration. Some 160,000 soldiers and civilians have died in the two Chechen wars. Eventually, Moscow succeeded in imposing a solution that restored relative calm. Chechnya has become a partly autonomous Muslim region in which the shari'a has become the law of the land. The demand for polygamy is now under consideration. The situation in Daghestan, Kabardino-Balkaria, and Ingushetia remains far more unsettled.

It is not clear to what extent the Chechen leadership truly believes in fundamentalist Islam. It could well be that they feel the need for an official ideology that could serve as a uniting force and counteract the accusations of the rebels that the Muslims in the ruling pro-Putin clique are apostates. The fact that Chechnya is now run to a large extent according to the shari'a as Ramzan Kadyrov, the leader, interprets it (women are forced to wear head scarves, for instance) has not diminished the opposition against him. The Russian policy of appointing more or less trustworthy satraps such as the younger Kadyrov offers no guarantee for the future. They must be quite aware that they will press for more and more independence and political concessions (and money) and in the final analysis cannot be trusted.

In Stalin's age, the problem would have been solved by exiling the rebellious minorities to some faraway parts of Russia, but this no longer seems possible. Since letting the northern Caucasus secede seems quite unthinkable from the Russian point of view, this area will remain Russia's soft underbelly. Even if the terrorist danger can be contained, nationalist-religious opposition is likely to continue. There is a traditional inclination in the Caucasus to engage in long wars. If there is no outside enemy, Caucasians seem to enjoy fighting one another. There are some forty nationalities and thirty languages in Daghestan alone, and the situation in other parts of the area is not very different. During the Soviet era the conflicts were suppressed, but the present policy of *divide et impera* will probably not lead to a lasting solution. The Islamists believe that if they can only succeed in defeating the Russians in a long, drawn-out struggle and expel the Russian civilians from the Caucasus, they might impose a Pax Islamica in the region.

Political Islam is bound to figure high in the years to come on the Russian domestic and foreign agenda, given the fact that the Islamist rebels are not the only problem facing Russia in the region and that, following NATO's retreat from Afghanistan, a flare-up in the central Asian republics at some future date seems more likely than not. Following its own misadventures in Afghanistan, Russia has no wish to be drawn again into the central Asian imbroglio, but at the same time it has no desire to give up its "zone of privileged interest." The views of Russian experts have diverged sharply, ranging from considering the northern Caucasus a lost cause to more optimistic appraisals. There have been studies predicting the Islamisation of Russia, whereas others, including Alexander Malashenko, have considered such predictions alarmist and misleading. Russian policy has been and probably will continue to be to leave all options open, but their number is limited and apparently shrinking.

TURKEY TO THE RESCUE

THE EU HAS BEEN NEGOTIATING with Turkey about a merger for about five decades, but Turkey's economic backwardness made this impossible during that time. More recently, the Turkish economy made great progress with 6 percent growth year after year, more than any other OECD country. With seventy million inhabitants, Turkey became one of the smaller tigers of the Western economies. It was hard hit by the recession of 2008–09 but recovered quickly. But there were other bones of contention. While America and Britain strongly supported Turkey's accession, those countries with sizable Turkish communities were opposed, fearful of a further invasion into their countries. Turkish elections became more democratic, but the views expressed by the majority were not democratic. It appeared that the Kemalist secular reforms had reached the end. They were abolished in part, and support for them outside the military high command, the judiciary, and some sections of the intelligentsia was quite weak.

The new Turkish ideology was shaped by and expressed the views of the lower-middle class and recent arrivals in the big cities from eastern Anatolia. It was a mixture of Islamism lite and Turkish nationalism. Turkey's policy had been beset by domestic unrest in the 1970s, when Turkey invaded and occupied northern Cyprus and the struggle with the Kurds intensified. But the main issue was the gradual detachment from the West, America as well as Europe. There have been hopes in some Western circles that a Turkey firmly anchored in a united Europe could serve an important role as a link with the Middle East. But these hopes gradually faded and there was soul searching—who had lost Turkey?

Probably no one had lost it, since its turn to the East had been a natural development in line with its traditions and history. Russia and later the Soviet Union had been Turkey's traditional enemy and contributed more than any other to the downfall of the Ottoman Empire. Even after the Second World War, Moscow schemed to seize the Turkish provinces Kars and Ardahan (as well as a say concerning the Dardanelles), and this was no doubt the main reason why Turkey joined NATO.

But as the years passed, the Soviet danger disappeared, the Soviet empire collapsed, and membership in NATO became unnecessary, even embarrassing, from the point of view of Turkish national interest. When at the time of the first Iraqi war America asked Turkey to be permitted to transport military units to Iraq, the request was refused. Islam had been discouraged under Kemal Atatürk and his secular successors, but, in the 1970s and 1980s, Islamist elements became stronger in Turkish politics, and the demographic balance changed as millions streamed from the underdeveloped east of the country to Istanbul, Izmir, and the West. Most of these newcomers were strong religious believers, hence the rise of AKP, the party with which they identified. According to a recent poll, about half of the Turks expressed the opinion that since their values were so distant from those of Europe, they could not really be considered part of the West.

When the idea of Turkey joining the European Union was first floated, there was considerable goodwill on both sides, but there had to be many postponements because Turkey was far from the economic minimum demanded from candidates considered for membership. In addition, a further democratization of Turkish politics was expected. Such democratization took place over time, but the political attitudes of the new leading class and their supporters were far from democratic, above all concerning the minorities in the country. True, the AKP, the ruling party, was democratically elected, but so was Hungary's in 2010, which engaged in a great deal of antidemocratic repression in record time. One could also refer to similar occurrences in Central Europe before the Second World War.

Washington had been initially among those strongly urging the EU to make Turkey a member. But such sympathy was not reciprocal. Opinion polls showed that the Turkish public turned steadily against America and its allies. As the country became economically stronger and as more of its exports went to the East and North, there was the feeling that too close a relationship with the West was not in Turkey's interest. Closer relations were established with the neighboring Arab countries, as well as with Iran and Russia.

Washington made strong efforts to woo Ankara. One of the first foreign trips of President Obama's was to the Turkish capital in April of 2009, where he made a highly laudatory speech. It did not help. Turkish support for joining the EU had been 73 percent in 2002. Six years later, it had declined to 38 percent. The mood had changed. The composition of the political elite had changed, and the anti-Westernism manifested itself not only in strategic treatises by leading Turkish politicians, such as the neo-Ottomanism and "strategic depth doctrine" of foreign minister Ahmet Davutoğlu, which has dominated Turkish foreign policy for the last decade, but also in the media. It said that Turkey belonged to about ten different regions from the Mediterranean to central Asia and should be active in all of them.

The new Turkish great-power status and the hatred against those standing in Turkey's way appeared even more strongly in Turkish popular culture, especially in Turkish pop and in such bestsellers, movies, and television series as *Metal Furtina* (or *Metal Storm*) and *Valley of the Wolves* (or *Urtlat Vadisi Irak*). In the former, Washington is carving up Turkey into a number of small states, as the Allies did in the Sèvres peace treaty after the First World War, and Turkey, allied with China, Russia, and Germany, detonates a nuclear bomb over Washington, D.C. In the latter, which was also widely shown to much acclaim to Turkish communities in Europe, American soldiers commit unspeakable acts of brutality against Muslims. A Jewish doctor pulls out Muslim hearts, selling them to aristocrats in New York, London, and Tel Aviv. American economic help to Turkey under the Truman Act is ridiculed and the question asked, "We sent you the elastic for your panties—what did you do for us?" There was a sequel, *Kurtlar Vadisi Filistin* (or *Valley of the Wolves*), about the Turkish ship that tried to break the blockade of Gaza in 2010.

Turkish leaders felt frequently offended by Westerners. Sometimes they were justified, such as in the case of the foolish Israeli behavior: for example, when a Turkish envoy was made to sit on a lower seat than an Israeli deputy foreign minister conversing with him so that the Israeli could look down on the Turkish envoy and when Israel refused to make amends in the case of the Mavi Marmara affair, the "blockade breaker" on the road to Gaza, however great the provocation might have been.

This drift in Turkish attitudes surprised many outside observers. There seemed to be no particular reason for the new friendship with Arab states or with Iran. The Arabs had been Ottoman subjects and had not shown much loyalty at the time, and Tehran was a traditional rival. It must have occurred to Turkish policy makers that if Iran was in possession of nuclear arms and Turkey was not, this could not be in Turkey's best interest. On the other hand, there was apparently the centuries-old Turkish feeling that the infidel Europeans could never be their true friends and allies and that Turkey belonged to Asia, not Europe. For this reason, Ankara seemed to be willing to forgive or at least to close its eyes to whatever the Russians, considered rivals of the West, inflicted on the Chechens but was not willing to appreciate American and European help to the Muslims in the former Yugoslavia.

Turkish Islamism is Islamism lite compared with Iran and the Arab jihadists, and Turkish policy makers realized that it was not in their best interest to burn all bridges, that if relations with the West should deteriorate too much they too would suffer. Even in decline, the EU was still an important trade partner, and Turkey might be better off in a toothless NATO than outside it. If Ankara aimed at great power (and not only regional power) status, it should not have retreated too much from the concept of Turkey's being a bridge able to act as mediator between Europe and the hostile Muslim world. Nor could the memory of Arab backstabbing in 1918 easily be forgotten.

Declarations made by leading Turkish spokesmen were quite often confusing. Recep Erdogan, the Turkish prime minister, in a clearly pro-European article in *Newsweek* in January 2011, maintained that Turkey had the vigor that Europe so badly needed. If so, how to explain the Turkish complaints about the wall built by Greece on one small section of the Greek-Turkish border intended to keep out illegal immigrants? This was considered another fatal obstacle to closer Turkish-European relations. A vigorous Turkey certainly could have prevented such infiltration or absorbed the immigrants into nonvigorous Europe. But on the contrary, Turkey opened its borders to most Middle Eastern countries, thus facilitating infiltration to Greece and other European countries.

Relations between Turkey and the EU will be one of the major issues facing Europe, irrespective of whether Turkey will be part of the European Union or remain outside. Turkey has influential friends in Europe. The foreign ministers of Britain, Italy, Sweden, and Finland published an open letter to their colleagues in December 2010 entitled "Europe, Look Outward Again," which summarizes their arguments. They say that the EU mission to bring stability, democracy, and prosperity to the continent is not yet finished. Greater dynamism is needed, and for this purpose they propose to bring Iceland and Turkey into the EU. It stands to reason that their interest is focused more on Turkey than on the other candidate. They mention first the importance of the free flow of capital, goods, service, and labor, and second the importance of strengthening the rule of law and common European values and standards.

This, they say, is apparent not least in Turkey, where EU-inspired liberal reform has been so successful, a country still in the midst of a far-reaching reform process. Furthermore, Turkey, like no other country, could advance European interest in security, trade, and energy networks from the Far East to the Mediterranean (Turkey has been active of late even in Mongolia—so far without outstanding success). In other words, if Turkey were to join the EU, Europe would be able to play a much greater role in world affairs. True, the authors concede that there may be something to the arguments of those who claim that Turkey still falls short of the "Copenhagen criteria." These guidelines, laid down by the European Council in 1993, define which countries are eligible to join the European Union. They refer in particular to the stability of institutions guaranteeing democracy, rule of law, human rights, and the respect for and protection of minorities. But whatever was decided in Copenhagen, the European foreign ministers, taking a more broadminded view, believed that "not accepting Turkey would mean that Europe is turning its back on the fundamental values and principles that have guided European policies for the last fifty years." There obviously was a clash of principles, but they trust that "the transformational capacity of enlargement" will lead Turkey to further democratization and the observing of human rights.

This appeal and the arguments adduced are of considerable interest. The foreign ministers represent countries that lacked major communities of Turkish immigrants and thus the experience of difficulties with their integration. Given the economic situation in Britain and Italy, along with the Finnish climate, it seems unlikely that there will be massive Turkish immigration in these countries. The authors are obviously impressed not by the declarations of Khaddafi and other Arab spokesmen that Turkey would act as a fifth column of Islam in Europe or by the Wikileaks revelations according to which successive American ambassadors to Turkey regarded Davutoğlu, the Turkish foreign minister, a very dangerous man who was responsible for pushing his country into a dangerous anti-Western direction. Nor were they worried by the declarations of the Turkish prime minister in Germany (which created much indignation in that country) admonishing the Turkish communities in that country not to assimilate. He also demanded the establishment of Turkish schools and universities in Germany.

Erdogan is known as a mercurial man, and not every word he utters should be taken that seriously. Gül, the Turkish president, on another occasion gave the Turkish communities in Germany different advice, encouraging them to integrate in German society. As for the negative appraisal of U.S. ambassadors, this was probably based on a misreading of Turkish politics or rather an ignoring of the fact that Turkey had been turning away from pro-Western Kemalism for a considerable time and that Islamism had made great inroads. Whatever the diplomats reported, the official line taken by Washington and by Europe was that Turkey had become more democratic, which was stretching the truth.

Davutoğlu represented the changes that had taken place inside Turkey. The AKP, the leading party, was supported by a majority in elections that were on the whole fair, but the majority to a considerable extent did not cherish democratic values and considered them Western, not Islamic, in inspiration. A rapprochement with Iran, Russia, and the Arab world was popular in Turkey, whereas Western values and the EU were not. The advocates of Turkey in Europe were arguing that Istanbul had become the most vibrant city in Europe, that the AKP was a liberalizing and democratic force. The Turkish press laws were about as democratic as those of Hungary, and the AKP was as democratically elected as Putin's party in Russia. But if Hungary was a member of the EU, and if there was a strategic relationship with Russia, why not treat Turkey equally?

True, public opinion polls were showing that Turks regarded the United States and Israel as the greatest danger to Turkey. Only 2 percent thought so about Iran. With all this there is little doubt that the Turkish government could overcome the aversion vis-à-vis the EU and "European values." Turkish foreign policy is "zero problems with neighbors" (except a very few), and to extend Turkish influence by soft power from Mongolia to the gates of Vienna. But there are limits to its rapprochement with Iran and the Arab world and also with Russia. Given the historical record, Turkey will not find it easy to enhance its influence in the Balkans, which it had ruled for centuries. Davutoğlu's policy is more neo-Ottoman in inspiration than Islamist; the mullahs in Turkey have no decisive influence on foreign policy.

Turkey's power and future prospects, both political and economic, should not be overrated. There is a strong inclination to do so (and to hubris in general) on the part of the AKP leadership. The projections according to which Turkey will be the second largest economy in Europe in the year 2050 seem to ignore among other things the state of Turkish education, which is about the poorest in Europe. Without radical improvement in this field, great advances in the economy seem unlikely.

The growth of Turkey's influence depends to a considerable extent on the country's functioning as a bridge and perhaps a mediator between "West" and "East." Burning the bridges with Europe and becoming an integral part of the "East" would be against the country's best interests and weaken its international position. Perhaps Turkey could act as a role model for the Arab world, but do the Arabs want such a model? Perhaps it could prevent a war in the Middle East. But this is far from certain. It could very well be that joining the EU would have a moderating influence on developments inside Turkey—in the very long run.

Whether all this would be in the interest of the EU in the

short and medium range is more doubtful. Turkey's interest is to expand its influence, not to accept and spread European values, not to "advance European interests," to quote the four foreign ministers, but rather its own. Who could blame the Turks, since all other European countries have behaved in a similar way? The vision of the future of Europe as expressed in the manifesto of the four foreign ministers seems to be based mainly on economic interests, such as the free flow of capital, trade and energy networks with the rule of law, with human rights and European values taking a secondary place; not to be flouted too blatantly if possible, but certainly not a decisive factor. Perhaps this is the shape of things to come—if a united Europe survives. But it is truly overly optimistic to believe that such an economic co-prosperity sphere could play an important part in international politics. On what foreign political issues would it agree and which aims would it pursue?

CHINA'S SHADOW—AND PRESENCE

CHINA'S RELATIONS WITH THE EU have grown enormously in importance during the last decade with the fast growth of the Chinese economy. Since the 1978 reforms, the Chinese GNP has grown by about 10 percent annually, an unprecedented trend in modern economic history. Europe is now China's biggest customer, having overtaken the United States. Chinese tourists in France now outspend those from all other countries, and 30–50 percent of luxury goods in Germany, France, and Italy are now bought by customers from China, leaving those from the Persian/Arab Gulf states and the Russian nouveaux riches far behind.

Chinese policy has become more assertive. Until the turn of the century, China regarded itself primarily as a regional power, but this changed as its massive demand for oil, gas, and many raw materials—a prerequisite for further growth—became clear to the rulers in Beijing.

EU policy vis-à-vis China has been defined as unconditional engagement, "a policy that gives China access to all the benefits of cooperation with Europe while asking for little in return. . . . The results speak for themselves." The study quoted further states that China treats the EU with something akin to diplomatic contempt. The Chinese know that the EU is weak, politically divided, and militarily nonexistent. The Chinese think that the EU needs China more than China needs the EU.

European prime ministers and foreign ministers have visited Beijing more and more often and bestowed great praise on the new China and its rulers. When Angela Merkel with half her cabinet went to Beijing in July 2010, the Chinese forgave her having received the Dalai Lama three years earlier, and she returned with a sizable number of contracts. Some major German firms had weathered the crisis owing to massive Chinese orders—BMW, for instance—stemming from what experts called an "insatiable demand" for top-of-the-range limousines. Germany was China's main trade partner in Europe, exporting and selling more than Britain and France combined.

When Hu Jintao, the Chinese president, visited Paris in November 2010, the French government made it a major affair of state. President Sarkozy and his wife went to the airport to greet him, an unprecedented gesture. Had the age of human rights been replaced by the era of the kowtow (three kneelings, nine times knocking with the head on the ground)? It was certainly very much in contrast to the situation two years earlier, when President Sarkozy had threatened to boycott the opening ceremony of the Beijing Olympic Games to protest China's treatment of Tibet. This time European values, human rights, and the fate of dissidents in China did not figure. France could not afford to lose major contracts in view of its worsening economic situation. The Chinese purchase of thirty-six airbuses was at stake, as well as major deals involving the nuclear engineering giant Areva and Total, the French oil company. Sarkozy also tried without much success to gain China's agreement in favor of a currency correction.

Not to be outdone by his German and French colleagues, David Cameron, the British prime minister, effusively complimented China on a visit in November 2010. In a speech at Beida University, he said that during the last twenty years China had changed out of recognition (he had been as student in Hong Kong in 1985). He quoted the Chinese national anthem and said that the Chinese people were standing up not only in their own country but in the world, that China had emerged as a great global power, that no issue of importance could be discussed without China, which was to reclaim later this century its position as the world's biggest economy. In recent years, China has been buying heavily into Africa as well as the European countries most heavily hit by the recession.

The EU was engaging with China not only in about twenty "sectoral dialogues" but also in a "strategic relationship," an important-sounding but in fact quite empty concept. It would have been very useful if the EU had coordinated its policy vis-à-vis China, but, on the contrary, the various trade partners were outbidding and competing with one another. As Timothy Garton Ash of the *Guardian,* writing from Beijing, reported at the time of the G20 meeting in Seoul: "I suspect China's leaders . . . chortle into their tea about the undignified antics of the Europeans who once plundered and humiliated their country. For today the Europeans appear like mendicants before the imperial throne, begging for business to lift their faltering economies."

The Chinese reaction has on the whole been polite, but gradually it became reminiscent of the famous letter sent by Emperor Quanlong to King George III in the eighteenth century. While sending King George III valuable presents, the emperor reminded him of his inferior status. After all, it was he, King George, who was "yearning after the blessing of our civilization," so he had to show obedience and be submissive. Or, in the language of the twenty-first century, Europe needed China more than China needed Europe. And in the twenty-first century, bilateral trade had doubled between 2004 and 2008, from 174 billion to 326 billion euros. But, as Duncan Freeman noted, China's exports to Europe were far larger than its imports and there was a European trade deficit of 169 billion euros. While Chinese exports to Europe fell during the crisis of 2008 and 2009 by 13 percent and European exports to China grew by 4 percent, there still was a European trade deficit of 133 billion euros. While the trade balance between Europe and China has slightly improved as far as Europe is concerned, the Chinese still export to Europe far more than they import. The EU complained about its lack of market access in China, as well as the violation of intellectual property rights, economic espionage (especially in Germany), and various discriminatory protectionist measures. But with all these complaints, China was the third most important export market for Europe. China was a customer that Europe could ill afford to offend at a time when other export markets were in jeopardy.

All of which explains the dramatic change in tone and substance within a few years. European leaders were pandering to Chinese nationalism, which had replaced communism as the main plank in the official ideology. Most European governments, as well as the EU foreign minister, had no compunction to take a very active part in the buildup of the Chinese armed forces. Bringing up democratization and human rights in this context would only harm relations between Europe and China. China had become much stronger and Europe weaker. But at the same time, it cannot have escaped the attention of the EU that China had profited more from the exchanges than Europe. China was appropriating European technologies and, with much cheaper production costs, was flooding the world markets. Individual European corporations, such as Nokia and Daimler, but also many others, have already suffered the consequences, and others will follow suit. In other words, European exports to China, while very welcome at a time of crisis, could not be expected to continue, let alone grow in the future, as the Chinese, often by stealth, were acquiring European know-how.

Having ignored or underrated China's potential earlier, EU leaders later on tended to overrate China's prospects and were not sufficiently aware of China's weaknesses. It was hardly in doubt that the Chinese economy would emerge as the world's largest and that, politically and militarily, China's weight in world affairs would also grow. But it was equally clear that a heavy price would have to be paid by the Chinese. Predictions of the economists range from impending collapse to China's emerging as having and producing the most of everything and buying up anything of interest in the rest of the world.

What can be taken for granted is that the differences between rich and poor in China will remain enormous and that, while different groups representing different interests are emerging, China will not be a democracy and does not want to be one. For Chinese ideologues, the story of European democracy acts as a deterrent because democracy leads to weakness and not to power. Nor has the record of European colonialism in China from the opium war onward been forgotten. Chinese control over the minority regions, Tibet and Xinjiang, will be maintained without much difficulty because there are so many more Han Chinese than Muslim Uighurs and Tibetans, and sooner or later Taiwan will be occupied by Beijing.

How far will China's imperial ambitions extend? According to historical evidence and despite current strong nationalist and even racialist impulses, despite premature hubris and triumphalism, despite major tantrums caused by very minor international incidents (such as in 2010, where there was a very heated dispute about naval rights near two islands that both China and Japan claimed were theirs), Chinese rulers are not on the whole interested in the occupation of foreign countries. They want stability rather than world domination, but stability on terms set by China that get the best deal for China through a predatory trade policy. This has created instability and will create more of it, distorting trade by keeping China's currency artificially low. In brief, China and the rest of the world are on a collision course. China claims to act in the interest of all fellow Asians, but Asians have not benefited so far from these actions. China proclaims that it wants to create international harmony, but so far the dissonances have been louder.

It is probably only a question of time until "A Short Story of the Antichrist" will be rediscovered. This is an amazing theological-political essay in futurology published in 1900, describing the Chinese (Mongolian) invasion of Russia and Europe and rule, or yoke, over them, written by a major Russian thinker, Vladimir Soloviev. In the essay the European governments, headed by Freemasons, are engaged in a final, decisive battle against the Muslims, and the Mongols, making use of this constellation, invade Europe and subjugate it. In the meantime, the Jews have settled in Palestine and Jerusalem has again become an imperial city. At this stage, Christ the savior appears in Jerusalem—but it soon appears that he is really the Antichrist, well disguised. But it ends well: the Mongol yoke lasts only half a century and is followed by a millennium of peace and a true spirit of Christianity.

To return to the real world: China has been very active in Africa, buying up or leasing locations where rare minerals are mined, which has caused apprehension in the EU, since it meant that the Europeans would find it more difficult in the future to obtain the raw materials they also needed. Other major Chinese activities have taken in place in Greece, Italy, Portugal, Spain, and other European countries that were hit hard by the economic crisis. Chinese emissaries promised to help these countries with their difficulties, buying local enterprises that had some promise but were strapped for cash. They also invested 400 million euros in Spanish government bonds and promised similar help elsewhere. It stands to reason that these purchases were not humanitarian in character but aimed at gaining maximum political influence at minimal financial investment. Some in the EU were quite worried by what they considered dangerous takeovers of strategically important European assets.

The growth of Chinese power—political, economic, and military—was bound to generate apprehension among its Asian neighbors and in all probability may induce them to look for a counterweight. China's new strong presence in Africa has also produced antagonism. China has never been popular in India and Southeast Asia. Chinese promises for the future Asian co-prosperity zone have been frequent and generous, but the skepticism among its neighbors is deeply rooted. So far, Chinese pressure has been sporadic and limited, but Chinese diplomats have not hesitated to point out to its neighbors that some countries are big, whereas others are small, and that they should draw the obvious conclusions that small countries should behave like small countries. Only time will tell how far these obvious conclusions will go.

What will Europe's place be in a new world order in which

China will be the strongest single power? The Chinese leaders are reported to have studied the major Western writings about the rise and decline of world powers. What lessons will they draw from them? They have also read Carl Schmitt, the leading German legal philosopher who served the Nazis until he fell in disfavor; he could explain to Beijing why *raison d'état* should always take precedence over democracy. Inasmuch as foreign policy is concerned, the lesson to be learned from the fate of the historical superpowers is quite obvious: *divide et impera.*

Since, unlike the Soviet Union, especially during the early years, China cannot hope to attract foreigners on the basis of an internationalist ideology, it will have to buy influence, with, it hopes, a minimum of investment. Such growing influence makes it easier, to give an example, to demand that the EU lift the embargo on the sale of arms to China. Direct interference in European affairs seems unlikely. While the present mood in Beijing is strongly nationalist, even chauvinistic, any Chinese expansion would affect the countries adjacent to it, not those more distant. On the other hand, China sees itself as becoming the main pillar of the world economy, and other countries will have to adjust to Chinese needs and interests.

This is the international harmony that Beijing has been preaching. Perhaps there will be a division of labor, with some European countries providing highly specialized products. Those who have little to offer to China may find themselves in a difficult position. Europeans complaining about American hegemony may remember with some nostalgia the bad old days. On the other hand, China may find the road to world power more difficult and demanding than it imagined and hoped. With growing wealth for a much larger section of the population, their appetite for more of everything may shrink, as has happened to other great powers before. The leaders may quarrel and the divisions inside the country may deepen. The history of the great powers teaches that there are an unlimited number of possibilities of how things may go wrong.

ISLAMOPHOBIA?

THE YEARS 2009 AND 2010 witnessed a new domestic political trend in many European countries. Political movements critical of Muslim immigration became stronger, even in traditionally very tolerant societies, such as Scandinavia and the Netherlands. These political trends caused a great deal of confusion among observers, who were further confounded by the fact that they occurred at a time of major economic upheaval. Surely at a time like this there were more important issues on the political agenda than the fate of relatively small immigrant communities? Nor could these communities be made responsible for the economic disasters that had occurred.

There were no easy explanations. But these anti-immigrant groups, while not achieving gigantic electoral victories, suddenly gained considerable political influence; without them, no stable ruling coalitions could be established in a number of countries. Perhaps it was, above all, the fact that the problems created by these immigrant communities had been neglected for too long.

The trend was frequently subsumed under the general designation of "right-wing extremism" or "xenophobia," even neofascism. But such labels were not very helpful; they could in fact be quite misleading. These movements were by no means right-wing in most respects. Furthermore, if opposition to the immigration of masses of people from abroad was made the yardstick for "right-wing extremism," it would be difficult to find a single Asian or African or Latin American or Middle Eastern country (with the possible exception of Kuwait and Qatar, which needed manual laborers) who were not "right-wing extremist." These countries wanted foreign laborers for limited periods, but none of them were ready to accept any significant number of foreigners wanting to settle in their midst. One could add to this list Japan and probably all but a handful of member states of the United Nations. Such an exercise shows the absurdity of affixing this label indiscriminately.

The issue, quite obviously, is far more complex, and a serious investigation ought to begin with the question, What does the left stand for, and what does *right-wing* mean in the contemporary world? The juxtaposition in Europe goes back to the age of the French Revolution. The left stood for the ideals of the Enlightenment, such as freedom, justice for all, democracy, and human rights. The left was progressive, open to new ideas; it was the party of the poor and oppressed. The right was conservative, the party of the privileged. It defended tradition and the existing social order and opposed social engineering, the consequences of which were unpredictable and possibly harmful.

However, the further removed one got in time and space from Paris in 1789, the more debatable these labels became. Was communism a movement of the left? Perhaps in some respects, but certainly not in others with its advocation for and justification of a ruthless dictatorship and the emergence of a new class. Was Nazism a party of the extreme right? Certainly in some ways, but not in others, because it did not want to preserve past traditions but aimed at revolutionary transformation—the leadership principle (where the leader of the Fascist regime, such as Hitler, holds a central role), its message of a political religion preaching racialist principles and the superiority of the Aryan race. In our time, with the emergence of such movements as jihadism, the old labels became often altogether meaningless; was Osama bin Laden a man of the left or the right? To ask the question was to invite ridicule.

To circumvent this dilemma, new labels such as *populism* were applied. But populism could be left-wing in some respects and right-wing in others at the same time, or it could turn from the one to the other with great ease. Some interpreted the anti-immigration movement as protest or discontent parties; others viewed it as a new radicalism of the center (similar theories had been developed at the time with regard to Nazism). Muslim spokesmen quite frequently called their opponents "racists," probably because racist attacks constitute a crime in various European countries. But this label too was hardly persuasive, because Islam is not a race and Muslims from, say, Kosovo, Nigeria, and the Philippines do not have genetically much in common.

In brief, no simple (or traditional) label could cover the various manifestations of anti-immigrant protest. The Swiss SVP (Schweizerische Volkspartei) initiated a plebiscite against building more minarets on mosques, but otherwise being an old-fashioned, conservative, patriotic party has nothing in common with neofascism. The Hungarian Jobbik, on the other hand, proudly regards itself as a successor of the Fascist Arrow Cross of the 1930s and 1940s. There has been hardly any Muslim immigration to Hungary, but anti-Semitism and anti-Romany (or Gypsies) figure prominently in Jobbik propaganda. Generally speaking, right-wing populism in Eastern Europe has little in common with such movements in the western half of the continent. In the Baltic countries, it is predominantly directed against Russia. The Italian Lega Nord considers southern Italy and Sicily almost as alien as it does the immigrants from North Africa. The originally neofascist Alleanza Nazionale in Italy led by Fini has tried to distance itself from its political origins. For the party of the "True Finns" that scored substantial gains in the 2011 elections, immigration was much less of a problem than relations with the EU.

The Flemish Vlaams Belang, which historically is rooted in the pro-German (and even pro-Nazi) separatist movement of the 1930s and 1940s but can now in no way be regarded as a neofascist party, as it is opposed to all foreigners, Walloons as well as Turks and Moroccans. Neo-Nazism in Germany, which has been relatively weak, has been preoccupied with anti-Semitism and "Zionism." It has regarded the radical Muslims as potential allies in its struggle and, for this reason, has found it difficult to make political capital from prevailing anti-Muslim moods. The French National Front has been anti-Muslim but has also collaborated with them on occasion, sharing certain beliefs, such as Holocaust denial. There has been a political axis encompassing Le Pen, the former head of the National Front, Robert Faurisson, a professor of French literature and the leading French Holocaust denier, and Dieudonné, a famous comedian, rabid anti-Semite, and idol of radical Muslims. In Russia, it is now difficult to discover with the naked eye the ideological differences between the Communist Party and the neofascists.

Political observers have been puzzled by the strong anti-Muslim feeling in Europe's most tolerant countries, such as Scandinavia and the Netherlands. The Norwegian Fremskrittspartiet collected 23 percent of the total vote, the Dansk Folkeparti 14 percent, the Dutch PVV 15 percent. The Swedish

Democrats also made notable progress in the last elections. Yet the reasons are not difficult to discern. These countries have been liberally accepting members of minorities claiming to be persecuted since the Second World War. Their earlier record, for instance vis-à-vis Jewish refugees, was much less impressive. The great majority of asylum seekers were not political but rather economic refugees hoping for a higher standard of living in these countries, aware of the fact that they would get state support even if they did not work. Many of them made no effort to learn the language of the country or adapt to its way of life.

Those opposing this kind of immigrant—there was much less opposition to immigrants from other parts of the world—were not persuaded by the accusations of intolerance and racism from people who thought tolerance and human rights aberrations on the part of a decadent and godless society. True, there were political refugees among them, as in Britain, but these quite often were radical Islamists under criminal indictment in their countries of origin. Among the younger generation of these immigrants, violence was quite frequent, and they were told by their preachers that assimilation was sinful because the unbelievers were enemies of Allah, as shown by their customs and laws, such as granting equality to women, gays, and Jews. To a significant extent, these immigrant communities were not believers in democracy, which they were told was incompatible with Islam. They were intolerant not only of Jews or gays but also of dissident sects within their own communities. They wanted to impose an alien belief system and alien laws (the shari'a) on the rest of the population.

This was the general background of growing anti-Muslim sentiment. Islamophobia in this context was a misnomer, since hardly any European native showed interest in the religion of the newcomers (Geert Wilders, who wanted to ban the Koran, was an exception). By and large, Islamophobia was a propaganda term intended to suppress criticism of and opposition to the demands and complaints of Muslim immigrants. There were a few Islamophobes, such as a pastor from Florida who burned the Koran in public. But European interest in the Muslim religion was truly limited; if there were a few radical opponents of Islam, there were thousands of converts, about five thousand annually in Britain, with similar numbers in other European countries. On the whole, there were no strong feelings about Islam as a religion.

Some radical Islamists were aware of this and, for this reason, also disliked the term *Islamophobia*. They would have preferred a term that would have connoted fear of and antagonism toward Muslims and that was racist in character, because racism is far more taboo in Europe (and often a criminal offense) than opposition to a religion.

Although there was little Islamophobia, there was a great deal of fear, but of terrorism, not of the Koran or the hadith. There was unease as the number of immigrants grew rapidly and as whole suburbs were taken over by them, and the earlier inhabitants—usually working class—were squeezed out. The media frequently reported crimes, not only drug-related, committed by immigrants from Muslim countries. Nevertheless, those convicted were permitted to stay by lenient judges. On other occasions, local authorities were putting large and expensive rented accommodations at the disposal of new immigrants. There was a growing feeling, justified or not, among large sections of the native population that certain parts of their cities had become no-go zones because of a lack of security. Jews living in cities such as Malmö or Anvers lived in fear of attack, and those in the Netherlands were told by a well-meaning former government minister that they should consider emigration, because there was not much of a future for them in the country.

But it was not just a matter of a few thousand Jews or other exposed minorities. There was the fairly widespread feeling of Europeans' becoming strangers in their own country. This, not hostility to Islam, was the reason for the underlying ethnic tension. The political elite would maintain that such fears were wholly unjustified, but their optimism was not shared by a majority, as shown in Germany by the fate of Thilo Sarrazin and his famous book.

Sociologically, most of the support for anti-immigrant movements came from the old working class and from the unemployed, whereas most defenders of immigrants were middle class or upper-middle class, such as the Greens in Germany. This is also true with regard to France, Sweden, Italy, and other European countries. Again, the explanation seems quite obvious: middle-class Germans (or Swedes or others) were much less likely at work or at their place of living to come in contact with the immigrants far from their ghettos and were not competing for work or housing with them.

Some parties belonging to the European extreme right have been doing exceedingly well, while others have stagnated, such as the late Jörg Haider's party in Austria, hence the frequent suggestion not to boycott these parties but to include them in the ruling coalitions, where their appeal would soon be eroded. But given the fact that immigrants will not disappear, it stands to reason that the tensions created by their presence will not disappear either and that, unless ways are found to integrate them in society, antagonism will persist.

It remains to be stressed that in most cases, such antagonism is not directed against foreigners per se but against those perceived as a danger to domestic peace and traditional values. This refers primarily to Muslim communities, or, to be precise, those elements in Muslim societies unwilling to adjust (it also refers to Gypsies moving—or being moved—from the Balkans to western Europe, but this would appear to be a social rather than political problem). Is the far right in Europe Islamophobic? Some of them are but Le Pen and Haider have sympathized with Iran and the Austrian right-wingers also with Khadaffi.

If further evidence is needed for the difficulties of finding precise labels for the political orientation of Muslim immigrants in Europe as well as for their opponents, one could point to the alliances entered by both sides. Radical Muslim groups have cooperated with the extreme right but also the extreme left. Such cooperation with Maoists, Trotskyites, or New Leftists may appear strange and unnatural, given Marxism's basic opposition to religion on the one hand and the firm religious beliefs, often fanatical, of the Islamists on the other.

But in political practice, this did not prove an insurmountable obstacle. Radicals on the left found it somewhat embarrassing, just as they could not easily accept the firm opposition of the Islamists to equal rights for women and gays, the open anti-Semitism (not just anti-Zionism) of the militant Islamists and their indiscriminate terrorism, and other beliefs that normally radical leftists would have thought reactionary, even Fascist. But the far left had been weak and isolated for very long and now saw a chance to gain power in alliance with a dynamic partner. They could always argue that this regrettable ideological backwardness of their new allies was inevitable in Third World conditions and would eventually moderate and disappear. As for their terrorist activities, their importance could be played down. What really mattered in the final analysis was the anti-American and anti-imperialist character of the religious radicals. Whether such political collaboration between apparent extremes would have any real and lasting political effect was yet another question.

WHY THE DECLINE?

WHY HAS EUROPE DECLINED FOR over almost a century? Why had it risen in the first place? Why, generally speaking, do great powers and civilizations rise and fall? There are many answers and explanations, and each case seems to be somewhat different. And when all the explanations have been adduced, there still remains the question of what role accident played.

Philo of Alexandria, a Hellenized Jew, who lived in the first century AD, summarized the experience gathered so far. Greece was once flourishing, but the Macedonians took away her power. Macedonia prospered but, divided, weakened and withered away. The Persians enjoyed good fortune, but one day Persia's great and mighty kingdom was destroyed. The Parthians, once the subjects of the Persians, now ruled over them. Egypt, their former master, shone in splendor for a long time, but, like a cloud, her great power vanished. In other words, the fact that empires and civilizations have come and gone has been known to historians for a long time.

Edward Gibbon put much of the blame for the fall of Rome on Christianity because it, among other things, opposed the institution of slavery. This has been doubted by others. Very often economic and demographic factors have been adduced, and it seems true that they have been of importance in some cases, but not in others. In the case of Spain, the responsibility of the decline in the sixteenth century was put on King Philip II and on economic decline. But the king, also known as El Prudente, was a very cautious man, and there was no economic decline at that time.

Britain was considered the leading economic power in the middle of the nineteenth century. Its steel output was greater than that of all other nations, and it had pioneered the railway and other crucial industrial inventions. But fifty years later, Germany had overtaken Britain, even though they had not shown great proclivity as merchants and industrialists. Why?

Montesquieu was among the first to emphasize the importance of climate for the rise and decline of nations and civilizations, but this seems to be more helpful in explaining Africa's lagging behind than the decline of Europe, which enjoys a moderate climate. Earlier, the decline of Portugal and the Netherlands was explained as stemming from their narrow demographic basis, since they were small countries and could not rule much bigger, distant territories for a long time. This may well be, but it does not explain why populations in certain countries expanded while others shrunk. Why did the population of the Mediterranean countries decline from the early eighteenth century whereas the north European countries, such as France, Britain, and Germany, increased? An argument that has been fashionable among the declinist school in the United States for more than two decades says that "imperial overstretch" might have been the main reason. This could be true (among other factors) with regard to the Roman Empire, but hardly for Europe in the twentieth century, which shrunk rather than expanded in the age of decolonization.

Very often, empires, countries, and civilizations have been

compared with human beings and animals going through the usual stages of life such as youth, maturity, old age, and decline. It has been said that countries, like people, lose their vigor and initial dynamism as they age. Thomas Mann, in his greatest novel, *Buddenbrooks,* deals with three generations of a family. The forefather was a successful merchant and laid the foundation for the prosperity of the family. His son consolidated this fortune steadily but cautiously. The cultured grandson was quite different, as his interest in the family business was virtually nonexistent. This could be seen as the mirror of the fate of greater collectives.

Those who tried to apply such kinds of theories about young and old peoples had their work cut out for them. They included Ernst von Lasaulx, a German nineteenth-century historian and philosopher, Oswald Spengler, and Moeller van den Bruck, an ideological precursor of Nazism who coined the term *Third Reich.* Moeller van den Bruck believed that the future belonged to the "young nations" such as Germany and Russia; others added Italy and the United States. But Germany, Russia, and Italy did not fare too well. In our time, China and India have been reinterpreted as young nations, even though they are among the oldest.

What is the role of accident? This was a question already pondered by Gibbon. What if the Saracens had won the battles of Tours and Poitiers in 732, and what if the Turks had prevailed at the gates of Vienna in 1529 and 1683? What if the European revolutions of 1848 had succeeded and the First World War had never broken out? Such outcomes were perfectly possible, and, had they happened, European history would have taken another turn. Counterfactual history is not a mere game. It shows that time and again accident played a decisive role.

Increasing luxury has been mentioned frequently as a cause of decline. People became lazy and lost their drive and enterprise, and countries no longer found enough young people to fight so had to employ mercenaries. This has been mentioned as an explanation even in the case of Holland in the seventeenth century, despite the fact that the Dutch lived relatively modestly compared, for instance, with the Italian aristocracy at the time.

What was the role of new religions or political religions or ideology in the rise and decline of nations? This was undoubtedly a factor of importance—why did intellectual elites lose their erstwhile patriotism, pride, and self-confidence and turn against the past and present of their country, away from an earlier feeling of historical mission? How to explain the loss of self-confidence even among ruling elites? Sometimes, but not always, it happened as a result of a lost war, and sometimes epochs of decadence were followed without apparent reason by a spiritual revival leading to a political renaissance. Perhaps it was, at least in some cases, a generational phenomenon, the younger generation getting bored with the tedium of decadence and decay. We call this the D'Annunzio phenomenon, the poet of a voluptuous lifestyle turning into a hero-aviator and an aggressive patriot (but, then again, he had always sympathized with ultranationalist views).

Many questions, no certain answers. One certainty seems to be the fact that, in order to attain or maintain superpower status, size is of importance, and this raises the question of Europe. What were the missed chances of Europe in history? What if Europe had united over the centuries? There were certainly some who wanted and even dreamed of it. The most poetic expression of this longing was provided by Novalis, the great German writer, in the beginning of *Christendom and*

Europe. "Oh what a beautiful, what a brilliant age it was," he wrote, "when Europe was one Christian land, when one great common interest united even the most remote parts of this continent, when one sovereign was uniting and guiding the great political forces." Relations between people were those of trustful children and even the wildest instincts and emotions were suppressed. Everyone was tending to his affairs quietly, with hope and without fear, everyone felt protected, and so on.

Not everyone would agree with such idyllic descriptions of the Middle Ages. But the feeling and the nostalgia certainly existed, and not only among the Romantics. Rousseau, and before him the French Abbé de Saint Pierre, had a plan for uniting Europe. Kant's famous treatise on perpetual peace rested on the basis of a federation of European secular free states. These men all believed in a European identity—on the impact of Greece, Rome, and Christianity and of the Renaissance, Humanism, and the Enlightenment. To a greater or lesser extent, they had all made Europe what it became, but it did not create a political Europe.

Two men did make famous attempts to unite Europe by force—Napoleon and Hitler (Hitler became an almost passionate European but only when he realized, in 1943, that the tide had turned against him). But even if they had won their wars this would not have worked. On the contrary, their aggressions strengthened European nationalism.

Why did Europe fail to unite in history, as only a few continents did? The various countries had different traditions, spoke different languages (Latin remained the language of a few), and there were different religions that were far more important at the time than they are now. The distances between the countries were great, and traveling was cumbersome and arduous. Europeans did not meet often and knew little of one another. This was true even regarding the state of affairs within most countries (France for instance) and it applied a fortiori for all of Europe. Unity came to Germany and Italy only in the second half of the nineteenth century. And so the nation-state developed: an "imagined community," according to some, but one with far greater emotional attraction than the European idea.

There were debates over whether feelings of national identity had developed only with the Hundred Years War between England and France, whether the phenomenon goes back to ancient times, or whether it only came about more recently, in the eighteenth and nineteenth centuries. These are interesting issues, especially inasmuch as the power of nationalism is concerned, but, whatever the answer, their relevance with regard to the present situation is limited. It boils down to the central question whether nationalism in Europe will wither sufficiently to make a united Europe possible. Even if this question is answered in the affirmative, it remains to be seen whether a united Europe will be able to play a substantially greater role in international affairs than at present or whether the afflictions besetting the countries of Europe at present, the listlessness and abulia, will reappear in a united Europe.

Historically, the most pertinent question is perhaps this: when did Europe lose its self-confidence? This loss began at the height of its power. Dismal visions among poets and philosophers and an end-of-the-world mood were not, however, always infectious, partly perhaps because there had been too many false alarms earlier on. Jean-Paul Sartre in the 1960s had been sounding the tocsin—Europe was dying a miserable death in its convulsions. Inspired by Frantz Fanon, the prophet of purifying violence, Sartre could not have been more mistaken, for the worst danger Europe was facing at the time was economic stagflation, which it overcame.

Going further back there was a bit of a panic before the First World War—the famous fin de siècle. In France it had started earlier, but it also ended earlier. All kinds of horrible disasters took place; poets and painters were in deep despair. Benedetto Croce, an astute observer, noted that the fin de siècle was more than a literary or artistic fashion. Something fundamental had changed: the decline of religion. Secular humanism could only in part compensate.

And yet it was not clear how deep the despair went. For optimism in a better future was still unbroken. Swinburne, the grandfather of the English decadents, hailed the new century in a poem entitled "1901":

> *An age too great for thought of ours to scan*
> *A wave upon the sleepless sea of time*

The mood was pensive rather than despairing. Europe was ruling the world, but was it really worthwhile? Kipling, the poet laureate, wrote in 1899:

> *Take up the White Man's Burden—*
> *And reap his old reward:*
> *The blame of those ye better*
> *The hate of those ye guard.*

Two years later there followed an even sterner warning against being drunk with power in his *Recessional* ("Lest we forget"):

> *Far-called, our navies melt away;*
> *On dune and headland sinks the fire:*
> *Lo, all our pomp of yesterday*
> *Is one with Nineveh and Tyre!*

Early on, Kipling, the bard of imperialism, realized that Europe's predominance would not last forever.

But statesmen acted as if it would last forever, hence the outbreak of the First World War, which Europe could ill afford. On the evening of August 4, 1914, Sir Edward Grey, the British foreign secretary, watching from his office in Whitehall the lights "springing out" in the dusk, told a friend, "The lamps are going out all over the Europe; we shall not see them lit again in our lifetime." These words have been quoted innumerable times, but, figuratively speaking, the lights have never gone on again. The world of yesterday had vanished.

The First World War broke Europe's self-confidence. True, it would hold on to most of its colonies a little longer. But the creditor of the world had become its debtor, and it was clear that, without the United States, the entente would not have won the war. Oswald Spengler's *Decline of the West*, published in 1918, was ready for publication in 1914, but it would not have received remotely the publicity and acclaim it did had it appeared that year; the war made all the difference.

Francesco Nitti, a former prime minister of Italy, said it all in a book published in 1922, *Europe without Peace* (also translated as *The Decadence of Europe* and *The Wreckage of Europe*). Europe's moral sense had declined or disappeared. The material damage that had been caused by the war could be repaired in time, but there had been an internal process of decomposition. Europe was divided into thirty states, each with its own nationalism. There had been a common feeling of solidarity and responsibility before, which now no longer existed. The Europe cobbled together at Versailles and the other Paris suburbs led to the Second World War, and this time it could be saved only with the help of America and the Soviet Union.

Intellectuals have been blamed for Eurodefeatism. George Canning wrote,

> *Steady patriots of the world alone*
> *The friend of every country but his own.*

Julien Benda wrote his *Trahison des Clercs* in 1927, but this was (which is now usually forgotten) an essay against chauvinism in France and Germany and only later acquired its present general meaning of a betrayal by intellectuals of their essential values. True, the anti-Western ideologies and regimes of the twentieth century exuded a strong influence on European intellectuals, both in the face of fascism and communism and up to and including manifest monstrosities. The story of intellectuals in politics in the twentieth century is very often an ugly one. Two further examples may suffice. During the cold war, a revisionist interpretation was influential in academia. While Stalin was not free from blame, according to this school of thought, both sides were to blame, and the West probably more so. After the collapse of the Soviet Union, this version was somewhat modified: both sides were guilty but behaved on the whole responsibly.

A somewhat similar debate developed in the 1990s, when, in the view of an influential group of academics, "Enlightenment fundamentalists" overdid their critique of Islam and were insufficiently willing to make concession to it. In addition, there was a subacute feeling of guilt in view of the imperialist record of Western powers, even though America had not been involved in the Middle East or Africa in past ages and European countries had been directly involved in the Middle East only for a short time in the late nineteenth and early twentieth century. The prevailing fashion of moral and cultural relativism in academe also played a manifest role.

The intellectuals had some influence as far as public opinion was concerned, but they had no power, and their impact should not be overrated. Similar attitudes existed after the Second World War, stemming from the alienation of intellectuals from society. But if a united Europe did not emerge after 1945 and if Europe was abdicated from a leading role in world politics, the alienation of the intellectuals was not the main cause.

EUROPE—SOME
CRYSTAL-BALL GAZING

DURING THE SUMMER OF 2010, before the immediate financial crisis was overcome but while the debt crisis was still in full swing, there was much talk on whether the EU would survive, and articles in leading journals had titles such as "Staring into the Abyss" (*The Economist*). The abyss was presumably a world without the euro and with a much reduced European social model, meaning the welfare state. There were sharp divisions in Europe between France and Germany, between north and south, between west and east. The French government survived street battles protesting the raising of the pension age from sixty to sixty-two. In Britain and the Netherlands, the proposals to raise the age to sixty-seven and even seventy hardly caused major protests. Compromises were reached as it was realized that protests were pointless if the needed money could not be found.

But the European malaise went considerably deeper. The CIA had predicted in January 2005 that if Europe's welfare systems were not reformed and revitalized, if there was no radical systemic change in the educational and tax system, Europe was doomed. Since Europe was aging quickly, it needed new immigrants, and, as a result, its Muslim population would rise to between 22 and 37 percent by 2025. The CIA also foresaw the collapse of NATO and of Israel and some other developments, and it predicted the emergence of a Catholic east Europe allied with the United States. In subsequent assessments of the National Intelligence Council (in 2008 and 2010), which were far less specific, Europe hardly appears at all. While in 2005 Europe had been written off, in 2010 it was revived even if as a "hobbled giant." Scenario 3, "Concert of Europe Redux," (2010) reads:

> Under this scenario, several threats to the international system—possibly a looming environmental disaster or a conflict that risks spreading—prompt greater cooperation on solving global problems. Significant reform of the international system becomes possible.... The US increasingly shares power while China and India increase their burden sharing and the EU takes on a bigger global role.

But this is not considered a likely scenario, nor is it made clear whether there will be a European Union by the year 2025. Having learned from bitter experiences, these recent essays in political futurism suffer from overcaution and vagueness and thus will not be of much help to policy makers. There is much talk of international order, but much less about international disorder, competition, and conflict, let alone possible violent developments. One of the assignments of the CIA is to predict coming events, but it should not be blamed for making frequent mistakes, because the future is a priori unpredictable.

On what grounds were the pessimistic projections for Europe based? On the one hand, no doubt, they were based on the assumption that in view of the aging population the welfare state would become more and more expensive. But more attention should have been paid to the question of whether

costs could be cut without abolishing the welfare state altogether. At about the same time, the EU semiofficial Eurobarometer survey published its own massive "The Future of
Europe" investigation, which reached far more optimistic conclusions. True, most Europeans had only a lukewarm interest
in European affairs. But when asked whether they wanted to
have more decision making at the national or the European
level, they came out decisively in favor of the European level.

What were the best ways to ensure the future of Europe?
The answer: comparable living standards as the key elements.
If so, the argument is returned to the level of the common
market. But the protagonists of the European Union have proclaimed for a long time that the EU is more than a common
market; it is also a union of values (without always making
clear what these values were). But was it willing and capable to
stand up and fight for these values, or at least defend them?

The crisis of 2008 did not spell the end of the EU, nor did it
bring the organization much nearer to solving the problems
besetting it. In addition to the problems confronting the EU
back in 2005, new ones appeared. There were, to begin with,
the internal dissension, the growing number of euroskeptics,
the growing distance between the EU elite and the people it
represented. At a time of economic crisis, Brussels wanted to
increase its budget by 6 percent. The demand was later reduced but a substantial sum was still demanded, the necessity
of which was not readily obvious to many European citizens.
It would have been easier to persuade Europeans of this need
if the leading personalities in Brussels had been of a different
caliber.

These internal problems quite apart, as well as the growing difficulties to gain a European consensus, there was also
the changing global situation—the difficulties of competing

on the world markets, China's increasing economic and political weight (and assertiveness), Europe's dependence on Russian and Middle Eastern oil and gas, America's great indebtedness, and, as a result, Washington's weakened international position. A rejuvenation of Europe was much needed, but it would hardly come from Waziristan and Yemen. "Europeans must tackle our demographic challenge," recommended *Project Europe 2030*. "If urgent measures are not taken, our aging societies will put unsustainable pressure on our pension, health and welfare systems and undermine our economic competitiveness." Quite true, but, according to historical experience, there are no measures that guarantee such results.

All this could have made for greater awareness of the need to strengthen the EU and its institutions. But it did not have this effect. Above all, the European mood did not change for the better. There was not much confidence in closer European cooperation, but there was equally not much confidence in going it alone. There were all kind of blueprints circulated about a green future and a digital future and a dozen other futures. Tours were arranged for young journalists in search of the coming future. But the enthusiasm had vanished, and Project Europe had run out of steam, admittedly not for the first time. Could it regain momentum in the foreseeable future?

The debate about Europe's standing in the world and its future prospects has been going on for a long time. Its most recent phase began with the publication of Robert Kagan's essay "Power and Weakness" (*Policy Review* 2002), which became known as the "Americans are from Mars, Europeans from Venus" essay. It begins as follows:

It is time to stop pretending that Europeans and Americans share a common view of the world or even that they occupy the same world. On the all-*important* question of power—the efficacy of power, the morality of power, the desirability of power—American and European perspectives are diverging.

The Mars/Venus metaphor became quite popular, even though classicists and historians had doubts. Mars was a complex figure and Venus by no means the goddess of peace. She was also Venus Victrix, the goddess of victory, and Roman warriors used to pray to her on the eve of battle. In any case, the history of Europe has been more martial than that of America.

The statements were not to be taken quite literally; Europeans and Americans occupy the same world, and Kagan conceded that "one cannot generalize about Europeans." But such exaggeration helped put into relief the basic differences in approach to world politics. Kagan notes that the end of the cold war exacerbated the disagreements. Europe has been militarily weak for a long time and America much stronger. Europe's greater tolerance toward threats and incapacity to respond to them has shaped European foreign policy: diplomacy, negotiations, patience, the forging of economic ties, political engagement, the use of inducements rather than sanctions, the taking of small steps, and others. As the then head of the European Commission, Romano Prodi, put it in a speech in Paris in 2001, Europe had a role to play in world governance, a role based on replicating the European experience on a global scale. Hence the basic reason for the divergence in views between America and Europe. America was powerful and willing to exercise its power unilaterally if necessary, while Europe saw its mission as spreading the gospel of law, civilization, and eternal peace.

What could be done to bring Americans and Europeans

closer? As far as the basic issues were concerned, Kagan was
not optimistic. Perhaps some of the major European countries
would have, deep down, a memory of what power was, international influence and ambition, but this would be building
on atavistic impulses. Perhaps the Bush Junior's administration (and even the Clinton people) could have ceased to regard
Europe as an albatross, payed more respect to multilateralism,
shown a "decent respect for the opinion of others," as the
founders put it. Kagan, who apparently did not want to end on
too pessimistic a note, said that a little understanding could go
a long way.

But it did not go a long way, as subsequent years were to
show. It was much easier to be optimistic about the state of the
world in 2001 (despite 9/11) than at the end of the decade. In
the meantime, the United States had become involved in the
seemingly unending wars in Iraq and Afghanistan, and Europe, while expanding, had been further weakened by internal dissent stemming largely (but by no means entirely) from
economic and financial issues that also threatened America.

As far as the United States was concerned, was it a case of
imperial overstretch, as some argued? Not really. The Soviet
Union did not collapse because of its military intervention in
Afghanistan, nor will the United States. It was, however, a
typical case of profound political misjudgment to enter a war
(or two wars) hoping that it could be won cheaply, with a
minimum of military investment. If the wars were deemed
inescapable, overwhelming force should have been applied,
resulting in a crushing defeat of the enemy, in a quick victory,
and in an equally quick withdrawal. It is quite possible that
such an operation would have presented only a temporary solution and that it would have had to be repeated after a number of years. But there was no such strategy in the White

House and the Pentagon, nor was the Iranian threat taken into account. If there had been a realistic strategy, it is not certain whether there would have been public support for any length of time, many Americans apparently not being from Mars.

In the case of Afghanistan, there was the justified fear that it would turn into a jihadist base for attacks (possibly with weapons of mass destruction) against unbelievers all over the globe. But given geopolitical realities, such a base could have also been established in a number of other countries. It would have been wiser if Washington had left the solution of the Afghanistan problem to her neighboring countries, which were equally, if not more, threatened. It would have been regrettable if as a result dissent would have arisen among Afghanistan's powerful neighbors (Russia, China, Pakistan, India, and Iran) as it probably will in the future. But such a development would not have caused strong headaches to policy makers in Washington; perhaps Washington might have emerged as an arbiter in such a constellation.

Kagan's views were widely discussed at the time but found few sympathizers. American policies even under Bush were frequently considered neoconservative (even though Kagan was not a Straussian), reactionary, neoimperialist, a recipe for perpetuating American hegemony at a time when the world was allegedly moving to a reduction of tensions and toward multipolarity.

Delusions were rampant at the beginning of the first decade of the new century. Writing in 2008 ("The End of the End of History" in the *New Republic*), Kagan noted that the earlier grand expectations that the world had entered an age of convergence had proved wrong; it was divergence rather than convergence that had prevailed. Charles Grant, a strong and persuasive advocate of a united Europe and head of the London-based Centre for European Reform, tended to agree with him. He still believed in 2010 that the EU should not leave it to China, Russia, the United States, and others to design the new world order. For their order, as he put it, might be illiberal or no order at all.

But how to achieve this aim of strengthening European influence? Europe's performance on hard security matters had been unimpressive. When it came to major and pressing international problems, the EU had been invisible or absent. The EU had some soft power, but not much, and its economic power was declining. Grant quoted an eminent Chinese commentator to the effect that a power needed guns and guts. Both were in short supply in Europe.

How to remedy the situation? Grant suggested that there was no point to build up European defense because too few countries were caring about it. European foreign policy should be made by a small group of states, for twenty-seven cooks in the kitchen were too many. A common energy policy should be made an absolute priority. All other things apart, this was crucial as far as Europe's relations with Russia were concerned. He stressed that leaders should lead and made a number of other sensible suggestions, warning (quoting David Milliband) against "stand[ing] aside and let[ting] others shape our 21st century for us."

Grant's observations were commented upon by Robert Cooper, whose ideas have been mentioned earlier. He made reference to the deployment of European forces in eastern Congo and Aceh and the fact that the success rate of piracy attacks off the shores of Somalia had been halved, but he admitted that Europe had failed to stand up to major powers. Cooper agreed that Europe was slow in making decisions but also that this had certain advantages, for this way Europe was likely to make fewer mistakes. Cooper certainly sounded much less optimistic than ten years earlier ("Failures are normal in foreign policy"): Aceh and eastern Congo were not manifestations of great strength, and, following the European defense cuts in 2010, it seemed unlikely that Europe would be able in the future to engage even in such minor expeditions. He observed that the world did not need another great power in the nineteenth-century mode. But since the world was saddled with such powers, how could Europe retain any influence at all, given their presence?

The EU represented the aspiration of a world governed by law. But Cooper left open the question how this aspiration could be achieved without some mechanism to enforce the law. Could Europe be a power without being a state? This, Cooper thought, remained to be answered, but it should certainly be tried. The view that this could be achieved in the contemporary world was stretching optimism to a far limit. And since, in their present mood, most Europeans did not want a state, it meant they were willing to accept that others would shape their twenty-first century, unless, by some miracle, the other powers would be somehow fatally weakened, in which case no one would shape the century—not a joyous perspective either.

There had been more participants in the debate about Europe's standing in the world in the years to come. But the certainty that the future Europe will not be the same inasmuch as its ethnic composition is concerned and that this could have an impact on its policy have not been on Europe's agenda. It will be discussed in the following pages.

The crisis so far has not given a real impetus to a policy of strengthening Europe on the international scene, which would include stabilizing the economy, building up a common defense, and of course attaining closer political cooperation. On the other hand, various quick (or not so quick) fixes have been suggested to remedy the situation in ways that would involve less of an effort. This refers above all to broadening the European base by expanding it, drawing in Russia and Turkey under the somewhat nebulous heading of "interdependence." Such a strategy rests on the assumption that if the European Union were to support Russian and Turkish foreign political ambitions and integrate them in a common European framework, this would greatly contribute to a much stronger Europe, including a European security treaty and a new stable and secure world order. The way to achieve this is a "trialogue," aiming to draw the two prospective partners into Europe by satisfying their political goals.

This policy rests on a mistaken assessment of Russian and Turkish political interests and their attitudes vis-à-vis Europe. The inclusion of Russia and Turkey would result in a very different Europe from the one now existing; it would mean a farewell to its advocacy of democracy and human rights as now interpreted in Europe. It is not clear what it would contribute to the security of Europe; neither Turkey nor Russia have the intention (or the power) to serve as the Janissaries of a continent for whom they have no high respect.

It goes without saying that good, progressively closer relations with Russia and Turkey are desirable and that there are minorities in these countries that share the aim of a rapprochement with Europe. It is possible that, in the course of time, liberalization will take place in Russia and Turkey, but this process could take generations. At the present time, most Turks and Russians have clearly expressed the view that, while they share certain interests with Europe, the European values are not theirs, that Turkey's future is in the East rather than with Europe, that Russia has a new *Westpolitik* and would be interested in extending its "sphere of privileged influence" in Europe, economic and political, but that the European theory and practice of democracy is not theirs.

In brief, the "interdependence" strategy is not realistic. If successful, it would result in a Europe that has little in common with the present. If Europe has become so much weaker, if its economy needs deep reform, its policy fresh major impulses, its defense far greater strength, the rescue can come only from within, a revival of the native political will. It cannot come from the outside, however intense and long the dialogue or trialogue. To paraphrase the *Internationale*—no higher being, no outside power can be of help—it can only be done by the Europeans, if they have the wish to do so.

PART TWO

REJUVENATION?

ENRICHMENT: A GUIDED TOUR

WHAT CAUSED STAGNATION AND DECLINE in Europe in our time? There was more than one cause, and some reasons have been mentioned earlier. One has to look back quite a few years, probably a few decades, to form an understanding. Was it inevitable? Perhaps not to this extent. When I first revisited London not long after the end of the Second World War, it was a pretty shabby sight. Much of the damage caused during the war could still be seen, especially in the City and the East End; people were not dressed well and the food in the restaurants was execrable. It was the age of austerity and there was still much rationing of food, textiles, and quite a few other things. But the mood was upbeat (the writers who came to be called the "Angry Young Men" were still in kindergarten). In 1951 the Festival of Britain took place on the south bank of the river Thames, with all kinds of impressive new buildings going up, such as the Royal Festival Hall and the Dome of Discovery. There was a great deal of entertainment. There were at the time, I believe, some eighty theaters in London, not counting the many music halls and cinemas. The movies produced during those years, especially by the Ealing studios, were funny, in particular those starring Alec Guinness. Anyway, I liked them much more than most recent productions. London was a very English city, with, of course, some enclaves—the Irish in Kilburn, Africans and West Indians in Brixton, Poles in Earls Court, Jews moving from the East End to Golders Green and Hendon. Television, the new and most popular medium, was showing heart-warming crime series such as *Dixon of Dock Green,* but crime was seldom violent, and most conflicts could be settled over a cup of tea.

During the next three decades, London became more prosperous. If a friend or a cousin from abroad came to London in the 1970s and asked to see what was new in the British capital, he would be taken to the Barbican, which was about to become a cultural center, with arts unlimited, galleries, the home of the London Symphony Orchestra, as well as countless restaurants, pubs, and bars. Or perhaps to Canary Wharf, once the West India docks and cargo warehouses but now about to become the new business and banking center—"vibrant" was the term to be used. Even a new city airport was planned for the middle of town. The Tate Modern opened in 2000; the old Tate Gallery had been established in 1897.

Paris after the war was different. Hardly anything had been destroyed, but virtually nothing new had been built either. There was no rationing. Many little shops were open until late at night, often owned by retired policemen and their wives, selling butter, milk, and eggs. Food in the restaurants was excellent. But the little Renaults and Citroëns in the streets were mostly prewar and less than impressive. Many of the prewar movie stars had collaborated with the Germans, some more, others less, but no great damage had been done to their careers; most were back dominating the screens again by 1948. But then the plays of Sartre and Camus had also been performed during the occupation. Thirty years later most of the small shops had disappeared and the cars were sleeker and faster. As in London, many small music halls and cinemas and theaters had disappeared. The visitors from abroad or out of town would be taken to the Centre Pompidou near the big indoor market in the fourth arrondissement. It opened in 1977, was not very fashionable (and the building's exposed pipes were an eyesore), but it was where the action was, with fifty thousand works of art. Or we would have taken the visitor to La Défense, a new business center with many skyscrapers, the impressive Arche and Palace, quite different from earlier such quarters. In the evening, we might be off to one of the venerable music halls; some had to go out of business in this age of television, but a few had a second coming.

In Berlin we would have shown him the Wall, but this was not really that new; if he was interested in architecture the choice was clear—the Maerkisches Viertel and the buildings designed by Gropius. Europe in 2011: the travel agencies promote vacations in Europe—"Europe is full of jaw-dropping attractions, including historical cities and historic ruins, majestic castles, alluring landscapes, beautiful rolling hillsides." One can easily add to the list cruising down the river on a Sunday afternoon, be it the Thames, the Seine, or the Rhine, all of which have been cleaned up to some extent. Breathtaking Capri or Portofino, walking *au bord de l'eau* with Nana Moskouri. Or hiking in the Black Forest, inspecting the Louvre or the Prado, or, for more middle-brow tastes, the Copenhagen Tivoli.

The year 2005 was not a quiet one in Paris and vicinity. Elsewhere, too, heated debates were under way about the future of the continent. More and more people took an interest in demography, which, as some nineteenth-century sages had predicted, was fate. According to some, the old continent would be largely Muslim by 2050 or by 2100 at the latest. But such predictions were not widely accepted, partly because most people did not think they would live that long, partly because demographic projections had sometimes been wrong. Somehow one would muddle through as so often in the past. Anyway, not long after came the recession, and people became preoccupied with far more immediate concerns.

Today, if the visitor were to ask where the action is, the decision would be easier. As the reviewer of my *Last Days of Europe* in *The Economist* put it, "In truth European cities such as London and Berlin acquired a new zip thanks to immigrants from around the world." Let us look for the new zip in Berlin Mitte with the new ministries, the center of the new capital. But Berlin has been a capital before, with many ministries from the Wilhelmstrasse to the Bendlerstrasse. If the visitor really wanted to see the zip concentrated, we would not have to rely on long explanation and abstract description; a short walk or bus ride would do in order to get a preview of the shape of things to come.

An excellent starting point would be Neukölln or Kottbusser Tor in Berlin or St. Denis or Evry in the Paris banlieue. In some ways, moving about has become much easier. There are fewer language difficulties; the argot of the banlieue (*verlan*), we are told by *Le Monde,* consists of four hundred words. True, in Kreuzberg (also locally known as SO 36, the old postal code) and in Neukölln, knowledge of Turkish could be more helpful than speaking German. Among the younger generation, Kanak Sprak is probably even more useful (for a taste see the translation of Snow White and Hansel and Gretel into Kanak Sprak). According to the experts, it consists of about three hundred words, a third of fecal or sexual origin, another third has to do with motorcars, and the rest is a mixture of various elements. Those mastering this language may be able to understand the dialogue in the famous American TV series *The Wire* without the benefit of subtitles. In Britain, hip-hop language, an interesting mixture of materialism and nihilism, has become fashionable. It also has a great deal to do with violence and pit bulls. Its origins are Jamaican, but hardly Islamic.

In London, we would advise our guest to stroll along Edgware Road, starting at Marble Arch, or, if our visitor wanted to venture farther afield, we would take a bus to Tower Hamlets (the old East End) or Lambeth, where the archbishop has his official residence, or to Lewisham. If our visitor has a special interest in Southeast Asia, we would take him to Brent in the north, or if he is interested in things African, we would take a taxi to Peckham. *The East Enders* has been the most successful soap opera on British television for the last twenty-five years, telling the life and little adventures of several families in this part of London. It pretends to take place in the present, but we would not recommend it as a realistic guide to the contemporary East End. For as the Commission for Racial Equality has rightly pointed out, this series is a sentimental re-creation of the East End of the 1960s, when the overwhelming majority of its residents were white working class. Today they are black and Asian, and only some elderly whites are left who could not find or were not given housing elsewhere.

Monica Ali's *Brick Lane* is probably a better guide to the contemporary West End. The author, who is of Bangladeshi origin, was a runner-up for the Booker prize, but she was bitterly attacked for a "lack of authenticity," painting too negative a picture of the community. They even threatened to burn the book. Mrs. Ali's knowledge of the Bengali language was less than perfect and she had studied philosophy at Oxford, admittedly not a typical East End career.

These parts of London offer much of interest, and the

guidebooks recommend their gastronomic delights. The sounds of Cairo and the sights and smells of Karachi and Dacca can be found in these areas. A Muslim writer named Aijaz Saka Syed, in an article in the *Arab News,* says that arriving in Brussels he observed that the capital of the new Europe "increasingly looks like Beirut, Istanbul or any other great city in the Middle East." He was most "pleasantly surprised" by the impact of the Arab and Muslim population and added that "it is not just in Brussels. Scenes like these are increasingly familiar . . . from London to Paris and from Berlin to Copenhagen to Amsterdam."

He reported that "the European media has been buzzing with talk of the 'Muslims are coming' and the 'demographic time-bomb.'" He advised his European colleagues not to get overexcited and "wish their immigrants away" but to accept the facts. Those who are "invading . . . Europe" are "transforming its profile forever." But they are needed to "rejuvenate" an old and exhausted continent forever: "Like them or hate them, Europe has to learn to live with its Muslims." Or, as Dr. Aidh al-Qarni, a well-known Saudi preacher, put it, "I expect, like many perceptive people living in Europe, that, Allah willing, the European continent will be an Islamic continent" (www .onislam.net, Oct. 31, 2010).

Returning to contemporary London, many of these scenes are charmingly exotic, the women in black in their hijabs, the halal butchers, the kebab palaces, and the couscous-eating places enriching the menus of the local restaurants, the Aladin cafés and the Marhaba minimarkets. The visitor will be offered fattoush and felafel, and he will soon realize that Mecca Cola has replaced Coca-Cola in these parts. Many of the placards and inscriptions are in languages and alphabets he cannot read (unless he happens to be a graduate of the nearby School of Oriental Studies). The corner shops sell Arab dailies, such as *Al Hayat, As Sharq, al Awsat, Al Quds al Arabi,* and others. There seem to be almost as many Arabic dailies here as English-language ones. They also sell periodicals in Bengali and Urdu, papers that I can read but do not understand. *Hürriyet,* the leading Turkish newspaper, has had a Berlin edition since about 1970. The editor thinks that Turks in Germany are better integrated than East Germans and that this is why the circulation of his paper is declining (although they can read the Turkish papers free of charge on the Internet).

The visitor in London will pass by mosques, the main one in Regents Park, but most on side streets or in the suburbs. Some cities now have more mosques than churches, Birmingham, for instance, or Bradford. The churches are bigger but emptier. He will pass by cultural centers and clubs financed by the governments of Saudi Arabia and sometimes also Libya. There are bookshops selling religious treatises but also secular literature. Sometimes, from under the counter, literature will be produced that is considered hate literature by the infidels.

Edgware Road (also known now as "Arab Road") is an interesting social mixture: Church Street market with its fruit and vegetable stalls is certainly not a place where the wealthy shop; they do so at Harrods in Knightsbridge, which belongs to the Qatari royal family. But the Lamborghinis and the Ferraris to be seen and heard here in the evenings belong to young Arabs. The Maroush restaurant is certainly not inexpensive (there are more branches since I wrote about it last), and the Arab and North African pop stars and the belly dancers are well paid. Hasir is recommended as the best Turkish restaurant in Berlin; the name does not mean "pig" or "pork" as students of Semitic languages may think—this would be singularly inappropriate. Widely used are hookahs, or water pipes (called *shishas* or *nargilehs* in Berlin). There are few Maseratis in the streets of Kreuzberg and Neukölln, but there is a restaurant named Baghdad in the Schlesische Strasse. The best Middle Eastern food in Paris is said to be in the Meurice with three Michelin stars; to say that it is not cheap would be an understatement.

Music is an essential part of the European Muslim scene, with Abdel Ali Slimani in London and Cheb Khaled (the king of the rai, a form of North African music) in Paris. The French rappers doing their rai were first on the scene (in Bobigny in 1984, to be precise), but they perform almost exclusively for their compatriots, whereas in London, young Englishmen and women also attend these sessions. There is less music in Neukölln, which in contrast to the Paris banlieue is still ethnically mixed (but there are hardcore rappers in Turkish Berlin too). There is a political and cultural contradiction here, because the Muslim fundamentalists, above all the Muslim Brotherhood, are strictly opposed to musical entertainment, not to mention belly dancers. But were they to try imposing their will in these parts of Paris and London, they would lose much of their popularity. The rappers of the banlieue have more followers among the young than the imams; they refer to Islam, Allah, and Muhammed in their music (often to the dismay of the preachers). Some of them predicted the riots of 2005; others called for calm. We shall return to this subject.

All this is a far cry from what these quarters used to be in the 1950s and 1960s, when they were British or French or German working-class neighborhoods. The locals have mostly moved out, and some of the neighborhoods have become a little more colorful (less in Paris than in London). Once upon a time, the red banlieue was the stronghold of the French Communists, but these days too have gone.

Such visits are an educational experience, but, folkloristic interest quite apart, they also provide a glance into the future. These quarters are spreading, and within a generation they will probably cover a much greater space of the big cities of Europe, a gradual process that can be observed, for instance in the Tiergarten section or Moabit in Berlin. In what direction will they expand? West of Edgware Road is Bayswater, but this has been Arab and Middle Eastern territory for a long time. To the south is Hyde Park and to the east is the West End, with its expensive shops. The Middle Eastern upper crust has moved long ago to Knightsbridge and Kensington, not far from their embassies. In Berlin there is no Turkish upper class, only a middle class, small for the time being, who have been moving to certain streets in Schöneberg but also to Charlottenburg and other parts in the west. But there are no Turkish middle-class concentrations.

True, northern parts of Neukölln have been embellished and apartments there are no longer cheap, in the same way you may have to pay close to a million dollars for an apartment on the Isle of Dogs (Seacon Towers, for instance), which is also part of the East End. But those settling in these gentrified areas are likely to be British yuppies rather than Pakistani or Turkish. The housing bubble has been pricked a little. Prices are still high, but you may find a two-bedroom apartment for $600,000 in what was a slum not long ago. However, many of the young people living here used to work in the City and have lost their jobs.

Great changes are taking place in the cities of Europe. Will they be all one-sided, affecting only the natives and not at all the newcomers? Perhaps the Muslim women will opt for colors other than black and perhaps the hijab will be reduced to something more symbolic? Perhaps their predilection for couscous will give way to fish and chips and bockwurst (and if

it does not, what harm will be done)? Perhaps mosque attendance will drop like church attendance did in western Europe.
Is the attractive power of the European way of life so small
that it will be overwhelmed by foreign customs and habits?
Could it be that the new immigrants stick to their old ways
imported from Anatolia or North Africa or Pakistan precisely
because they still are a minority, fearful of losing their identity,
and that once they no longer feel under siege but constitute a
majority, their societies might open up to outside influence irrespective of the warnings of their religious leaders?

A hundred years ago, a visit to Commercial Road in the
London East End or the Grenadierstrasse and the Scheunenviertel in East Berlin or Belleville and the Marais in Paris or
New York's Lower East Side would have shown a scenery that
was quite strange and not particularly pleasing to the eye—
the Jewish immigrants from eastern Europe in their new European or American surroundings, the little synagogues, the
cheap eating places, the sweatshops, the foreign language newspapers, the men and women in strange, outlandish clothes.

But there are major differences in these waves of immigration. There is, to begin with, the scale of immigration. Only
tens of thousands came to western Europe at the time, not
millions. The immigrants of a century ago made great efforts
to integrate socially and culturally. Above all, they wanted to
give their children a good secular education at almost any
price, as Chinese and Indian immigrants are doing today. The
rate of intermarriage was high within one generation and
even higher within two. No one helped them; there were no
social workers or advisers; no one gave them housing at low or
no rent; "head start" and "positive discrimination" had not yet
been invented. There was no free health service or unemployment benefit. There was no social safety net—it was a ques-

tion of sink or swim. There were no government committees
analyzing Judeophobia and how to combat it. The immigrant
Jews entered the trades and the professions, and their social
rise was quick and spectacular. They made a significant contribution to the cultural and scientific life of their adopted countries. Some strove to maintain the old way of life of the east
European shtetl, but the majority wanted assimilation and ac-
culturation.

Some observers argue that such comparisons are unfair
because the Jews arrived in countries where few natives had
gone beyond primary school, whereas the Muslims landed in
an unprecedented educated Europe. But this is a flawed argument: present-day immigrants came indeed from countries in
which the educational level was particularly low—but why
was it so low? It was certain that this was not because of Western imperialism, but the actual cause was a hotly debated issue. In the final analysis motivation was and is the decisive
issue, the wish to learn, to better oneself. If such eagerness
does not exist, outside help is bound to fail.

Many present-day immigrants live in societies separate
from those of the host countries. This is true for cities large
and small. They have few if any non-Muslim friends and they
seldom meet them except at work. Their knowledge of the
host language is rudimentary. Their preachers tell them their
values and traditions are superior to those of the infidels and
that any contact with them, even with their neighbors, is undesirable. Their young people complain about being victims
and being excluded, but more often than not their social and
cultural ghettoization is voluntary.

Do they identify with their new homeland? One day you
are told that they are Muslims (or Turks or Nigerians) who
happen to live in Britain, France, or Germany. On another day,

the polls say that they are more patriotic than the natives; perhaps there are rapid changes of mood and conviction. They get their politics, religion, and culture quite often from Arab and Turkish television channels. They may identify on the local level, rooting for a hometown soccer club such as Hertha BSC or Liverpool. If Germany plays Sweden as during the recent world championship they will hoist in Berlin the Turkish and the German flag. But if France is playing Algeria (or if Germany plays Turkey), the boys from the banlieue and Neukölln will not join in singing the national anthems and they will not applaud the French and German teams. However, they have no wish to go back to Turkey or Algeria. This is their country and they show it. No one should have any doubt about it.

But why focus on Muslim immigrants? There are many others in the big cities of Europe. About five hundred thousand Indians live in London as well as a great many Sikhs. But what a difference between, say, Southgate in North London and Southwark south of the Thames. Southgate is strongly Indian. Only 10 percent of the population is now native English, it is relatively prosperous, there are few run-down council estates, and the crime rate is not higher than elsewhere. There are countless shops and restaurants on the Broadway. South of the river is a very different picture. When my older daughter went to school in Peckham, it was a sleepy, lower-middle- and working-class quarter well described in Muriel Spark's 1960 novel *The Ballad of Peckham Rye*. Today it is predominantly African and Caribbean. Despite massive investment by the government and the EU, it is a slum, shabby and run-down, a center of gun and knife crime; few English live there anymore, except those who cannot afford to move out. The Labor Home Secretary called it a no-go zone. True, some courageous outsiders still venture there. Clint Eastwood chose the Heygate Estate for the background scenes in one of his recent violent movies, but he provided his own security. The well-meaning critics who warn against media hysteria do not live there.

About 250,000 Russians live in London now, but they will not be found in Peckham. Paris was the center of the Russian emigration in the 1920s and 1930s; today it is London and it has much less to do with Russian literature and the arts than with income tax regulations. Foreigners living in London do not have to pay taxes on money earned outside the country, which explains why a dozen Russian billionaires make their home there and also countless millionaires. They have been buying up the most expensive buildings within the epicenter in Kensington Park Gardens—according to estimates at least three billion dollars were invested in these purchases, about as much as all the buildings bought by Americans and Middle Easterners put together.

Or take Paris—what difference between the Muslim black African suburbs, Clichy-sous-Bois, where the riots of 2005 started, Choisy, Ivry, Vitry, on the one hand, and the Asian Paris on the other, including the Chinese and Vietnamese quarters such as Belleville, the third and thirteenth arrondissements. Much of the great difference has been explained with reference to unemployment, especially youth unemployment. But this leads to other questions—why unemployment among some ethnic communities and much less among others? Some claim that it is the result of ethnic and racial discrimination. There is some eagerness to believe this. But is it true?

EUROPE—A CULTURAL THEME PARK?

WHAT KIND OF NEW EUROPE is emerging as a successor to the old continent? This, of course, is an open question, if only because it depends not solely on events in Europe but also on events in other parts of the world. Will Europe turn into a cultural theme park, a kind of sophisticated Disneyland for well-to-do visitors from China and India, something like Bruges, Venice, Versailles, Stratford on Avon, Rothenburg ob der Tauber, but on a larger scale? Some such parks already exist. When the coal mines in the Ruhr were closed down, the Warner Bros. Movie World was opened in Dortmund, which introduces Batman but also the Agfa Museum of German Film History. Indeed, Essen was selected in March 2006 as the European capital of culture for 2010. Former cultural capitals of Europe have been Glasgow and Antwerp.

This could be a Europe of tourist guides, gondoliers, and translators who say, "Ladies and Gentlemen, you are visiting the scenes of a highly developed civilization that was once leading in the world. It gave us Shakespeare, Beethoven, the welfare state, and many other fine things." Even now, there are guided tours in Berlin to the slums and the areas considered slightly dangerous ("Kreuzberg, the most colorful district—two hours"). Cambridge University has become a must for many educated Chinese tourists because of a famous Chinese poem about it. But Louis Vuitton, Hugo Boss, and Gucci attract an even greater number of visitors from the Far East, and a knowledge of Mandarin has become a virtual must for those working in the most expensive shops of Europe. Some nine hundred thousand Chinese tourists came to Western Europe in 2004. In 2010, their number had risen to 2.4 million. They have overtaken the Russians as the highest spenders on luxury goods.

My vision of a European cultural theme park apparently inspired a well-known Croatian writer, Slavenka Drakulić, to envisage open-air museums all over Europe called Euroskansen (following the lead of a Swedish open air museum), which will provide the main source of income for the old continent. In 2050, guides will tell schoolchildren how Europeans once lived. Ms. Drakulić's idea of wholesale self-musealization seems overblown, and her explanation of why it came to this (the pursuit of endless profit) more than a little simplistic.

This scenario of European theme parks may appear fanciful at the moment, but, given current trends, it is a possibility that cannot be dismissed out of hand. Tourism has been of paramount importance in Switzerland for a long time. It is now of great (and growing, by 4 percent annually) importance in France, Italy, Spain, Greece, Portugal, and some other countries. In several European countries it is becoming the most important single factor in the economy and the main earner of foreign exchange. More than fifty million Chinese now travel annually to overseas destinations. Soon there could be a hundred million.

Having solved one way or another its political, social, and economic problems, and being able to compete again in the world markets, getting its act together at least to some degree, could Europe find a place in the new world order? It would be a more modest place than in the past, but still respectable. This is the best-case scenario. But what if the general decline continues? European conditions under the impact of massive waves of immigration could become similar to those prevailing in North Africa and the Middle East. These and perhaps some other scenarios in between the extremes seem possible at the present time. What appears impossible is that the twenty-first century will be the European century, as some observers, mainly in the United States, claimed even in the very recent past. As they saw it, a united Europe had not only caught up with the U.S. economy but was likely to overtake it very soon. The countries of Europe were living in peace with one another and their neighbors; they had established a way of life, a model more civilized and humane than any other. True, it was not exactly a political-military superpower, but through its "transformative power" acting as an example, it was changing the world. In brief, the rest of the world was becoming more and more like Europe, moving toward an order that was more just and humane than any previous in the annals of mankind. But Europe did not overtake America. On the contrary it found it more and more difficult to compete with China and India. The character of power in world politics did not radically change and the predictions of yesterday seemed more and more detached from the facts of the real world.

Looking back thirty or even fifteen years, attenuating circumstances could be found for engaging in what now appear to be mere pipe dreams. In 1945, as the guns fell silent, many thought that Europe was finished and would never recover. But recover it did, and, within a decade, the various economic miracles took place. The recovery was not only economic. European living standards were not only higher than ever before, but welfare states were established to provide essential health services, free education, and unemployment pay, among other services. European countries lived in peace with one another, borders were gradually removed, and there was no war or danger of war, except perhaps on the borderlands of Europe such as the Balkans. Europe was on the road to world power, but of course it never arrived there. Somewhere along the road it had lost steam.

Europe had been divided during the cold war. The wall came down with the collapse of the Soviet empire and the countries of Eastern Europe became free. Seen in retrospect, there was at one time good reason for optimism. True, Europe had not reemerged as a major player in world affairs but had to rely on soft power with all its limitations. However, it had made great progress toward close cooperation. Common institutions had emerged and there seemed reason to believe that given a few more years there would be a common European foreign and defense policy, so that the old continent would again play a role in world affairs commensurate with its history and its economic power. But there were danger signs even in the 1970s, when the great boom slowed down and unemployment began to appear. The terms *euroskepticism* and *eurosclerosis* go back, after all, to the late 1980s. But they referred to the rigidity of the European labor market and, generally speaking, to the economic situation with its ups and downs rather than Europe's political future. It was only in later years that a significant change in European attitudes took place. Progress toward further unification stalled despite the introduction of a common currency, the euro, and other seemingly important measures. The European enthusiasm, which had once been so startling and positive, declined.

More important yet, there were demographic warning signs. The experts were sounding the horn in the 1990s. A number of works by Alfred Sauvy, the best-known French demographer of his generation, and his disciple Jean-Claude Chesnais attracted some attention (Chesnais's *The Twilight of the Occident* and *Revenge of the Third World* and Sauvy's *The Aging of Nations*). As Chesnais put it, Europe was old and rigid, so it was fading. One could see this as the natural cycle of civilization, perhaps something inevitable. In Germany, the studies of Herwig Blog, a distinguished professor and head of the professional organization of German demographers, got at long last a hearing with his work *Die demographische Zeitenwende,* which in turn inspired a leading journalist, Frank Schirrmacher, who published the *Methusalem Komplott,* discussing the problems of a graying society, which for many months headed the German bestseller list.

Dark predictions were made in Russian right-wing circles in the 1980s concerning the future; the specter of alcoholism, the greatest social evil, was conjured. Attention was drawn to the fact that ever fewer children were born, that there was a mass flight from the countryside, and that life expectancy (especially of men) in the Soviet Union was steadily declining. But Russia has not fully woken up to its demographic prospects even today. Though life expectancy among men has risen slightly and the number of births now exceeds the number of deaths, the rate of reproduction, 2.1 births per family, has not been reached. Recent developments only mean that the population of Russia is graying and the process of absolute shrinkage has been slowed slightly. Furthermore, the rise in the birthrate has probably occurred mainly among the non-Russian minorities.

It should have been clear that the face and the character of Europe were changing. There had been guest workers, millions of them, who played a vital role in the economic miracle of the 1950s. But these had been mainly Europeans such as Italians, Spaniards, Portuguese, and Yugoslavs who eventually returned to their countries of origin. They were replaced by millions of new immigrants from Asia, the Middle East, and Africa; some of them had come as political asylum seekers but most had been in search of a better life for themselves and their children. Unlike the earlier guest workers, they had no intention to return to their homelands. But many of them had no desire to be integrated in European societies like earlier immigrants. This created increasing social, political, and cultural problems, which were, however, considered by and large manageable until, at about the turn of the century, it was suddenly realized that these newcomers constituted about a quarter (sometimes a third) of the population of the inner quarters of many European cities and that they were a majority among the youngest generation. In Brussels, for instance, more than 55 percent of the children born were of immigrant parents.

In the Ruhr region in Germany, more than half of the cohort under thirty will be of non-German origin within a decade or two. In the foreseeable future, perhaps in the lifetime of many of those attending kindergarten now, they will constitute the majority. Thus almost overnight what had been considered a minor problem on a local level was becoming a major political issue, for there is growing resistance on the part of the native population, which resents becoming strangers in their own homelands. Perhaps they are wrong to react this way, but they have not been aware until recently of this trend; no one had asked or consulted them.

In brief, by the turn of the century at the very latest, it should have been clear that Europe was no longer on the road to superpower status but that it faced an existential crisis, or perhaps more accurately a number of major crises of which the demographic problem was perhaps the most severe. This began to be recognized almost immediately, but again there was confusion because the crisis seemed intractable—it had been discovered too late.

These were not exactly strong hopes, and they certainly do not explain the illusions of some foreign observers who continued to claim that the twenty-first century would be Europe's. They said that Europe had a vision of justice and harmony very much in contrast to the American dream, which no longer existed. The European vision was the emphasis on the collective in contrast to the narrow stress on individualism in America. It preferred the quality of life to amassing money. Americans had to work harder than Europeans, had fewer holidays, lived not as long as the Europeans, and, generally speaking, enjoyed life much less. If Goethe had once written "Amerika, du hast es besser" ("America, you've got it better"), this was no longer true at all: Europeans were selfless. *Europa hat es besser*, it was argued. According to a recent poll, 95 percent of Europeans said that altruism, the wish to help others, was their highest value. Or, as another observer put it, power politics was a thing of the past. Europe's main weapon was justice and the law. Coming from Europe, this idea would spread all over the world and would become the main instrument in world affairs.

We are not concerned here with comparisons between America and Europe, the merits and demerits of their respective ways of life, but with the state of Europe on which her American friends, it would soon appear, were so sadly misinformed. How to explain the depth of such confusion? The motivation and underlying assumptions were different. They had much more to do with the situation in America than the

European realities. Tony Judt, author of a massive history of postwar Europe, said, "Europe's emergence in the dawn of the twenty-first century as a paragon of the international virtues: a community of values and a system of inter-state relations held up by Europeans and non-Europeans alike as an examplar for all to emulate. In part this was the backwash of growing disillusion with the American alternative." Some Americans, unhappy with the state of their country, transferred their hopes and expectations to Europe, which they believed was closer to their ideals. Tony Judt did not live to see how differently things in Europe would turn out.

The eulogies of Europe and the rosy prophecies were written by critics of the foreign and domestic policy of the United States, and in particular of George W. Bush's presidency. Whether their critique of the United States was correct or not is irrelevant in this context. What matters is the psychological motivation. They came to see in Europe all (or at least many) of the things they were missing in America, and they came to believe that the European model was not only preferable but that it was going to prevail. As Mark Leonard wrote in a long essay entitled *Why Europe Will Run the 21st Century,* "As this process continues we will see the emergence of a 'New European Century'. Not because Europe will run the world as an empire but because the European way of doing things will have become the world's." And slightly more cautiously, Tony Judt said that "the 21st century may yet belong to Europe." Their deeply held convictions about the state of America apparently blinded them to the seriousness of the European crisis. They failed to understand that their image of postwar Europe was a thing of the past. By 2006 some of them had retreated from their erstwhile optimism, but others had not. There was still a strange fixation on the rivalry between Europe and America, which ignored the fact that other centers of power were emerging that would constitute a major challenge and also very serious competition. It took a few more years for a more realistic appraisal to prevail.

But it would be unfair to focus on the imperfect knowledge or understanding of some American observers. The illusions were shared by many leading political figures in Europe. As the year 2000 was solemnly rung in as befitting the beginning of a new century and millennium, it often seemed business as usual. It was the last year of Clinton's presidency in the United States. In Russia, Putin was appointed, Greece joined the European Union, and Milošević was overthrown. There were a few disasters, such as the tragic loss of the Russian submarine *Kursk* and the explosion of a Concorde on Charles de Gaulle Airport in Paris. Real Madrid won the European soccer championship, and, for the first time in history, Spain won the Davis Cup in tennis.

At the end of March that year, the heads of European governments and prime ministers met in Lisbon to discuss their strategy for the next ten years. Among the main issues on the agenda were full employment and the creation of a European space institute for research and innovation. The general consensus was that Europe would become the most competitive and dynamic economy in the world, able to sustain permanent growth with more and better places of work and greater social cohesion. This, as it was stated in the final communiqué, could be achieved through the transition to a European economy and society based on science, the modernization of the European model, the investment in human beings, and the combating of social marginalization. All schools should have access to the Internet and multimedia by the end of the year 2001, workers should be taxed less, peace should prevail in the

Balkans, and a political solution found for Chechnya. Altogether, twenty-eight main targets were defined as well as 120 secondary aims.

The year 2000 was a very good one for Europe. Economic growth reached 3 percent, much more than during the years before and after. But it was a false dawn. When five years later the statesmen met again for an interim review, they had to admit that progress had been quite limited, and even this was a euphemism, because unemployment had grown and labor productivity had not significantly increased. There had been no quantum jump as expected, and the goal of becoming the most dynamic sphere in the world economy seemed more remote than ever. Though the Europe of fifteen had become a Europe of twenty-five (and was to become the Europe of the twenty-eight with Croatia joining in July 2011), it had not become a more closely knit union. On the contrary, the centrifugal trends had become stronger as manifested in the vote against a common European constitution, first in France and later in Holland.

There was a rude awakening. One seemed further away than ever from a common European foreign and defense policy. The earlier Euro-optimism had given way to a wave of Europessimism, the expression not just of a changing mood but of the belated realization that the continent faced enormous problems with which it had not yet come to terms. The issue at stake was not Europe's emergence as the leading superpower but its survival. In 2006, the official EU institution in Brussels still believed that the European Union of 2020 will look much as it does today. But even if this should be true, it left open the question how the rest of the world would look that year and what the specific weight of Europe would be in that world.

EUROPE AGING

THE WORLD IS AGING, AFRICA and some other regions exception apart. Europe is aging even faster.

My maternal grandfather, a miller by profession, was born in 1850 and lived in Upper Silesia; he had six children. Three of his six children had no children of their own, two had two each, and one had a single child. This, in a nutshell, is the story of the rise and decline of the population of Europe. The average European family had five children in the nineteenth century, but this number declined steadily until it fell below the reproduction rate in the major European countries before the outbreak of the First World War. There were brief periods when the trend went in the opposite direction, for instance the baby boom after the Second World War, when the birthrate in all European countries rose above 2.2 and in some, such as the Netherlands, Ireland, and Portugal, above 3.0 (these numbers represent children per household). But this lasted for less than a decade, and, since the late 1950s, the decline has continued except in the last few years when there was a slight increase partly (or largely) as the result of immigration.

At present, the total fertility rate for Europe is well below the reproduction rate. In Italy and in Spain, to give another example, about half as many children are born now than forty years ago. If this trend continues (and it is difficult to think why there should be a lasting reversal), in a hundred years the population of Europe will be only a fraction of what it is today, and in two hundred, some countries may have disappeared.

It is certainly a striking trend, considering that only a hundred years ago Europe was the political, economic, and cultural center of the world. Africa consisted almost entirely of European colonies, and India was the jewel of the British empire. Germany, France, and Russia had the strongest armies in the world, Britain the largest navy. The European economy was leading the world; America was making rapid progress, but it still had a long way to go and few were taking notice. Politically and culturally, only London and Paris, Berlin and Vienna counted; there was no good reason why European students should attend American universities, which were behind the European in every respect (except perhaps in the field of dentistry, which was not yet a university subject).

There were clouds on the horizon; for instance, the Russian Revolution of 1905. But in Russia, too, there was considerable economic progress. There were tensions between the European powers, but there had been no war for several decades and such a war seemed unlikely. The confidence of Europe was unbroken. World population in 1900 was about 1.7 billion; one out of four lived in Europe. Europe's population was about six times the size of the United States, which was 76 million at the time. Then the First World War broke out, with its horrible devastation and its many millions of victims, followed by revolutions, civil war, inflation, and mass unemployment. Europe had become considerably weaker, but it was still the center of the world.

All the while the population clock was ticking away, but

few paid attention because in absolute figures the population of Europe continued to increase, since people were living longer. But Europe's population grew much more slowly than in other parts of the world. If the population of Europe had been 422 million in the year 1900, it was 548 million in 1950 and 733 million in 2008. In fact, there were frequent false alarms concerning the danger of overpopulation. When I went to school in Germany (which was before and after the Nazi takeover), the teachers talked at great length about lebensraum, the need for more space. The famous bestseller of that period was Hans Grimm's *Volk ohne Raum* (*A People Devoid of Living Space*). The author had lived for many years in South Africa, and he thought, like many others, that agriculture was the most important pillar of the national economy and the health of the nation. This was wrong even at the time (before the great technological revolution in agriculture), and Hitler too had accepted that, for building up and maintaining a big modern army, heavy industry was more important than growing potatoes and tomatoes. But even after the Second World War, the talk of European overpopulation found for a while influential supporters, such as the Club of Rome, which published a report in 1972 with a circulation of thirty million copies about the limits of growth, which preached precisely this gospel.

What was the reason for the steady decline of the birthrate in Europe? This is not an easy question to answer, because the trend took place all over the continent in north and south, in west and east, in Catholic and Protestant and Orthodox countries, in very rich and relatively poor—that is, in countries of very different character. For this reason it does not come as a surprise that there is no unanimity among demographers. The birth-control pill played a certain role, but probably not a decisive one; more important was the fact that more and more women accepted (or felt compelled to accept) taking full-time jobs and did not want their careers interrupted by pregnancies and taking care of their babies. To give but one example, half of female scientists in Germany are childless. Most important, in all probability, was the fact that the institution of the family had greatly declined in value and esteem. Families became outmoded; many wanted to enjoy themselves and not be tied down by all kinds of obligations and responsibilities. Thus the apparent paradox that at the very time when Europeans could afford to have more children than at any time in the past, they had far fewer children.

Given this decline, what were the predictions for the future? According to the estimates of the United Nations and the European community ("World Population Prospects" and "Eurostat"), the population of France will only slightly decline from about 60 million at present to 55 million in 2050 and 43 million at the end of the century, but the number of ethnic French will decline more rapidly. A similar trend has been observed in the UK. According to the official projections of the Office of National Statistics in 1998, the UK population was to peak at about 65 million in 2051 and after that slowly decline. According to the official projection of 2008 it would reach 77 million in 2051 and 85 million in 2083. How to explain the discrepancy? It would be the result of immigration—Indian, Pakistani, West Indian, and Bangladeshi. According to the same projection, white Britons would be in a minority in less than fifty years if the present scale of immigration were to continue.

The projections for other European countries would be similar unless immigration is taken into account. Thus the population of Germany, 82 million at present, will decline to 61 million in 2050 and 32 million in 2100. The decline of Italy and Spain will be more drastic. Italy counts some 57 million inhabitants at present. This will shrink to 37 million at mid-century and to 15 million at its end if present trends continue. The figures for Spain are 39 million at present, declining to 28 million in 2050 and to 12 million at the end of the century. All these projections do not take into account immigration in the decades to come.

Later projections in 2008 and 2010 present a somewhat different picture, with decline proceeding more slowly: the UK will have a population of 77 million in 2060, but the percentage of elderly people will be about twice what it is now, followed by France with 72 million and Germany with 71 million. The population of all these countries will decline fairly sharply in the years thereafter. The total European population will peak in 2035 but later on decline, slowly at first, more rapidly thereafter. Aging will be a major social problem with the median age at present about forty, and, according to the projections, forty-eight in 2060.

What will be the ethnic composition of the major European countries? By 2008, 55 percent of the children born in Greater London were not of British background. In cities such as Birmingham and Leicester, the non-British element will be in a majority by 2020, with London following somewhat later. As for Britain, various projections have been made. All seem to agree that by the end of the century at the latest, the "white British" element will have fallen below the 50 percent benchmark, even if the emigration of the British from the UK dramatically declines and the intermarriage between various ethnic groups substantially increases, which cannot be taken for granted.

The projected losses for Eastern Europe according to UN projections are even more massive. The numbers below represent how much the population of each country will shrink by 2020.

Ukraine: 43%

Bulgaria: 34%

Latvia and Lithuania: 25–27%

Russian Federation: 22%

Croatia: 20%

Hungary: 18%

Czech Republic: 17%

Once societies age beyond a certain point, the number of those able to produce children falls rapidly and the decline gathers momentum. For the first time in history, there are (or soon will be) more people over the age of sixty than under twenty in major European countries such as Italy, Germany, Spain, and Greece. The other factor that has to be taken into account is that the relatively slow decline in countries such as France and Britain will be the result of the relatively high fertility rate among the immigrant communities—West and North African in France and Pakistani and Caribbean in Britain.

There has been a worldwide decline in fertility; the fertility rate has halved, broadly speaking, in the Third World from 6.2 children in 1965 to 3.4 in 2000, and, according to UN and other projections, the world population in 2100 will be approximately eight billion, and then it will decline. (It is seven billion at present). However, in the regions closest to Europe, such as North Africa, black Africa, and the Middle East, there will be no decline in the near future. According to these projections the population of Turkey will be 100 million in 2050, that of Egypt 114 million; there will be 45 million Algerians and 45 million Moroccans. The biggest rise will be in the poorest countries. According to these projections, by 2050, Yemen will have a larger population than the Russian Federation, and Nigeria and Pakistan will each have a larger population than the fifteen original countries of Europe that joined the EU a decade ago. Germany, at present the fourteenth most populous country, will have fallen behind Congo, Ethiopia, Uganda, Vietnam, Turkey, Egypt, Afghanistan, and Kenya.

Russia has at present a population of 141 million, but it might be overtaken first by Turkey and subsequently by other countries, including perhaps even Ethiopia. Yemen (as Paul Demeny pointed out), which had about 4 million inhabitants in 1950, now has some 24 million, and, according to projections based on present fertility rates, will have more than 100 million. At the same time, the population of Russia will be shrinking annually by 2 percent, which is to say that within fifty years its population will shrink to a third its present size. There is, in Demeny's words, hardly any historical precedent for such a precipitous demographic collapse.

Common sense finds it difficult to accept such projections, and this for good reasons—not so much with regard to the Russian demographic collapse but concerning the growth of Yemen. Yemen is a poor country, with much of its territory consisting of desert (only 3 percent of the country is arable) and little water. The prospects for agriculture are limited, and, while a certain amount of industrialization will no doubt take place, the idea that the Yemeni economy could sustain a population of more than 100 million defies even the most fertile imagination. The population of Yemen (and of other countries in a similar position) will grow less because there will be neither work nor food. Similar considerations apply to Egypt. But at the same time, it seems certain that even if there is a dramatic decrease in Yemen's fertility rate, the population of that country will increase considerably, many will look for work outside their native country, and there will be a far greater population pressure on Europe. For more fortunate countries such as Turkey, on the other hand, the projections for 2050 and beyond seem quite realistic. It also seems quite realistic that Europe's share of the world's population will be no more than 5–7 percent in 2050 in the lifetime of many of those living now; it was 25 percent in 1900 and 12 percent in 1950.

The same considerations apply to projections beyond the year 2100. According to the UN projections for the year 2300, the population of Europe will have fallen to a mere 59 million. Many European countries will be reduced to about 5 percent of their present population, and Russia and Italy to 1 percent, less than the population at present in the cities of Novosibirsk or Torino respectively. While such a possibility cannot be ruled out, projections for long periods ahead cannot possibly take into account scientific and technological developments. We do not know what progress medicine will make and how long people will live in two hundred years (at present life expectancy is rising by about 2–3 months annually). On the other hand, pandemics or wars or natural disasters may have an impact that cannot be calculated. Nor do we know the impact of future technologies on labor productivity and how much manpower will be needed to keep the economies going. New ideologies or religions may appear that could influence population growth or decline.

Some have argued that if Europe will still be a continent of any importance two hundred years from now, it will almost certainly be a black or brown continent. Others have predicted that at the end of the twenty-first century Europe will be Islamic. Such predictions are based on the higher African and Middle Eastern birthrate on the one hand and the need for massive immigration into Europe on the other. But since the birthrate of immigrants to Europe is also substantially decreasing, the change in the ethnic composition of the population may well be slower than assumed until recently. Most projections seem to agree that the number of Muslims worldwide will increase twice as fast as that of non-Muslims and then level off.

At present, Europe counts about 317 million people of working age (between fifteen and sixty-five). If there is no immigration into Europe, this figure will shrink to 229 million by 2050. However, this estimate may well be too high because not all members of this age group are in fact working or are able to work for various reasons, so the actual figure could be closer to 160–70 million, about half the present number. On the other hand, the number of elderly and old people will be considerably higher than at present. This is bound to create a major social problem, but, given technological developments, it cannot be predicted how many people of working age will be needed to keep the economy going. It can be taken for granted that the number of those in the service sector will at least have to remain equal and probably will have to grow in order to provide essential services.

According to a scenario published in a report by the UN, *Replacement Migration*, no fewer than 700 million immigrants into Europe will be needed for the period between 1995 and 2050 to restore the age balance and maintain industries and services in Europe. But such figures belong to the realm of fantasy, for it is not known how many workers will be needed or where they will come from. India and China are aging too, and the birthrate is falling even in Bangladesh. At present, the European problem is unemployment among young immigrant workers and the fact that many of these people lack the necessary skills to participate in the workforce.

It is unlikely that Europe will be Muslim at the end of this century. Muslims may become the majority in some cities and provinces, and it goes without saying that the Muslim element will play a far greater role in European politics and society than at present. But many of the new immigrants to Europe are not Muslim in the first place—they come from India and Southeast Asia, from West Africa, from the West Indies, and other parts of the world, which I will discuss more later. While it is true that many Muslim immigrants have resisted absorption and integration, it is not certain that this will continue with equal intensity for future generations.

Russia is one of the countries whose ethnic composition will probably change greatly as the result of immigration. It had 148 million inhabitants in 2005, including about 15 million immigrants. Without massive further immigration in the years to come, their number will have decreased to about 110 million by 2050. Vladimir Putin envisages the immigration of more millions into Russia in the near future. But they could come only from China and the Muslim countries of central Asia and the Middle East, since people from other countries have never come, nor do they want to now. This, for obvious political reasons, may be thought inadvisable.

There are factors that cannot be measured. Within a generation or two, the institution of the family may be even further weakened; in Germany, the sharp decline began with the generation of 1968. The Frankfurt school, which belittled the function of the family from both a social and an economic point of view, provided the ideological rationale. But the family declined also in societies in which the existence of the "critical school" was hardly known. One prominent economist said that "homo economicus" would have no children. What are the consequences if young people find that with the disappearance of the family their parents are their only relations? It will be a lonelier and sadder world.

Two questions remain to be answered, however briefly.

Could the projections be wrong? And is it possible to reverse these trends if that is deemed desirable?

Historical experience tends to show that "natalist policies" are not very successful, at least not in the long run. Under Hitler, Mussolini, and Stalin, larger families were strongly promoted by the propaganda machines of these regimes and a variety of incentives were promised and given to large families. But this did not affect the long-term trend of the birthrate. East Germany under the communist regime provided a wide range of services to working mothers, and many complained after the unification of Germany that many of these services were discontinued. But this had no lasting impact on the birthrate. Democratic societies such as France and Sweden adopted policies likely to reduce the financial burden of having children, including generous parental leave before and after the birth of the child, tax reduction, cash payments, and various other incentives, including the possibility of working only part-time. Some have suggested that when two candidates apply for the same job (and other conditions being equal) precedence should be given to a mother over a childless woman. Altogether, Sweden spent ten times as much on such incentives than countries like Italy and Spain. But after a short-lived upsurge, the number of births went down again. A downturn in the economy was held responsible. But in Italy, where the birthrate went down even more, prosperity was thought to be the reason for the decline. In brief, Sweden (and also France, which provided a variety of incentives) cannot serve as a model. At most, it can be said that, but for these measures, the birthrate would have declined even more.

There are bound to be minor ups and down in the European birthrate in the years to come, but the basic trend is downward, and, while a radical turnabout is always possible, it is difficult to even imagine its causes.

What can be predicted with near certainty is that the decline will continue in the foreseeable future. If there are more deaths than births, a whole generation will be missing that could have produced children. By and large, the predictions of the demographers have been accurate with only a minor degree of error.

THE NEW EUROPEANS: DEMOGRAPHY—FATE OR FALSE ALARM?

UNTIL QUITE RECENTLY, MOST THINKING about the future of Europe, political, social, economic, or cultural, ignored demography. It can be found even today. Some Marxist and also conservative writers commenting on the future seem to believe that the Europe of a generation hence will be more or less the same as contemporary Europe or that of a generation ago. A visit to a school could have acted as a corrective, but few politicians, sociologists, or philosophers tend to visit schools, let alone kindergarten.

Few countries in Europe were ever ethnically homogeneous, but the minorities within their borders were not that remote from one another in outlook, mentality, and origin; they had not come from distant countries or even continents. The migration before the First World War of Poles to west Germany and northern France or of Jews from eastern Europe had been on a relatively small scale. Moreover, these new immigrants had been eager to adopt the values and the way of life of their new home countries. Quite frequently, they even changed their names in order to be more easily integrated.

Immigration on a massive scale after the Second World War was the result of political-territorial changes, such as the expulsion of Germans from eastern and southeast Europe and then, ten years later, as the result of Europe's "economic miracle," in which Europe prospered and needed additional labor. But the newcomers were mainly from inside Europe, Italians and Yugoslavs who went to Germany, Spanish and Portuguese who came to France. The great majority of these did not stay, but instead returned to their countries of origin as the economic situation there improved. During this period, major European countries recruited workers abroad to do the work that European workers were not willing or able to do.

The next wave of immigrants was the result mainly of the disintegration of empires—West Indians, Pakistanis, and Indians who went to Britain. Indians who had been expelled by Idi Amin from Uganda also settled in the United Kingdom, while North Africans migrated to France. There was also an influx of Turks, mainly to Germany and to a lesser extent to other European countries such as Austria and Belgium. But it was generally assumed that this was a temporary phenomenon, that these "guest workers" (as they were called) would return to their home countries after having made some money that would enable them to be economically active in their native towns or villages. However, in actuality, only half of the two to three million guest workers who came to northern Europe in the 1960s returned. The others stayed on, legally or illegally, and in many cases brought relatives and brides to join them, and the host governments were not willing to enforce the law against them. Major foreign communities came into being— and this at a time when the economy worsened after the oil crisis of 1973 and as unemployment increased.

European governments stopped issuing labor permits, and, as a result, the number of immigrants to Europe should have declined or even come to a standstill, and the number of foreign workers should have decreased, but this did not happen. The higher birthrate of Asian, African, and Middle Eastern immigrants aside, there were a number of reasons that had not been taken into account by the authorities. The number of dependents that were brought legally and illegally from countries such as Pakistan, Turkey, and North Africa was considerably larger than had been assumed. Secondly, illegal immigration increased considerably and became an organized business. Illegal immigrants were smuggled from the Middle East through the Balkans and Eastern Europe or over the Mediterranean to Italy, from North Africa by way of Spain.

Lastly are the political asylum seekers. In 1983, there had been a mere eighty thousand of them; by 1992 their number had risen to seven hundred thousand. In 2009, 317,000 applications were made, mainly by refugees from Somalia, Iraq, and Afghanistan; Britain replaced France and Germany as the most popular destination. These figures are not very high, but they are probably quite incomplete. In countries such as Italy and Greece there were, according to estimates, hundreds of thousands who had entered the country illegally and had never applied for official recognition.

In the beginning the authorities had been quite liberal in their approach, even though the majority and probably the great majority of immigrants were not political refugees but "economic immigrants" in search of a better life for themselves and their children. Among the political asylum seekers there were Islamists or even terrorists who were in danger of being arrested in their native countries, but for reasons that had nothing to do with the struggle for democracy and freedom. As far as can be ascertained, some illegal immigrants and also asylum seekers were criminals and aimed to establish criminal gangs (specializing in the drug trade, prostitution, car theft, etc.) in their new home countries. There were genuine political refugees among them, but all asylum seekers, legitimate and illegitimate, were supported by a powerful lobby of human rights associations as well as churches, which provided legal and other aid. These organizations said it was scandalous and in violation of elementary human rights to turn back new immigrants and that in case of doubt mercy should prevail.

Gradually, the attitude of the authorities became considerably harsher. Entrance permits were often denied, but these rejections frequently remained a dead letter, because many asylum seekers from Africa and the Middle East had destroyed their papers, claiming they had been lost. Their stories could seldom be verified, and, once they had entered European territory, it became virtually impossible to deport them. The Schengen accord abolished border controls and permits all European citizens and legal immigrants to move to all EU countries for ninety days, although it does not automatically permit immigrants to work in Europe, contrary to popular belief. According to this accord, if an immigrant had put foot on one European country, he could move freely to another.

Germany was the target of most asylum seekers by far—some two million between 1990 and 2000, followed by the United Kingdom, the Netherlands, and France. The number of asylum seekers real and bogus began to decline after 2002, following the introduction of more stringent measures. The ethnic composition of the immigrants also changed. More recently, the majority has come from Eastern Europe and the former Soviet Union, as well as from Afghanistan and Chechnya.

This, very briefly, was the historical background of the emergence of Muslim communities. The present (2011) official

or semiofficial figures for Muslim communities in Europe are
as follows:

> France: about 5 million
> Germany: 4.2 million (the number was 15,000 in
> 1961)
> Britain: 2–2.5 million
> Netherlands: 1.0 million (having more than doubled
> during the last 25 years)
> Sweden: 0.5 million (having tripled over the last
> 25 years)
> Denmark: 0.2 million (25,000 in 1982)
> Italy: 0.9 million (120,000 in 1982)
> Spain: 1.0 million (120,000 in 1982)
> Greece: 0.5 million
> Belgium: 0.6 million
> Austria: 0.4 million (80,000 in 1982)

To those numbers should be added about sixteen to twenty
million Muslims in the Russian Federation, both legal and illegal residents, as well as those making their home in Bosnia
and Albania.

All these figures are estimates. In a few cases, they might be
too high. According to some sources, the number of Muslims in
France could be as low as 3.5 to 4 million (five million was the
estimate of the French Ministry of Interior for the year 2000).
But most figures are probably too low. The number of Muslims
in Spain, which had for years the highest immigration rate in
Europe, could be closer to 1.5 million, and in Italy there are
thought to be between 1 and 1.5 million, perhaps half of them
illegals. The PEW Forum published an interesting study on the
future of the Muslim population in Europe and elsewhere but
seems not to have taken illegal immigrants into account.

To what extent is it legitimate to talk about Muslim "communities," since they come from different parts of the world? There is a strange habit to regard them as a monolithic bloc, which is far from true. Turkey is the country of origin of the great majority of Muslims living in Germany, and Turks constitute 50 percent of those living in Austria and Greece and 40 percent of those in the Netherlands—and almost as many in Belgium. But among these Turks there are hundreds of thousands of Kurds, who, to put it cautiously, are not on the closest of terms with the Turks.

Most of the French and Spanish Muslims are of North African origin, as well as half of those in Italy and Belgium and perhaps 40 percent in the Netherlands. There has been considerable, mostly illegal, Muslim immigration from Albania to Italy. A sizable proportion of the illegal immigrants have continued to move to the north, but it is impossible to say how many. British Muslims come mainly from Pakistan (45 percent) and Bangladesh (15 percent or more).

In brief, these communities in Europe are anything but monolithic. Other than France, they have no common language. Few of them have a command of Arabic. But even though their number is relatively small, their political influence is growing. Thus the Muslim Association of Britain (MAB) is thought to be Arab-dominated. The great majority is Sunni, but there are also Shiite congregations (among Turks in Germany) as well as Alawites (especially in Germany), Ahmadiya (considered heretics by mainstream Muslims), and a variety of mystical (mainly Sufi) orders and groups.

Religion is important in the life of the Muslim communities. The number of mosques in France has grown from about 260 twenty years ago to 2,350 or more at the present time. There are a few great mosques in cities such as Paris, Marseilles, and Lyon, but the majority are small prayer rooms, and the same is true with regard to Germany and other European countries. Germany had some 700 small mosques or prayer rooms in the 1980s, but now there are more than 2,800. There were 584 "certified mosques" in Britain in 1999, but the real number is about 1,800 at present; in Birmingham, England's second largest city, there are more mosques now than churches, albeit the mosques are much smaller. It could well be that there are now more practicing Muslims in Britain than church-going members of the Church of England. Statistics from 2010 in a number of European countries, including Norway and the Netherlands, tend to show that mosque attendance is declining, especially among the younger, after a few years in Europe. But as the mosque is replaced by the street gang and spiritual impulses by a political religion, it is too early to draw far-reaching conclusions from this trend.

How orthodox are European Muslims? Estimates vary considerably. Mosque attendance on Friday prayers is thought to be as high as 60 percent in some places and as low as 10 percent in others, with the older generation, as usual, more frequently represented. A majority of young Muslims, British-born, do not understand the sermons given in languages such as Urdu, Bengali, and Arabic.

In a poll among Turks living in Germany, 7 percent made it known that they were very orthodox, whereas 27 percent said that they were not very religious or not religious at all. (But other polls produced different results with much higher figures for orthodox believers, much depending on the definition of "religious.") The length of the stay of Muslims in Europe seems to be of not much relevance in this context, whereas education and income are of significance; those with higher education and higher income tend to be less religious than the rest. In a recent survey in France, 36 percent said that they were strictly observant, but a far larger percentage observed individual commandments such as fasting during Ramadan.

Some mosques are more orthodox than others. A certain proportion has the reputation of being the most "militant" (i.e., a reservoir for the recruitment of terrorists), such as the mosques at Finsbury Park and Brixton in London, but these are not necessarily the most religiously orthodox. The religious orientation depends more on the personality of the imam, or preacher. Recruitment and training of militants is carried out in a variety of organizations in the general orbit of the mosques. Many mosques constitute something like an archipelago with a variety of social organizations such as sport clubs (for men) and schools, kindergarten, and other institutions. The more monolithic the communities (such as in Germany), the more likely the emergence of a self-sufficient separate society, and the less the need, therefore, to learn the language of the country.

Muslim immigrants are not evenly distributed over the various European countries. The main concentrations are in the big cities and the old industrial regions. In the United Kingdom they are found in London (and within London in certain boroughs such as Towers Hamlet in the East End) as well as in the Midlands (towns such as Bradford, Burnley, Oldham) and Birmingham.

In Germany, Berlin has the biggest Muslim community, but percentagewise they are even more strongly represented in the Ruhr/Rhein area (Essen, Dortmund, Duisburg, Solingen). Some cities have a non-German population of between 25 and 30 percent.

In France, the strongest concentration is in the banlieue, the outer suburbs of Paris (such as Seine/St. Denis), with strong concentrations in southern France such as Toulouse, Lyon,

Nice, and the Côte d'Azur. But they are also found in the old industrial cities in the north; many of the inhabitants of the Lille conurbation are Muslim.

In Spain, the main concentrations are in southern Spain and Madrid, but also in Catalonia. In Sweden, Malmö, with such quarters as Rosengard, is the most Muslim city in Scandinavia. There are also substantial concentrations in north and northwest Stockholm, such as Tensta, and in eastern Göteborg. The influence of the Muslim Brotherhood is strong among the Islamic community in Sweden following the influx of Saudi preachers who are radical and anti-Western.

The Muslim communities are considerably younger than the non-Muslim population. About half of the Muslims in western and central Europe were born there. While Muslims constitute only about 15 percent of the population of Brussels, they are 25 percent or more of the cohort of those under twenty-five. The respective percentages in the major Dutch cities are higher. According to projections the proportion of foreigners (most of them Muslim) in the year 2015 will be more than 40 percent in west German cities such as Cologne, Düsseldorf, Wuppertal, Duisburg, and many others. Altogether, the number of Muslims in Germany will double during the next decade, while the native German population will decrease as the result of the low birthrate and emigration.

The problem facing western European societies is more often than not that the second and third generation of young immigrants, those who were expected to integrate and become equal members of these societies but who, on the contrary, revolted against their country of adoption. The reasons usually given are poverty (two-thirds of British Muslims live in low-income households), inadequate and overcrowded housing, ghettoization, unemployment (especially of the young), lack of education, and racial prejudice on the part of their non-Muslim surrounding—all of which are said to lead to a lack of social mobility, crime, and general marginalization of the Muslim communities. By implication or directly, it is argued that it is the fault of the state and of society that these and other evils have taken place. However, Muslims who have a successful career in business or the professions say almost without exception that their ethnic identity did in no way hamper them.

To what extent has ghettoization been enforced by the outside world and to what degree was it self-imposed? That new immigrants congregate in certain parts of a city is a well-known phenomenon. It can be studied, for instance, in London, where traditionally Irish (Camden Town, Kilburn), Jews (East End and later Golders Green), Australians and Poles (near Earls Court and Olympia), Black (Brixton), Japanese (South Hampstead), and other newcomers settled at first in certain neighborhoods. They were motivated by the wish to be among people who spoke their language, to have ethnic food shops, travel agencies, clubs, and other organizations. The Russian emigration into the Berlin of the 1920s congregated in Charlottenburg, while poor Jews from eastern Europe settled in the eastern part of the city.

A similar process took place among Muslim immigrants, but there was a basic difference. Earlier immigrants did not receive any help with their housing from the state or the local authorities, whereas in the second half of the twentieth century such aid became the rule rather than the exception. For this reason, there was little incentive to move out from lodgings that, however inadequate or displeasing, were free or inexpensive. When eastern European Jews first moved to Whitechapel toward the end of the nineteenth century and the beginning of the twentieth, there was no mayor of London who went out of his way to help them. They and other immigrants had to fend for themselves, facing incomparably greater difficulties (the absence of a health service and other social assistance) than present-day immigrants. Muslim newcomers apparently like to stick longer with their coreligionists than other groups of immigrants, and they are encouraged by their preachers to do so. This is true even with regard to India, where there is more ghettoization than in Europe; even middle-class Muslims seem to be reluctant to leave the areas where members of their community live.

The sites around Paris where many of the French Muslim immigrants live and that exploded in November 2005 were uncomfortable and aesthetically displeasing, but they are not slums like the London East End of the past. Yet it was precisely in these quarters that, in the words of a foreign visitor, Theodore Dalrymple, (in "The Barbarians at the Gates of Paris," *City Journal,* Autumn 2002) an "anti-society" grew up, infused with a burning hatred of the other France, with deep distrust and "alienation." This hatred, in Dalrymple's words, manifests itself in the desire to "scar everything around them" with graffiti. "Benevolence inflames the anger of the young men," and, while they enjoy a far higher standard of living (or consumption) than they would in their parents' country, that is no "cause of gratitude—on the contrary: they feel it as an insult or a wound," even as they expect it as their due.

"Barbarians" seemed a harsh, perhaps even racist term, but was it wholly unjustified? One of the major gangs in the banlieue that had been involved in various criminal and terrorist activities, such as the abduction and murder of Ilan Halimi in January 2006, proudly called itself the Barbarians.

Housing has been mentioned as perhaps the main reason

for the Paris riots of 2005, youth unemployment as another. It amounts to 30 to 40 percent in France and Germany and not much less in Britain and the Netherlands. As a Berlin head teacher put it, "We are creating an army of long-term unemployed." The rate of dropouts is very high among Turkish youth in Berlin and also in other European countries, and it is much higher among boys than among girls. Only 3 percent of Muslim youth make it to university in Germany, and many of these graduates do not stay in Germany but return to Turkey because prospects for employment are better there.

Their language skills are low on the whole, which is not surprising because Turkish or Arabic is spoken at home, books are not found in many households, and the use of German (or English) is discouraged by the parents, who often do not master the host language. Boys are sent to a madrassa, religious schools where the Koran is taught, but are not encouraged to study other subjects. Girls are often forbidden to go to school beyond the age of sixteen, let alone attend universities, because they might be exposed to undesirable influences. When a Berlin school decided, after consultation with students and their parents, to insist on the use of German as the sole language of instruction at school, it came under heavy attack by the Turkish media, even though most pupils and their parents favored it. Some well-meaning local protagonists of multiculturalism joined the protest because they believed this policy was tantamount to cultural repression. But how to expect the social and cultural advancement of a young generation unless it masters the language of the land?

Racism and xenophobia have been adduced as factors responsible for underachievement of Muslim youth. But Muslims are not a race and this fails to account for the scholastic successes of pupils with an Indian and Far Eastern background who score higher in many subjects than the average German or British student. Nor does it explain why Muslim girls acquit themselves much better than the boys. Could it be connected with the fact that girls are not allowed to go out unaccompanied, whereas the boys spend most of their time in the street? Indian pupils in British schools have been doing twice as well as Pakistani students and those from the Far East have been outpacing almost everyone else.

There are a variety of explanations, but the idea sometimes voiced that it is all the fault of the state or society is not plausible or very helpful once one proceeds to remedy the situation. Young people are told day in and day out that they are victims of society and that it is not really their fault if they fail. As a result of these failures, a youth culture of violence and crime has developed that has little to do with religion. Despite attendance at Koran schools (more in Germany than in France and the UK), these young men are not well versed in their own religion. They may go to the mosque on Fridays but will drink and do drugs, despite the religious ban. The main influence on them is neither the parental home nor the imams but the street gang. The parents have little authority: their way of life does not appeal to the offspring, they are not assertive enough, they work too hard and earn too little. Old-fashioned Islam is of no great interest to many of them either; a well-positioned imam in Britain said that "we are losing half of them."

Only a few charismatic religious leaders who preach extreme action may have a certain following among young males. To understand the scenes in the schools and streets of Neukölln and the banlieue, a textbook on juvenile delinquency could be more helpful than the Koran.

School has little authority; in France and the UK, language is less of an impediment, but, in Germany, the pupils often quite literally do not understand what the teacher is saying, and there is no effort to understand either teachers or pupils from other countries with different native languages. Many teachers fail to impose their authority, because if they dare to punish pupils for misbehavior or make any demands on them, they are accused of racism and discrimination. The streetwise pupils are adept at playing the race card.

Muslim youth culture varies to a certain extent from country to country. High Street sports gear and machismo is common, and the body language of young Muslims expresses aggression. They want respect, though it is not clear how they think such respect has been earned; perhaps it is based on the belief that "this street (or quarter) is ours." In France and the UK, hip-hop culture plays a central role. The texts of their songs express strong violence, and often sadism. The street gang usually has a territorial base. Turks in Berlin have their own gangs and the same is true of Arabs, who arrived later in Germany, as well as the Kurds. Sometimes the street gang is based on a certain village or district in the old country where the (extended) family originated. There has been a great deal of fighting between these territorial gangs. In Britain, it has been quite often black against Indians (or Pakistanis) or, as in Brussels, Turks against Africans.

Street gangs lounge about aimlessly and often engage in petty crime. In Britain, they have largely replaced the Afro-Caribbeans as drug pushers, though the key positions are usually not in their hands. Dealing in stolen goods is another way to earn the money needed for their gear, hashish (heavier drugs are sold but seldom consumed), as well as other entertainment. Teachers do not dare to interfere, and local police are reluctant to make arrests, since judges will release those who have been arrested, especially if they are underage. Some proceed to more serious crime.

This is a theme that the European Muslim communities

have been very reluctant to deal with. Crime figures are difficult to obtain, but all experts agree that the percentage of young Muslims in European prisons far exceeds their proportion of the population. This also goes for cases of rape, which in many gangs have become part of the rite of passage, especially in France and to a lesser degree in the UK, Scandinavia, and also Australia. The victims are by no means always non-Muslim girls and women who dress immodestly, but also sometimes young Muslim women. The hijab does not always offer protection.

This rise in European crime cannot, of course, be explained entirely with reference to immigration, but there is no doubt that it is one of the main reasons. The head of the London metropolitan police made it known that 80 percent of the crime committed on the London underground was carried out by immigrants from Africa. The head of the Berlin police announced that one out of three young immigrants in this city had a criminal record. Such statistics mentioning ethnic or religious background are forbidden in France, but the high number of young Muslims in French prisons is no secret.

The account of Kirsten Heisig, a Berlin judge, became a bestseller in Germany in 2010. Judge Heisig was a strong believer in multiculturalism, but her experience in courts dealing with juvenile offenders in Neukölln, a heavily Turkish quarter, was depressing. She was no hanging judge, but, on the contrary, went out to visit schools and families, trying to help change the milieu in which the many young offenders were growing up. In the end, in the face of her failure, she gave up and committed suicide in July 2010.

How to account for the great aggressiveness of the youth gangs? Their lack of achievement undoubtedly adds to the general discontent. The issue of identity (or lack of it) is frequently

mentioned in this context. Many of the young (second) generation do not feel really at home in either their parents' homeland or in the country in which they live. They don't consider
themselves accepted in Europe and may curse the host country in all languages, but they feel even less at home in Turkey,
North Africa, or the Indian subcontinent and have no wish to
return there.

Sexual repression almost certainly is another factor that is
seldom if ever discussed within their communities or by outside observers. It could well be that such repression (as the
French psychoanalyst Tsvetan Todorov has noted) generates
extra aggression, an observation that is also shared by young
Muslim women. Young Muslim men cannot freely meet members of the opposite sex from inside their own community.
Homosexuality is considered an abomination, yet in fact, according to many accounts, is frequently practiced, as it has
been all through history. The rejection of society manifests itself in many ways, beginning with the defacing of walls of
buildings to the torching of cars (which has become custom-
ary in France). In extreme cases there is an urge to destroy everything at hand and to attack all responders, including the
firefighters and ambulances rushing to the ghettos to deal
with an emergency.

Socioeconomic factors have been held responsible, and, in
this respect, there have been interesting similarities with young
black males in the United States. If only more jobs were offered, it is often maintained, everything would change for the
better. It would, of course, make a certain difference, but many
studies have shown that when such jobs were offered (as in
the Clinton years in the United States), the takers were predominantly Caribbean immigrants or from Latin America and the
Far East. There is enormous reluctance, as Orlando Patterson

of Harvard has put it, to accept cultural explanations for the
plight of young black males. As in Europe, these findings do
not apply to black girls. "Why were [the young males] flunk-
ing out? [The] candid answer was . . . what sociologists call
'cool-pose culture,'" which was "too gratifying to give up. For
these young men it was almost like a drug, hanging out on the
street after school, shopping and dressing sharply, sexual con-
quests, party drugs, hip-hop music and culture." The young
males found "this subculture immensely fulfilling [and] it also
brought them a great deal of respect from some white youths."
Nor was it clear why unemployment should more or less automatically lead to a life of crime and drugs; there is high unemployment in Pakistan and India, in North Africa and Latin
America, but less crime and drugs.

NATIONALISM VS.
THE EUROPEAN UNION

THE REASONS FOR THE FAILURE so far of the European project
and for the crisis Europe now faces are manifold and cannot
be reduced to a few wrong decisions taken by European heads
of state and by bureaucrats in Brussels. The decision to introduce the euro without stricter political and economic controls
was certainly a mistake; if the time was not right and there
was insufficient agreement to make such far-reaching decisions, the idea should have been shelved. The real reasons for
the present crisis, of course, go considerably deeper; what was
said at one stage of its history about France ("We have created
France, let us now create Frenchmen") was true a fortiori with
regard to Europe. Europe had been created, but where were
the Europeans, where was European solidarity?

The idea, and the need for, solidarity is as old as the hills. It
can be found in the Bible and all through antiquity and the
Middle Ages. It can be found in Christian, Muslim, and Jewish
religious teachings and among the early socialists and Communists (Ernst Busch's famous song in praise of solidarity:
"beim Hungern und beim Essen . . . nicht vergessen," text by
Bertolt Brecht, music by Hanns Eisler).

But there was not that much international solidarity in the

twentieth and early twenty-first centuries, except sporadically on the occasion of major natural disasters. The tendency in international affairs was centrifugal, toward splits rather than union, even in Europe, with Yugoslavia in the recent past and Belgium at the present time as prime examples. It is difficult to account for this trend. The argument that it is not of much consequence because in a united Europe all small groups would find their place is not very convincing. For if these groups, putting their interests first, had not been able to coexist harmoniously within a smaller framework, why should there be greater harmony in a bigger one such as Europe? Such a Europe would be like a mosaic of very small stones; to put it together might exceed the patience and strength of Sisyphus.

The decline of solidarity also manifested itself within societies. There was less support for the welfare state, only 36 percent in 2010 compared to 58 percent in the days of Margaret Thatcher. In 1992, 58 percent of the British thought that the government should spend more on social benefits; twenty years later their number had shrunk to 27 percent. At the same time, only 36 percent were in favor of redistributing income from the rich to the poor, compared with 51 percent twenty years earlier. This mood will probably change with the increase in unemployment.

These trends are surprising because income inequality had substantially risen in most European countries (as in the rest of the world) while, on the other hand, satisfaction with the health service, education, and other services was higher than ever before.

Explanations are not easy. Perhaps they have to do with the fact that there was great indignation about the abuse of the social services, especially for payments made on behalf of new immigrants who were not working (for instance, women in

Islamist households who were forbidden to leave their homes unaccompanied). Generally speaking, there is the feeling that immigrants received a disproportionately high part of the social budget, which had to be covered by the heavily taxed native sons and daughters. Nevertheless, few people in Europe were willing to abolish the welfare state, which had become in a short time a permanent fixture, a self-evident part of the western Europe's way of life.

How to explain the lack of international solidarity which had shown itself so blatantly at the time of the outbreak of the First World War and, in fact, ever since? Was it the fault of the conflicts inherent in a capitalist world order? But Marx and his followers, legitimate and illegitimate, up to the age of the anti-globalists, had been teaching that capitalism was breaking down not only social bonds such as the family but also national borders. Why then the growing strength of nationalism and the nation-state?

The reluctance to bail out bankrupt countries such as Greece mirrors the resistance to support those who abused the social services at the domestic level. But was it not illusory to expect the growth of a United States of Europe, with all its components responsible and trustworthy, overcoming hallowed national traditions, adjusting their way of life, making far-reaching concessions, surrendering much sovereignty, and all this within a few decades?

It was unrealistic to expect a quick change in mentality. It would have been far more preferable if such a difficult process had had a century or two or even three to unfold. Unfortunately, seldom in history have timetables been adhered to according to needs.

Post–Second World War Europe has frequently been named a postnationalist continent, but this designation is only partly correct. It is true that all the major European countries (and most of the smaller ones) have learned the lessons of two devastating European civil wars, and military conflicts have become virtually unthinkable. But at the same time, the loyalty of the individual and the group is still to the country of birth and to the nation. And while even such loyalty has become weaker, as has become the willingness to make sacrifices on its behalf, it is still much stronger than any pan-European sentiment or cosmopolitanism.

European nationalism as presented by the philosopher Jürgen Habermas is not a political reality. Habermas believes that Europe needs a constitution and, on this basis, a constitutional European nationalism. But such a constitution should not be imposed; the people should freely decide on it. However, there is no reason to believe that at the present time a European majority (and perhaps not even a significant minority) would vote for such a constitution. In some respects, these Vernunfteuropäer remind one of the "Vernunftrepublikaner" of the Weimar Republic, who were decent and honorable people who fully endorsed parliamentary democracy yet did not particularly love it and felt only a limited duty to support it. These were not the people to mount the barricades for a united Europe, like Victor Hugo and Giuseppe Mazzini might have done, and in any case they were outvoted and outgunned.

European solidarity and national feeling could perhaps develop over a longish period (in ten years, according to Wolfgang Schäuble, a leading German politician, and in fifty years, according to Habermas) because of dire necessity and economic and political pressure—in other words, as the result of a deep crisis. But whether in a real emergency Europe will still be strong enough to engage in such a break with its past is uncertain.

. . .

Why should the appeal of nationalism and the nation state be so much stronger? The idea of a United States of Europe seemed, after all, a promising and exciting beginning and should have generated enthusiasm. Nationalism had developed organically over generations, but according to some of its students it was a relatively recent phenomenon—of the nineteenth century. But it could apparently draw on deep roots: the idea that it was *dulce et decorum* ("sweet and honorable") to die for one's *patria* went back, after all, to Roman times. The *patria,* the clan, the family, the culture, the common language all provided ties that the larger units could not give.

Few people have been willing to die for humanity rather than for narrower causes. Experts discuss the magnetism of the nation and nationalism, the motives and the strength of its claims on individuals. But whatever the outcome of their discussions (and there was no doubt that chauvinistic nationalism was bad), the loyalty to the nation, to its values and interests, has proved stronger than any other ideology or emotion, however rationally convincing.

Particularly among sections of the intelligentsia, there was a strong feeling that Europe (and one's own country) had no future except within a wider European framework. But such recognition was and is far from universal. That some compromises should be made was beyond doubt, but that the interests of the nation should always be subordinated to the higher interests of the European Union seemed abhorrent, not only to the euroskeptics but to the majority of citizens.

The historical differences between the peoples of Europe are great—in their culture, mentality, and way of life; the languages they speak; their interests; the way they look (despite the

intermingling of various ethnic groups); in short, in their national character, to use a dubious term. There are, of course,
considerable differences even within countries, not only in Italy,
Switzerland, or Belgium but also in major countries like Germany and France, and satisfactory solutions have not been found
everywhere. But the very fact that it was so difficult to find a way
toward national unity indicates how much more difficult the
road would be toward a European national feeling and solidarity.

All these difficulties have been compounded in recent years
by the influx of immigrants from overseas. These problems
indicate that tomorrow's Europe, united or disunited, will be
very different from the one we have known. The great majority of people would agree with the proposition that they should
be their brothers' keepers, but such solidarity does not extend
to people toward whom they have no feelings of kinship.

Not long ago, a writer for *The Economist* complained about
a conventional wisdom that considered contemporary Europe
as washed-up, aging, economically stagnant, a continent des-
tined inexorably to lose ground not only to a dynamic United
States but also to China and even India. Such complaints about
misreading the state of Europe could frequently be encountered in speeches, books, and official declarations that were
replete with optimism. But then the mood began to change,
and the speeches and the literature now dealt incessantly with
the great strides made by China and India and the pitiful performance of Europe.

Conventional opinion, like conventional medicine, is not
always wrong, nor is the phenomenon of rise and decline in
any way unprecedented. History is the story of countries and
civilizations rising and declining. Great powers wax and wane.
Not one has lasted forever, and some have disappeared. They
have declined for a great variety of reasons, some for economic causes, others because they were defeated in war, some

because over time they were exhausted and lost their will or spiritual strength and no longer cared whether they reproduced themselves. Gibbon wrote that the ancient Greeks thought that Rome prevailed over their country because of "fortune," that is to say, mere accident. It was at least in part by good fortune that the eastern Roman empire lasted for a thousand years after the western part had disappeared.

The question of why nations have declined can be discussed endlessly. When the story of the decline of Europe in the twentieth century will come to be written, it may well be asked why European dominance lasted so long. Migration may have played a certain role in the decline of nations, but, by itself, migration has as often strengthened as it has weakened nations. Both medieval and modern history is a history of migrations—as examples, think of European migration to North and South America (Italian and Spanish), of the Huguenots migrating to Germany and other European countries, of Polish migration to France and Germany in the early twentieth century, of Russian immigration to France after 1917, of Jewish emigration from Eastern Europe, of Chinese and Indian emigrants establishing major communities in Southeast Asia and even Africa. Very often these were the more enterprising elements who left their native countries for whatever reasons, and both sides benefited. The immigrants worked their way up in society, and the countries that absorbed them profited from the skills and talents of the newcomers.

Strong, self-confident societies have almost always been able to absorb such waves of immigrants and to make the best of it. There always were initial difficulties; even in a country of immigrants like the United States, it took a long time before the Irish and the Jews, let alone the "yellow peril," were accepted. Sometimes the new immigrants found it difficult to accept the laws and the way of life of their new countries; some, for instance, refused to serve in the military. There was almost always a certain return migration, but the majority remained in what became their new homes, and, after a few generations, they became part and parcel of it.

This is true also for our own time. Mention has been made of the contributions of the Indian immigration to Britain; of the Chinese, Vietnamese, and Korean to the United States and other parts of the world; of the Sikhs and the Armenians; of the Cypriots; and of a considerable variety of other people. Polish guest workers are welcome all over Europe, and Filipinos all over the world. In an age of aggressive nationalism, some ethnic minorities did find themselves under pressure: Idi Amin threw the Indians out of Uganda, and Gamal Abdel Nasser expelled Greeks, Italians, and other Europeans as well as the Jews from Egypt, even if they had lived there for generations. The Chinese minorities found themselves under pressure in Southeast Asia. But these were relatively small groups, and it was only in Europe that the issue of Muslim immigrants became a major political problem. Integration did not work, partly because it was not wanted by the newcomers. Multiculturalism led to the emergence of parallel societies and frequently had negative consequences.

Inevitably, this led to soul-searching: whose fault was it and what could be done to remedy it? One of the reasons for this was, of course, that the countries of Europe were not accustomed to absorb millions of foreigners who were rooted in a wholly different culture and who had no particular desire to trade in their old way of life and accept the ways of their adopted countries. This is not a specific European feature. It can be found all over the world, excepting only countries who depended largely through long periods of their history on a flow of immigrants, including North America, some Latin American countries, Canada, and Australia. Elsewhere, dislike of foreigners, even of those close in language, religion, and culture, has been deeply rooted and widespread. Even the fate of the Palestinian refugees in the Arab countries has often been an unhappy one. They were frequently kept in camps, sometimes expelled, and only rarely given citizenship, even though there was no dearth of speeches in which solidarity with these persecuted brothers and sisters was stressed.

But there were other reasons as well. To begin with, Muslim immigration to Europe was largely unplanned and uncontrolled. It continued a long time even after it should have been clear that the guest workers had no wish to return to their countries of origin and long after it appeared that there was no work for them. To a certain extent this immigration was a consequence of the imperial past. Algerians had a right to settle in France, and West Indians and those expelled from Uganda in Britain. But this right did not extend to other immigrant groups, the majority of whom had been born long after the imperial power had given up their former possessions and these countries had gained independence. Nor did it apply at all to those who went to Germany or Sweden, Austria, the Netherlands, or Belgium.

There was, and to a certain extent still is, a school of thought in some European countries that maintains that the failure of integration was the fault of European societies, which had not shown sufficient goodwill toward the immigrants and had not invested enough funds in helping with their housing and in other respects, including education. But European societies had never been asked whether they wanted millions of new neighbors in their country. They had the right to vote on all kinds of issues, domestic and foreign, but about this very essential issue, no one had ever consulted them. Governments and corporations had initiated it. Would they have acted differently had they foreseen the consequences of their policy?

Even this question cannot be answered with certainty. Some

might have been more cautious, inasmuch as immigration and granting the right of asylum was concerned. Others might not have cared, believing that their countries (and Europe in general) had no particular contribution to make anymore, that they had more or less fulfilled their historical mission (if there ever had been one), and that maintaining their social and cultural identity was not a matter of paramount importance in the modern world. Suffering from exhaustion, perhaps the time had come to hand the torch of civilization over to other people, religions, and ethnic groups.

In some cases, such as in Scandinavia and in the Netherlands, a bad conscience dating back to the 1930s, when refugees from Nazi Germany were in most cases refused asylum, even though they were racially or politically persecuted, might have played a role. In Germany too there was the fear of being painted with the racist brush if Germans rejected immigrants. It is difficult even in retrospect to establish what the authorities in these countries were thinking—that uncontrolled immigration did not involve major problems; that the economic, social, and cultural problems would be solved; that the immigrants would one day disappear or be well integrated?

All this is not to say that self-confident European societies should have closed their gates hermetically against all immigrants. On the contrary, given its low birthrate, Europe needed immigrants to maintain and expand its economy, which was the precondition for the maintenance of the welfare state. But they needed a literate workforce, positive in its attitude toward the country and its society. This workforce should have been directed to productive labor rather than to being recipients of welfare services from the day of their arrival. Preachers and agitators inciting their fold against the decadent and sinful Western way of life should not have been welcomed and supported by the state. They should have been given equal rights, but also expected to behave in accordance with the law of the land, as well as the values and prevailing norms. If these laws and norms were not according to their convictions, they would have been free to leave; this, after all, had been the case all throughout history. Christians from central Europe and Jews from eastern Europe had gone to America precisely because they felt discriminated against or persecuted.

However, the European governments and societies were no longer self-confident. They were no longer willing to clean their streets and perform similar menial jobs. Among the establishment little pride was left of belonging to a certain nation (or to Europe); a cultural and moral relativism had prevailed. Such societies were not in a position to provide guidance and a compass to newcomers but were highly permissive. Newcomers to these countries were bound to gain the impression that prevailing laws and norms could safely be ignored.

Such tiredness, coupled with cultural and moral relativism, was bound to have far-reaching consequences, and European societies now will have to live with them. Illegal immigrants to Japan or China, to Singapore, or to virtually any other country would have been sent back within days if not hours to their countries of origin. The United States faced a similar problem with Mexican immigrants, but these people did not want to impose the shari'a. Illegal immigrants to Europe were permitted to stay. But even if the authorities had taken a harsher course, this would have affected only a minority, because most members of the immigrant communities are by now citizens of their countries of adoption or were born there and have as much right to live there as anyone else.

Combined with the other threats facing Europe, there is now a gradual realization how this will affect the continent's future. It almost certainly means the end of Europe as a major player in world affairs. Misfortunes could befall other continents too. Of course, a great number of cosmic disasters could happen elsewhere. Some have been described in works of science fiction, others are listed and discussed in a recent work by Richard Posner (*Catastrophe; Risk and Response,* 2005). They range from a pandemic to a collision with a comet, global warming, and bioterrorism. But chances are that in such a case Europe also would be affected—it would not be an occasion for schadenfreude.

The Chinese economic megaboom may come to a halt or at least decline as the result of the weaknesses of crony capitalism and China's deficient infrastructure as well as its public health system; continued state opposition to political reform could lead to the alienation of the masses. The Indian boom may come to a sudden end for a variety of reasons. Only a relatively few of the population have benefited from it, leading to enormous disparities between rich and poor and between cities and countryside, and this could lead to bitter old-fashioned class struggle and political conflict. The enormous economic power of the United States, as has become only too clear, rests on uncertain foundations, beginning with the country's great indebtedness. There have been foreign political setbacks and a growth of domestic tensions.

All these disasters might happen, but they would in no way benefit Europe. Its economy is largely export-oriented, and, as its domestic market continues to shrink, it will be even more so in the future. Setbacks affecting its major export markets would almost certainly cause another crisis in Europe.

Uncontrolled immigration was, to repeat once again, not the only and not the main reason for the decline of Europe. Its threat is not immediate, but long-term. But taken together with its other misfortunes, it is leading to a profound crisis. A miracle might be needed to extract Europe from these predicaments.

DEPOPULATION

No one can say with any certainty whether European unification will make much (or any) progress in the years to come or how the European economy will perform. Until quite recently the further EU expansion was widely discussed. The founding statement of the "Eastern partnership" (2009), which was to include six former Soviet republics, among them Ukraine and Georgia, said that it was to support political and socioeconomic reforms facilitating approximation toward the European Union. But such approximation would hardly cause great joy in Moscow, nor would the leading EU countries want to be saddled by the domestic and foreign problems of these six countries. It is unlikely that much will be heard of the "Eastern partnership" in the near future.

But the demographic problems can be foreseen with a reasonable degree of accuracy, and it is to these that we shall turn first. Even population projections are based on certain assumptions, and, as Chesnais, the French demographer, has noted, demographers working for bodies like the United Nations often err on the side of political correctness and optimism because they do not want to shock and they play down political implications. Estimates by individual experts are often more reliable.

However, even the UN's projections, which are based on the assumption that the birthrate in Europe will rise in the years to come, have reached the conclusion that, by the year 2050, the old European Union will have sixty million fewer inhabitants and that the whole of Europe, including Russia, will be diminished by 130 million. More important, after 2050, population decline will be far more rapid because by then the average age will be much higher. For instance, the number of births in a country like Germany will be only half of what it is today. If one does not factor in further immigration into Europe—and there is every reason that immigration will be smaller for both political as well as economic reasons (unemployment)—countries with a low birthrate such as Italy and Spain will have substantially shrunk, as pointed out in some detail earlier on.

Such shrinking can be observed even now in parts of Europe. In Russia, for instance, thousands of villages in European Russia have ceased to exist, not to mention the exodus from Siberia and other parts of northern Russia. In Spain, the rural depopulation began in the post-Franco era, affecting also Andalusia and very poor regions such as Estremadura and gathering speed in recent years. Unsuccessful attempts have been made to resettle new immigrants in deserted villages. There is a sizable Latin American immigration (especially of Ecuadorians and Colombians) to Spain, but these immigrants move to the cities where there are better-paid jobs.

In Britain, Manchester and Newcastle have lost 20 percent of their population in the last forty years. About one hundred thousand people leave London each year. While London housing prices are still astronomical, houses can be bought for next to nothing in the inner cities in the Midlands and in the north, where the old, traditional industries have disappeared. It is particularly in these parts that large Muslim communities exist.

In Germany, depopulation has especially taken hold in the eastern part of the country, where the younger people have left. Two thousand schools have closed down in recent years, there are few shops left and even fewer doctors, and it seems only a question of time until the last ones in many villages will also leave. But the shrinking is not only limited to the countryside. The number of inhabitants in small towns and some bigger ones is also rapidly falling. The prices of houses have gone down, and deserted streets can be seen here and there. Halle, Rostock, Cottbus and Magdeburg lost 16 to 20 percent of their inhabitants during the last decade, including most of their young generation.

Who will take care of this aging population? Who will work in the economy to ensure the economic health of the country so that pensions to the elderly can continue, as well as funds for health and other services? At one time, it was believed Eastern Europe could provide this labor force, but the number of those who came from the East was small, and it is going to dry up even more because birthrates in Eastern Europe are as low (and even lower) than in the west.

There is a great and growing reservoir of young unemployed in North Africa and the Middle East, about 25 percent, and population growth there is outpacing economic growth. Some one hundred million jobs will be needed during the next ten years to solve this problem, but they are unlikely to be created. The unemployment issue in North Africa and the Arab East (the "youth bulge") has been called a time bomb, and there is the question whether it will explode in the Middle East, Europe, or perhaps in both regions.

Political considerations quite apart, it would be pointless to invite immigrants from these parts unless they are highly skilled at a time when unemployment among young Muslims in Germany, France, and other European countries amounts to

30 percent to 40 percent. The presence of unskilled and unemployable young workers, who sometimes also lack drive and motivation, would only aggravate present ethnic tensions without helping solve Europe's economic and social problems.

South Asia, Southeast Asia, and the former Soviet central Asian republics could be a more promising source of labor. But so far European countries have made little effort to attract immigrants from these areas, nor is it certain how many skilled workers and technicians would be willing to move to Europe at a time when the economy in their own countries is picking up. Germany for a short while tried to attract computer experts from Bangalore and other centers of India's high-technology industry. But the German offers were not very attractive and there were few candidates. Spain for a while renewed its interest in immigrants from Latin America; tens of thousands had come in recent years, especially from Ecuador and Colombia. But this was before the unemployment index in Spain had risen to almost 20 percent.

How likely is a rise of the birthrate in European countries? The birthrate has been falling for the last 150 years, and a reversal seems unlikely now. The dictatorships of the 1930s and also Soviet communism tried, through various premiums and inducements, to pursue natalist policies, but without significant success. In Russia, it has been suggested that members of families with children should be given preference in state employment. In France and Sweden family-friendly legislation (providing for long holidays after childbirth) has caused a slight increase in the birthrate, and it seems likely that other countries may follow their example. But even in France and Sweden, the birthrate remains below the reproduction rate. The French birthrate increased to 2.0 in 2010, but it wasn't specified in what sections of French society this sudden increase took place. In brief, short of developments that cannot be foreseen, the prevailing trend will not be substantially reversed.

Chinese and Japanese and, of late, Indian birthrates have also significantly decreased, and the same is likely to happen eventually in the Middle East and North Africa. It seems equally certain that the birthrate of the immigrant communities in Europe, at present significantly higher than that of the local population, will also decline. But the impact of this decline will be felt only in a generation or two, not during the next decades, since the growth rate of the immigrant population will be considerably higher than that of the native population for at least one generation.

For more than a decade, the term *Eurabia* has caused a great deal of commotion. It refers to the warning that, if present trends continue, Europe will become an extension of Arabia (or North Africa) within two or three generations. But others have maintained that such trends do not exist and that the use of this term is either motivated by propaganda or the product of a feverish, alarmist imagination. *Eurabia* is, in all probability, a misleading term simply because of the wide variety of Muslim communities in Europe. Most Muslims in Germany are Turkish (or Kurdish), in Britain are Pakistani or Bangladeshi, in France hail from North or West Africa, in the Netherlands are mainly Turkish or Moroccan, and in Russia are Turkish, Iranian, Kurdish, and more—but certainly not Arab.

However, it is useful to recall that those indignant about the use of this concept seem unaware that its origins are by no means Western but rather Muslim. Among Arab public figures and writers, the idea that Muslims would be a majority in Europe goes back a long time. One early example is the speech made by Houari Boumediene, then president of Algeria, in the United Nations General Assembly in 1974, in which he argued that, in view of the high birthrate of Muslim women (and the low rate of European women), such a development was more or less inescapable.

To give a more recent example Muammar Khaddafi, the then Libyan leader, wrote in an article (published in *Al Shams* on June 8, 2010) that statistics about the number of Muslims in Europe were incorrect and that their number was much greater than officially given; the Muslims will inherit Europe, and Turkey will join the EU as a "Trojan horse." Boumediene and Khaddafi are not among the most authoritative demographers of our generation, and their predictions may well be wrong. But no special training is needed to note that important demographic changes are indeed taking place in Europe.

TOWARD A UNITED EUROPE

AFTER THE NEW EUROPEAN CONSTITUTION had been voted down in France and the Netherlands, Europe decided to take a lengthy pause for reflection—there was little else that could have been done. Some were saying that a new initiative toward closer cooperation must come from a new activist core consisting of Germany and France and perhaps also Spain and Italy (although France had just voted down the constitution). It was clear to almost everyone that the original federal idea of the United States of Europe, which one way or another had been the aim of the founding fathers after the Second World War, was no longer feasible once the European Union consisted of twenty-seven members.

Some suggested a new plan D, but it was also clear that the real problem was not finding new wording that would put at ease those fearing a surrender of too much sovereignty or even of losing their identity. The real problem was that a new push could come only on the basis of a new psychological orientation, a new mood, and a new attitude toward Europe. Basically everyone was in favor of some kind of Europe, but there was no agreement where its borders should be. Above all, whenever the interests of the nation-state and Europe collided, the interests of the former always came first. This emerged on every occasion, and just one recent illustration should suffice.

A new treaty in December 2007 was intended to "enhance the efficiency and democratic legitimacy of the Union and to improving the coherence of its action." It was a more or less elegant way to circumvent and overcome the opposition to closer European unity that had manifested itself in the various votes in earlier years against a European constitution. It was well phrased, but how would it be able to affect the real situation? There were deep divisions on economic and other issues.

The often-quoted "European model" meant above all the welfare state. Opinions of leading economists concerning its future (social Europe) range from bleak pessimism—the prediction that the welfare state is dead and cannot be resuscitated—to relative optimism and the assumption that through a mixture of modest cuts of benefits and modest tax increases the essentials of the welfare state can be saved. Every European country had to cut benefits for two decades. This was initiated by conservative governments (Margaret Thatcher in Britain, Helmut Kohl in Germany, Carl Bildt in Sweden), but the Social Democratic governments that came after, such as Gerhard Schröder in Germany, had to follow the same policies as well. The services provided had become permanently more expensive. This was in part the result of more people living longer and the higher costs of medical services. It was also the result of slow economic growth or stagnation. When the welfare state had first been conceived, its expenditures had been considerably less, and economic growth more substantial.

Governments could increase taxes, but taxes in most north European countries were high in any case (close to 50 percent), and further increases would slow economic growth and create more unemployment. The policy suggested by the far left—soak the rich—was also unsatisfactory in European circumstances. It is true that at a time of economic crisis, growing disparities in income were difficult to justify. Such criticism also applied to the EU bureaucracy in Brussels. Why should members of the European parliament, not to mention business leaders who had failed, receive pensions that were many times higher than the average? But there were not enough rich people to be soaked so as to make a decisive difference overall. On the other hand, if companies or individuals were squeezed too hard, there was the danger (even the probability) that they would transfer their activities to countries with lower taxation.

The only alternative was a political-social covenant between all those concerned to show moderation and to accept the necessity, however painful, of cuts in order to preserve at least some of the essentials of the welfare state. Such agreement seems easier in some countries than in others. In Sweden and to a certain extent in the Netherlands, such a compact worked, despite much grumbling. Beginning in 1996, the welfare state was reformed in Sweden; heavy cuts were made but the essentials preserved. Taxation remained high, but, following some deregulation, Sweden ranked high as far as private-sector efficiency was concerned, as well as in business creativity. The great crisis of 2008 hit Sweden less severely than most other European countries, and its recovery was quicker. In the circumstances, sneering in the United States and elsewhere about the failings of Swedish socialism was factually incorrect and misplaced.

In Germany and especially in France, there is considerable resistance to giving up any of the achievements of the welfare state. However, the exigencies of the economic crisis made changes imperative, despite violent protests and demonstrations, such as those against raising the retirement age in France from age sixty to sixty-two. Populists put the blame on global-ization and the vagaries of the market economy. But they have no answers to the problems facing Europe—economic nation-alism is unlikely to solve the problems.

The general European situation quite apart, there is the generational problem for which no answer has been found. As more people live longer and as the labor force shrinks, the weight of expenditures for the elderly rests more heavily on the young, and this burden of young taxpayers supporting elderly retirees is likely to grow. A compact between the generations will be needed not only in Europe but in all developed countries.

At the height of the 2008 economic crisis, all European countries cut spending on health, education, and other social services. In the UK and other countries, hospital wards were closed, fewer postmortems were carried out, and many other services were restricted or cut. In Britain, following the reform proposals by the conservative-liberal coalition, the opposition argued that the government meant eventually to privatize the health service. In Germany, the main bone of contention was Hartz IV, a scheme to reform and reduce government social aid, which had been proposed by the Social Democratic gov-ernment and came into effect in 2003 and 2004. This affected above all support for the unemployed. Full unemployment pay was restricted to a period of twelve months, eighteen months in the case of those over fifty-five, who were far less likely to find a new job. These measures helped to cut spending as long as unemployment was relatively low, but with the crisis of 2008 and the rise of unemployment, the spending situation again worsened.

The German government introduced a *Sparpaket* ("saving parcel") in order to reduce spending in most social programs, including subsidies for families with young children. The insurance companies suggested a reduction of the income of physicians by 2.5 percent, but since the income of German doctors was lower than in most other European countries, this led to threats of strike and eventually to strikes. The same happened in Greece in 2011, where pharmacies also closed down. In the UK, the income of general practitioners had been very low for many years, with the result that fewer and fewer students of medicine opted for a career as general practitioners, and the government was compelled to look for doctors in other European countries, and even Africa and Asia, with sometimes very negative results for the patients and no savings for the government. Eventually, the government was compelled to increase the remuneration of general practitioners.

Critics correctly argued that the European austerity regimes were a threat to the welfare state, and worse: they endangered the vision of a good society. These austerity measures hit virtually all European countries (rich Norway being one of the few exceptions), but affected most of all were those countries hardest hit by the recession, not only Greece, Spain, Ireland, and Iceland but also the poorer European countries such as Romania.

The welfare-state critics from the left argued, not without justice, that the poor were the prime victims of the economic crisis. Was it the fault of the Greek workers rather than the bankers that their country had sunk deeper and deeper in debt and that severe spending cuts had to be made to reduce the mountain of debt? There was no denying the justice in these complaints, but once a crisis had arisen that threatened the national economy (and that of Europe), what alternative measures could be suggested to rectify the situation?

Cutting the exorbitant payments made to bankers once the

immediate crisis was over was one such measure. The banks
that had been on the verge of collapse were saved only through
the intervention of the state (and thus the taxpayers). But the
funds that could be retrieved by cutting the bonuses of the
bankers were not remotely sufficient to compensate for
the cuts affecting the welfare state. This left open the basic
question: how much welfare state could Europe afford, especially for a country (or countries) in a state of acute crisis?

Giuseppe Eusepi and Luisa Giuriato, Italian economists,
reached the conclusion even before the outbreak of the economic crisis of 2008 that, given Italy's growing debt that had
accumulated over decades, there was no way the welfare state
could be maintained as it was. What if there was a spectacular
upturn in the European economies in the years to come? But
the forecasts are not optimistic, and the International Monetary
Fund predicts growth of only 1.5 percent even as far out as 2015.

What these economists predicted for Italy may apply to
most of Europe; if so, what will be the political consequences
of the gradual disintegration of the welfare state? The social
programs were based on a social contract, and if the contract
ceases to exist, political conflict seems inevitable. It would not
be just a matter of unfulfilled expectations, it would mean giving up a way of life to which citizens of Europe have become
accustomed. It would mean a substantial decline in the standard of living and the quality of life. Depriving citizens of services that were taken for granted could lead sooner or later to
a political earthquake, and even a lethargic Europe could witness violence. No one can predict what form protests will
take—probably a populist reaction that could turn left as well
as toward the authoritarian right and that could see the end of
the political parties and the parliamentary system as Europe
has known it since the Second World War.

INTEGRATION AND EROSION

To inspect the Muslim heartland in Europe where a Muslim majority can be expected in the course of the present century, one ought to take a walk in one of the cities of the Ruhr and then leave by way of the Autobahn, either straight west in the direction of Eindhoven (Holland) and beyond or in a northwesterly direction toward Nijmegen and Utrecht and the British channel. Starting at Dortmund and Duisburg, one passes through northern France and southern Belgium, the major Dutch cities (Amsterdam, Rotterdam, Utrecht), and the old heavy industry and textile centers, such as the conurbation of Lille/Roubaix/Tourcoing, with more than 1.5 million residents.

In addition, one might visit the enclaves in Britain such as Bradford, Burnley, and Oldham (and not to forget Birmingham) or Malmö in Sweden and also a number of cities in southern Spain and southern France. Some of these regions are gradually coming to resemble parts of North Africa and the Middle East. I doubt whether Georges Simenon, who was born in Liège about a hundred years ago, or Henri Matisse, who was born near Cambrai, would recognize the scenes of their childhood.

Such demographic changes have occurred elsewhere. In

the United States, New York no longer has a "white" majority, nor has Los Angeles, and in a few years the greater Washington, D.C., area and San Francisco will also be in this category. In the Washington area, the northern Virginia suburbs are mainly Latino and Far Eastern in background, now the fastest growing population there.

But there is an important difference, inasmuch as the United States is a country of immigrants and accustomed to the coexistence of various ethnic groups. New York, Washington, and Los Angeles have had black mayors in the past or have them now. Furthermore, while America may no longer be a melting pot, intermingling of ethnic groups there is far more frequent, and, by and large, no group wants strictly to impose its religious law on others. There are social tensions, but no calls for jihad. The business of ethnic America is to make a comfortable living and not to fight, except perhaps turf fights among gangs and the criminal underworld.

There are ghettos in America, but there is also a black and Latino middle class moving out of them. As for the immigrants from the Far East, they have been doing better than almost any other group in business and education. Immigrants from Muslim countries, mostly educated and middle class, have also been doing much better than their counterparts in Europe. According to some evidence, immigrants from Palestine have been doing best of all.

Is the trend in Europe toward disintegration? It would be an exaggeration to argue that immigrants from Pakistan and Turkey, from the Arab East and North Africa, have been a uniform failure, socially and economically. While there are only a few reliable statistics, it is reported that there are 5,400 Muslim millionaires in Britain. Among the list of Russian dollar billionaires, we find Mikhail Fridman, the head of the Alfa Group;

Roman Abramovich, the head of Millhouse Capital Investment Company, but also Vagit Alekperov, the head of Lukoil (7.8 billion dollars); Iskander Makhmudov, of Kuzbas oil (3.3); Suleiman Kerimov, of Sberbank (3.1); and the owner of London's Arsenal football club, Alisher Usmanov, of Orgasmetal (1.6). There are wealthy Turks in Germany and wealthy North Africans in France.

A small Muslim middle class is developing in Europe. But it is also true that, for the time being, the ghetto prevails, as does unemployment among the young generation and dependence on handouts from the state and the municipalities. The Muslim religious leadership is trying hard to keep their flock together, but this can be achieved only if the ghetto persists and only if there is little if any contact between the faithful and the infidels. The young are indoctrinated from an early age, and many of those in Germany, the Netherlands, and Scandinavia know no more of the language of the land than is necessary for daily use.

Educators in Europe who have closely followed the education of young Muslims believe that the efforts should be concentrated on the very young, with the aim of their acquiring language skills and a general education. The younger generation has developed a subculture of their own, expressed, for instance, in their songs and language and sometimes imitated by their white contemporaries, who think it cool. While a deep knowledge of German, French, or British culture cannot be expected from most candidates for citizenship—many of the natives would fail such examinations—it stands to reason that a working knowledge of the language as well as of the laws and way of life should be a precondition for citizenship.

Regions in which Muslims will be a majority might see a demand for autonomy. Separatism, the demand for full independence, is unlikely, be it only for the depressed economic situation in these areas. Muslims will be the new authorities on the local and regional level, but they will expect the state to accept responsibility for the social well-being of the inhabitants. Perhaps, in due time, these Muslim societies will produce an elite group of entrepreneurs, of scientists and technologists second to none, the Einsteins and the Nobel Prize winners of tomorrow, providing a major economic and cultural impetus to these societies. But, at present, it is difficult to see even the beginnings of such a trend.

It is unlikely that the demand to introduce Muslim religious law (the shari'a) as the new law of the land will be pressed very strongly. In any case, exemptions will be granted to the non-Muslims, though even now German and British courts have accepted the stipulations of the shari'a in civil actions. There have been demands for radical Islamisation in some circles (for instance in the UK), but there is no unanimity about this within the Muslim community.

Even in Germany, there is division within the Turkish community between Turkish Sunnis and significant other minorities, such as the Kurds (at least half a million) and the Alawites. Kurds and Alawites have been pushed aside by the official Turkish and Arab organizations negotiating with the authorities, but this could well change in the future. There are important differences between Islam as practiced by Moroccans and Turks in the Netherlands and Belgium, between Pakistanis in Britain and Muslims from the Middle East in Britain, even between those of Algerian origin in France and those from Morocco. This list could be lengthened, and there have been complaints that political and religious leaders from one country (or one sect—for instance, Turks in Belgium and Arabs in Britain) have acquired influence out of proportion to the size of the ethnic group to which they belong. It will be up to the Muslim communities to find a common denominator; there will be a struggle for influence and power, and the outcome is not at all certain.

Eurabia does not apply to Germany, Britain, or to other European countries. Turks are not Arabs, and their attitude toward them is not always friendly. The gang warfare in the streets of Muslim Berlin between groups of Turkish, Arab, and Kurdish adolescents does not reflect any particular closeness between these communities.

Nor is it certain how strong the impetus toward religious fundamentalism and radicalism will be in the future. There is much reason to assume that it will lose momentum. The radicalism of the young generation may manifest itself in religious terms, but it is doubtful whether it will be mainly religious in inspiration.

Facing the temptations of Western societies, this process of erosion is inevitable—the question is how quickly it will proceed. Among many Muslim intellectuals, there is the growing dissociation from a religion that has, under the impact of radical interpreters, become more primitive and identified above all with political violence directed against innocent civilians. Among women, however orthodox, there is increasing demand for an Islam that gives them more rights than the fundamentalists are willing to grant.

As for the young men, a leading Berlin imam has said the road to the mosque is long and the temptations many. This refers to drugs, crime, sex, and other seductions of the decadent West. Decadence is attractive and infectious. In Britain and France, young Muslims are now substantially involved in not only trading but also consuming drugs. Many young Muslims, who threaten to beat up their sister unless she dresses modestly with a hijab, will by no means disdain Western pornography.

According to Saudi authorities, of the 2.2 million Internet us-
ers in the Saudi kingdom some 92 percent wish to access forbidden or indecent material, which almost always does not
mean atheist Web sites but refers to pornography (*Arab News*,
October 2, 2005).

Such figures may not be unnaturally high in comparison
with other countries, as the Saudi authorities have pointed out.
But it certainly points to the deeply ambivalent attitude toward the forbidden on the part of the young Muslim male, the
attraction becoming even stronger because of the seductive
attraction of what is forbidden ("They close doors and we get in
through the windows," is a frequent comment). There is furthermore in Arab medieval literature something like a Kama Sutra
tradition, which will no doubt be rediscovered one of these days.
According to the Koran (16.90), *fuhsha,* which includes pornography, open and hidden, is strictly forbidden by Allah, who says
one should not even go close to it. But according to *Google Trends*
data assembled over many years, seven out of the top ten countries from which searches for the word "sex" came were
Muslim—including Iran and the Gaza strip.

The temptations are many and significant; the Beatles
played a modest part in the downfall of the Soviet empire. In a
similar way Arab pop (such as Fun-Da-Mental, Natacha Atlas,
Akhenaton, and IAM) is helping to undermine Muslim fundamentalism. However many fatwas against all types of music
that the mullahs publish, they are losing the battle in most
countries, just as they are losing the battle against soccer. In
the 1980s, musical entertainment and CDs of all types were
strictly banned by the Muslim Brotherhood in Egypt and elsewhere, and, as late as 2003, the performances of Lebanese-born
Nancy Ajram, who is probably the best-known belly dancer in
the Arab world, were banned by the Egyptian parliament on

all state television channels. But she and her colleagues can still be watched on hundreds of thousands if not millions of video clips and on countless private TV satellite channels, such as Rotana TV or Nagham or Melody Hits, which broadcast twenty-four hours a day and reach a very wide audience.

An Arab pop scene has emerged in the Middle East and among the Muslim communities in Europe in defiance of all the bans and fatwas. The lyrics of some rappers contain lines from the Koran and nationalist slogans: "I am a soldier in the army of Allah," from Malcolm X and Louis Farrakhan. There is a fair amount of sexism, antiwhite racism, and praise of gang rape, but mostly it is entertainment. However, with the events of 2011 in the Arab world, political radicalization has set in. Thomas Burkhalter has drawn attention to the growing number of religious and even military symbols on the clips of the rappers, as well as violent, sexist motives.

The first generation of rappers in the Muslim world was democratic and liberal by the standards of time and place. The second generation that played a notable part in the events of 2011 was more radical and closer to the Islamists. To give but one example: El General, the most prominent Tunisian rapper, turned in his "Allahu Akbar" against a world in which the Jews ruled and the Muslims were slaves. Arabs, he promised, would rise again in all their glory. He declared war against all those who rejected Islam and offended it. El General was widely praised, and his music played by European media, which were not aware of his politics—or did not want to know about it.

What makes the subculture of gangsta rap and hip-hop suspect to Muslim fundamentalists are the Afro-Caribbean, non-Muslim inspiration of this music and perhaps also the fact that some of the leading figures of this scene are not Muslim by origin but Italian (Akhenaton), Copt (Mutamassik), or even

Jewish (as with Natacha Atlas, who is Muslim but who has a Jewish great-great-grandfather). As for the cultural level of this subculture, the Beirut professor who argued that the worst aspects of Western mass culture have been copied, but not the best, may well be right. Fundamentalist leaders found it easy to ostracize Western ideologies from liberalism to Marxism, but they have been powerless vis-à-vis the pop scene and soccer. Movies featuring the music of Samira Said and Nancy Ajram were banned, but this did not affect the popularity of this kind of music (the previously mentioned Lebanese singer Nancy Ajram has sold thirty million albums). The situation in Pakistan was similar; banned under several governments, from Ahmed Rushdi, the most popular Pakistani singer in his time, onward, Pakistani pop survived and even spread to neighboring countries.

There is nothing in the Koran about street gangs, but this phenomenon (as well as gang warfare) in the Muslim streets in Europe is quite important and has been insufficiently studied so far. These gangs have appeared in many parts of the world, and various factors have been adduced to explain this phenomenon, including dysfunctional families, personal traits, human instincts, child abuse, urbanization, identity politics, and exposure to violence in the culture in which they grew up. Ethnic factors do play a role, and some cultures are more prone to violence than others. There has been generational conflict in many societies, but whereas in Germany, for instance, it was directed against the tyrannical father and teacher (the youth movement of the 1900s), among the Islamic minority it is now directed against "the other." In the European Muslim communities, gangs may have economic motives (drug trafficking) as well as psychological (satisfaction through display of machismo and protection of the turf).

These gangs are usually found among the second and third generation of immigrants, and this is connected to the retreat of the state, which in democratic societies no longer has a monopoly on violence. In authoritarian regimes, short shrift is made with troublemakers irrespective of age and gender. In contemporary democratic societies, these people do not have much to fear. The police are under strict restraints, as are teachers at school and judges at court. Perpetrators are bound to be released within days if not hours, and their very arrest turns them into heroes among their comrades.

The gang phenomenon had an important political dimension in the past (for instance, among Latinos in South and North America and the South African gangs in Soweto and elsewhere), and the same is true today. But as far as contemporary gang ideology is concerned, how much of it is Islamism, and how much is hip-hop culture and gangsta rap? It has widely been reported from various countries that the young enforcers of the shari'a have also been dealing and consuming drugs, engaging in sex practices not at all legitimate according to their religion, and listening constantly to rap music, which is also in contravention to strict Islam. While some Islamists have gone out to the gangs and the prisons to try and convert them, the gangs have also invaded the mosques to find and recruit new members. It is not at all clear who will prevail in this competition.

While all this has been predominantly a young male preserve, girls have also participated in some of these activities, particularly in school. This too has apparently to do with the urge to gain respect, or at least not to be considered "whores" (*Schlampen* or *putains,* terms frequently used with regard to German girls) by the young males if the girls choose to stand aside during an attack.

There have been mutterings on the part of young British and French Muslims about the formalistic and joyless character of their religion, the endless parrotlike repetition of prayers. As one young British Muslim said, in an interview that expressed the probable thinking of many of his contemporaries, their religion demands too much of them. They would like to do what their secular friends do, to have boyfriends and girlfriends, to go occasionally to the cinema, to watch television, to play video games, and not to live in social and cultural isolation.

The young will not engage in theological disputations with the imams; it is far more likely that they will quietly drop out or limit their religion to lip service out of respect for their parents and families. The next cultural war will not be between believers and infidels but within the camp of the believers, where erosion of religious belief will proceed not so much in open defiance but in stealth. However, such erosion of religious orthodoxy and fanaticism will certainly not affect all Muslims; there will be fanatics who, for all one knows, may redouble their militancy.

Political coexistence may be easier to achieve than social coexistence. Most political parties will compete for Muslim votes, and local branches might be taken over by them. There are certain common interests, and there could be coalitions. In some places the Muslim vote could be decisive even now (as shown, for instance, by the victory of the socialist PvdA [Partij van de Arbeid] in Holland in 2006, where half of the counselors nominated and elected were of Muslim origin), and it will be even more important in the future. Would Neil Livingstone, the erstwhile mayor of London, have been elected without the Muslim vote? Muslims have a quarter of the representation in the Brussels provincial parliament. There is the danger of polarization; local elections in London's East End showed an increase in the xenophobic vote (the British National Party) on the one hand and the Trotskyite-Islamist groups on the other. Islamists are reported to have taken over in 2010–11 the Labor constituency in Tower Hamlets in London's East End.

The establishment of ethnic parties is unlikely to succeed, as such attempts in Spain have shown. On the other hand, as has been argued earlier on, the growth of Muslim communities that have failed to integrate to any significant degree is bound to generate a political backlash, as witnessed by the growth of anti-immigration parties and the accommodation by virtually all major political parties to prevailing anti-immigrant moods among the population.

An anti-Muslim backlash has indeed begun, starting on a regional basis; Antwerp in Belgium serves as an example, and so does the Black Country area in Britain as well as Barking and Dagenham (white working-class neighborhoods), parts of Birmingham, and certain electoral successes of the National Front in France. It has also taken place in northern Italy and virtually all other European countries, including those that were traditionally the most liberal, such as the Scandinavian countries and the Netherlands.

Works of political science fiction have presented scenarios in which Muslims (and Jews) have been expelled on twenty-four hours' notice from Belgium. Following the French riots in November 2005 a French political thriller in a similar vein appeared, *Le songe du guerrier,* by Clément Weil-Raynal, about a right-wing backlash. A backlash, and not only in France, seems likely, but the more extreme scenarios less so: that these extreme forces will come to power seems about as likely as Russian fantasies about France becoming a radical Islamic state with a small Christian minority resisting underground—to be eventually saved by Russian armed forces. (Elena Chudinova,

Mechet Parizhskoi Bogomateri [*The Mosque of Paris Notre-Dame*] Moscow 2005).

Political speculations frequently rest on the assumption that there will be a monolithic Muslim bloc, which, as has been stressed earlier on, does not correspond with the facts. With all the religious-political radicalization of recent years, there are many centrifugal trends, internal competition, and rivalry inside this community. In many ways, it is a race against time. It is partly a question of the durability of fanaticism, as such waves, inspired by religions or secular religions, do not last forever. The fanaticism of Muslim communities in Europe should not be overrated; there are sympathies for the so-called militants, along with frustration and aggression and the desire to manifest the discontent, but the majority do not want to die a martyr's death but prefer a quiet and reasonably comfortable life.

How to promote the peaceful trends in the European Muslim communities? It is above all a question of raising the level of education of these communities, of inducing them to think for themselves, and of lessening their dependence on guidance by fundamentalist imams. A backlash against fundamentalism among Muslim communities should not be ruled out, as this has happened in most religions. But even if a moderate Islam prevails, Europe will no longer be the same.

The policy of the secular forces in Europe will be based on a certain amount of appeasement, however difficult many may find this to accept (if terrorists have become "militants," then why not prefer the term *accommodation*?). *Appeasement* is a term that is in disrepute, and rightly so in view of its historical connotation going back to the 1930s. But having failed to take a strong stand, which may have prevented the present crisis when it was still possible to do so, what are the alternatives now as immigrants of Muslim background become the majority in certain cities and regions?

Accommodation means, among other things, refraining from criticizing basic beliefs and practices of the other side. If a religion has 1.2 billion adherents, it is not advisable to talk openly and candidly about its negative aspects; quantity in terms of Marxist doctrine becomes a new quality. Some believe that the quaint observations of Prince Charles that the Muslim critique of materialism helped him to rediscover the sacred Islamic spirituality could be a model for the peace makers on how to make friends and influence people in an age of tensions. Horst Köhler, the former president of Germany, has been criticized (in 2010) for making statements in a similar vein. A certain amount of self-censorship is already practiced by Western politicians and media, and there may be more of it in the future, such as, for instance, the decision of a European television network in addition to *al Jazeera* not to screen a program about the situation of persecuted Christians in the Arab world or, in general, playing down the unfortunate fate of Christian minorities in recent times in the Middle East.

Accommodation may mean that citizens in certain regions of Germany and elsewhere will be well advised to acquire a working knowledge of Turkish or Arabic, just as the residents of Southern California and some southern states in the United States have acquired a smattering of Spanish. The *Times Atlas of the World* says about Germany: "currency, Euro; language, German and Turkish." This is a premature statement, perhaps, but it could be true at some future date. *Accommodation* also means a more nuanced approach by European authorities toward the Muslim communities in their midst, which, as I have stressed repeatedly, are anything but monolithic. There is no reason why the authorities should treat them as if they were

an integrated whole, which they have never been. The British
example of dealing with the "moderate fundamentalists," as if
these were the only authentic representatives of the Muslim
community, has not been a great success, but rather it strengthened the anti-Western elements. Governments and local authorities should deal with all kinds of Muslim groups. The
decisive issue is, of course, How far should accommodation
go? How much tolerance should there be toward those not
believing in tolerance?

I have also emphasized in these pages the importance of
education. Yet it is precisely here that the German approach
has been least successful. According to alarming reports, normal teaching has virtually broken down in some Berlin schools
attended by immigrant children from Muslim countries. These
schools, according to many reports, have become a blackboard
jungle of Arabs fighting Turks, Turks combating Kurds, Muslims versus immigrants from Russia and the Balkans and everyone against the Germans.

Could it have been any different? Muslim children often
come from patriarchal families with hardly any education,
where they are likely to be beaten for even light violations of
the strict rules prevailing. Their encounter with progressive
education must have been a cultural shock. The teachers know
little about Islam and its way of life and their anti-authoritarian
training does not help. Eren Uensal, the spokeswoman of
the *Türkischer Bund,* a political activist group in Berlin, has
stressed that a certain measure of authority on the part of the
school and its teachers was absolutely essential. At one time
some Muslim parents in Britain sent their children to Jewish
schools because discipline there was said to be stricter.

The situation in the Paris banlieue is no better. The French
authorities made special efforts over the last decade to improve

education in the banlieue. There is a program called Second
Chance for those trying to catch up at a later age, and there are
schools classified ZEP (*zone education prioritaire*) and ZUS (*zone
sensible*), where there are programs for the prevention of violence. But the results are not impressive. The number of dropouts is several times higher than elsewhere, the achievements
of many pupils are poor.

What could be the solution? Send them to the soccer fields?
Perhaps a Baden Powell is needed to establish a new Boy Scout
movement; but if he should arise, he will probably be an Islamist. Concessions have to be considered. What should the
curriculum be in state schools? There have been questions
from the immigrant communities whether Dutch children of
Muslim origin should be taught that much about Rembrandt,
who after all was not part of their tradition. Should young
Muslims in Italy have to study the Renaissance, learn to appreciate all kinds of paintings of saints and Madonnas of another
religion, or read Dante, who wrote nasty things about the
prophet Muhammed?

Goethe wrote respectfully about the common features of
Orient and Occident, and he is also the author of the *West-
Östlicher Divan* (*Poems of the West and East*), but he is still not part
of the Turkish heritage (there was an exceedingly silly debate in
Germany in 2010 whether Goethe was an admirer or critic of
Islam). On the other hand, why should children of Moroccan
origin in the Netherlands be taught the history of the Ottoman Empire, which means little to them? It will not be easy to
find common denominators.

An educator at the London School of Economics, Ahmed
Iftikar, pondering the low grades of children from Muslim
families in British schools, put part of the blame on the fact
that they were spending too much time learning the Koran by

heart in mosque schools and had little or no time for doing their homework. Nor could the children identify with their non-Muslim teachers. He said special Muslim schools were needed to improve the situation. Will the situation improve with time? Research in Germany indicates that the second generation of pupils from Muslim families is in fact doing worse than the earlier generation. But what would be the religious-political orientation of separate Muslim schools? Would they not perpetuate the divisions in society? An improvement in the education of young people of Muslim background will not solve their problems if jobs cannot be found for them after graduation.

Accommodation does not imply accepting Muslim religious law and customs that are unacceptable to non-Muslims, such as a denial of the equality of the sexes. It is against this background that tensions and conflicts are bound to arise. Tolerance toward minorities has not been one of the distinguishing features of Muslim societies in modern history; the Armenians have not fared well in Turkey, or the Copts in Egypt, or the Baha'i in Iran, or even the Shiites or the Ahmadiya and Ismailiya in Pakistan, Muslim sects who were persecuted by the Sunni (or Shia) majority, though they are Muslims. The status of Christians in Indonesia, one of the most tolerant Muslim countries, is still problematic, and in Malaysia the Chinese have been made second-class citizens. There has been an exodus of Christian Arabs from Iraq and Palestine and lately also from Egypt. If this trend does not change in the course of the coming decades, the prospects for peaceful coexistence in Europe will be less than bright.

CONCLUSION

EUROPE 2020, EUROPE 2030

What role will Europe be playing in the future world? Individuals as well as committees have been pondering this question. The Reflection Group, submitting its report to the European Council in Brussels in December 2007, introduced it with the following words:

> Our findings are reassuring neither to the Union nor to our citizens: a global economic crisis; states coming to the rescue of banks; ageing populations threatening the competitiveness of our economics and the sustainability of our social models, downward pressure on costs and wages; the challenges of climate change and the increasing energy dependence; and the Eastward shift in the global distribution of production and savings. And on top of this, the threats of terrorism, organised crime, and the proliferation of the weapons of mass destruction hang over us.

That is a fair summary of the threats facing Europe, even if it is quite incomplete, but then it was written before the full extent of the last economic and financial crisis and its consequences were realized. The commission then asked, "Will the

EU be able to maintain and increase its level of prosperity in this changing world? Will it be able to promote and defend Europe's values and interests?" It replied, "Our answer is positive."

Such an optimistic answer is refreshing and it may be politically necessary, but is it realistic? Europe, once the center of the world, has been witnessing a shift of world power since the end of the Second World War. It was cushioned from feeling the full consequences—political, economic, and military—because it was under the protection of the United States. America was a superpower, and, for some of the time, the only superpower. But now and in the years to come America will face its own crisis, and Europe, to a far larger extent, will be on its own.

The misguided Western literature about the twenty-first century being that of Europe had its counterpart in the works of a new breed of East Asian latter-day Spenglers, such as Kishore Mahbubani, a Singapore professor of public policy, representing his country at one time at the United Nations. In his view, the two centuries of Western domination was an aberration that has now come to an end, with Asia again taking center stage ("irresistible shift of power"). Mahbubani believes that Asia has to teach the West a great many things, above all perhaps the importance of good (that is to say, strong) governance and the importance of regulators of the economy who are stronger than the banks and the industries; on the other hand, Europeans may not be that enthusiastic about economic arrangements in Singapore, and all other Asian countries, that do not provide for unemployment benefits and a minimum wage. Asia can take a leading role in maintaining global security as well as climate change. It can show new models of elementary and higher education. Asia will not only outproduce the West, it also has the moral and ethical values that will guide the world in the years to come.

There may be more realism in these Asian exaggerations than in the earlier European and American fantasies, but they are still dubious. The rates of economic growth in China and India have been most impressive, but they cannot continue without causing enormous harm to their own countries and the world at large. They are generating internal and external conflicts that cannot indefinitely be swept under the carpet. The distance between poor and rich in the BRIC countries (Brazil, Russia, India, and China) has grown at an alarming rate (as it has in the United States and many European countries), and this cannot continue without social and political consequences in the long run. As a result of China's growing political clout and assertiveness, its neighbors feel threatened and draw closer together. Asia may well teach Europe and America a thing or two about stronger governance and better education, but moral and ethical values, freedom, and human rights should better be kept out of these discussions.

Julian Assange, the founder of Wikileaks, was the intellectual hero and moral guide for many in Europe in 2010. He and his followers truly believe that, *grosso modo,* everyone should know everything of importance, that keeping secrets is wicked, and that secret diplomacy is the source of all evil. They apparently have not heard of the debate, since ancient times, about the *arcana imperii* ("the state secrets"). The idea that the "goal of the art of government might be the longevity and stability of the commonweal," which had been obvious to political thinkers of the seventeenth century such as Corvinus, would have been rejected as altogether reactionary had the fighters for total freedom of information known about it. Such old-fashioned ideas were rooted in a time when people were stupid and could not be trusted but were apparently outdated in an enlightened world like ours, when peace and goodwill are prevailing between nations.

At the same time Carl Schmitt, the legal and political philosopher, and, to a lesser degree, Leo Strauss, became the heroes of China's young intellectual elite. Schmitt was the protagonist of the strong state, the primacy of the state and the *raison d'état* over the law. In this confrontation between anarchism and authoritarianism on the international scene, there could be few doubts as to who would prevail. As the European economic crisis continues and various cuts and austerity programs become imperative, preserving the democratic order will become more difficult.

Beyond any shadow of doubt, Asia will be a major agent of change in the new world order. What will Europe's role be? Asian diplomats quite often refer to the European Union with a mixture of condescension and incredulity. Europe, as they see it, is a spent force, a customs union that never seriously intended to become a global power. They find it strange that Europe seems to be unaware of its reduced status in world affairs and that it has not come to terms with it. They are not even offended by Western admonitions to pay greater attention to human rights; they simply ignore them.

The Reflection Group, one of the informal European think tanks, is more optimistic, and they say, "The EU can be an agent of change in the world . . . and not just a passive witness." But with one major stipulation: "If we work together." It could be an overly optimistic estimate, because even if the European states acted together, their influence might not be that great. When the Italian city-states at long last got together in the nineteenth century, it was too late to make a united Italy a major force even by European, let alone global, standards.

But what are the prospects of working together? There is,

of course, awareness that European nations share common interests—even euroskeptics do not deny this. But what price should be paid for a closer union? How much do European countries have, after all, in common? Could not Latin America serve as a model? The Latin American countries live in peace with one another and cooperate to a certain extent; they even established a common market of sorts called Mercosur, with free transit of goods with no customs. Not all Latin American countries belong to it, but it may well expand.

Two hundred years ago, Simón Bolívar had more ambitious plans for unifying the continent, but it did not happen, even though these countries had much more in common, including (with the exception of Brazil) a common language. Bolívar's dream collided with the Latin American realities of his time and the lack of enthusiasm for his ideas. In the end he set himself up as dictator, but this didn't help his cause either. What prevented a Latin American union? Perhaps it was not considered necessary. Perhaps the union that would have emerged would have been too large and unwieldy, and the longer the separate states existed the stronger the vested interests in a status quo would have become. There have been recent attempts to establish a closer political framework, the last of which was called UNASUR (Union of South American Nations) in 2010, but substantial progress is not expected in the near future. Nor have similar endeavors in other parts of the world led to the emergence of strong regional groups—either in Africa or the Middle East (the African Union, with its fifty-three members, or the Arab League, with twenty-two).

But the European situation is different in many respects. Poor in raw materials and lacking energy resources, it will find it difficult to maintain its standard of living and social achievements unless it is united. Unlike Latin America, its geopolitical location makes it far less exposed to political pressures, since it is distant from the centers of world power and not attracting a stream of immigrants anymore. The fact that progress toward greater unity has been slow is not surprising, given that nation-states have been in existence for centuries.

But this has become more urgent than ever for a variety of reasons, above all because in the years to come Europe may no longer count on an American safety net. Unless there is stronger economic governance there will be recurrent crises, the imbalances between the countries will increase, and there will be a return to economic nationalism and protectionism. There could be even worse consequences. Unless it has a common energy policy, Europe will no longer be master of its own destiny and will find it difficult to compete in world markets. Without a common defense policy, Europe will count for even less on the international scene. It will be unable to cope with regional conflicts, let alone the spread of weapons of mass destruction—and these are among the tasks outlined in the European security strategy. Europe may be able to carry out minor police functions, but not war fighting.

By 2020 or 2030 proliferation of weapons of mass destruction and the emergence of failed states not too distant from European borders in North Africa and the Middle East may well constitute real threats, and Europe may not be able to count indefinitely on NATO. But there is at present no political will to provide the necessary defense for the dangers ahead. France has suggested including Russia into future European defense planning, but this will not be met with universal enthusiasm on the part of the other states. Also, according to most reports, the Russian defense forces, its nuclear forces perhaps apart, have not been in the best of shape.

Europe depends for more than half of its energy supply on

outside sources, and this dependency may increase in the years to come. The Baltic countries and Sweden, Bulgaria, Slovakia, and a few others are totally dependent on Russian supplies. There have been plans for years for lessening this dependence on Russian oil and gas, while Russia, on the other hand, has taken a variety of steps to lock in and if possible increase this dependence. However, the results have been more than modest so far, and the prospects for the future are not reassuring. One of the main projects is support for the Nabucco pipeline, leading from the Caspian Sea by way of Turkey and then by way of the Balkans to Austria and western Europe. It would compete with the proposed Russian South Stream pipeline, leading under the Black Sea and Bulgaria and to western Europe. Preparations on Nabucco, the Turkey-Austria pipeline, began in 2002, and it is expected to be operational by 2016–18. But Nabucco will pass through politically exposed regions, such as the Balkans and the Near East, and Europe will remain vulnerable.

European energy security will not be strengthened unless Europe makes a determined effort to increase substantially the use of other sources of energy. Some countries, such as France, have made greater efforts in this direction than others. Germany's decision to liquidate its nuclear facilities within the next six to nine years will increase its dependence on Middle Eastern and Russian imports and, at the same time, make German industrial production costs more expensive. Various European action papers are replete with such terms as *vigorous, stable, efficient, competitiveness, prime importance,* and *partnership.* But, overall, progress in reducing Europe's economic and political dependence during the next decade is not encouraging.

Looking ahead, there are, broadly speaking, three likely scenarios for the European Union: that it will fall apart, that it will try to muddle through as before, or that it will become far more unified and centralized than in the past. Muddling through is probably not a serious option for more than a number of years, unless one considers a split, with some countries opting out of the EU and the major economies staying on, or the abolition of the euro. But a European Union without a common currency would not amount to much of a union.

When the EU was established (and in particular when it was enlarged and when the euro was introduced), its founding fathers did not fully realize the problems created by the disparities of the various economies, rich and poor, north and south. The individual EU countries retained to a large extent their economic sovereignty. They could in practice (if not in theory) run deficits in their budgets and set their own tax rates (almost a dozen countries adopted a flat tax rate, something that would be unthinkable in Germany or France). Leading banks were not regulated, which, as the result of greed and ill-advised speculation, as well as the action of spendthrift governments, led to the financial and economic disasters of 2008. The experience of the recent past has shown what should have been clear from the beginning—that an economic union was impossible without a far larger measure of political union. But this would have involved a price that many did not want to pay—the surrender of hitherto sovereign rights.

By 2010, there had been some progress. France was pressing for the gradual establishment of a European "economic government," and the then French finance minister Christine Lagarde announced there would be much stronger fiscal and economic coordination among EU countries. This meant a violation of all the existing rules (the treaty of Lisbon had said no bailouts of member countries) because this was the only way the Eurozone could be saved. A European stabilization mechanism was established as a permanent bailout fund, but there would also be "strict conditionality," meaning telling countries what actions they had to take on taxes, spending, and economic policy.

After some delay, the German government joined forces with other EU members, but when it came to the interpretation of what an "economic government" would mean, there were considerable differences between Germany and France. Would the European governments have to submit their annual budgets to the central government before their adoption? According to the Lisbon treaty, it was by no means clear whether any single government could be overruled.

With all this, the emergence of a European economic government now seems likely, but it is equally clear that it would take a long time to negotiate the rights of such a government, such as how quickly it would be able to act and many other important questions. If such a central economic administration were to come into existence, it would be in some ways a political government. This would be a great step forward, but how would it function? Would it not face all the difficulties confronting a coalition government, based not on two or three political parties but on twenty-seven? Or would it be independent of the individual nation-states, which at the moment seems difficult even to imagine?

In the Lisbon treaty of December 2009, changes were introduced as to how member states would vote in the EU's Council of Ministers. Voting was to be based on the population of each country, which meant in practice that most small countries lost half of their votes, whereas a country such as Germany would double its share. There would be similar changes affecting the election of the European Commission. The rights of the European parliament, on the other hand, remained restricted. Over the years the EU has adopted some ninety thousand laws, of which roughly eighty thousand could not be changed by the European parliament, let alone by national governments. They include, to adduce a frequent (but not atypical) example, the size of strawberries for sale in shops.

There was the danger that the immense preoccupation with such details would not promote the cause of European unity, and many of the laws could probably not be enforced, given the lack of a mechanism for legal control and adjudication. The danger was not just overbureaucratization and being swamped by unimportant detail. Such practices would cause resentment throughout the continent because the great variety of conditions in the twenty-seven member states ensured that strict regulations covering all of them without distinction were bound to lead to absurdities. If, on the other hand, the EU were to send out hundreds of thousands of diaries to schoolchildren that gave the dates for Ramadan but did not mention Christmas, and if some European countries such as Italy and Poland then protested, who would decide what ought to be done? The basic problem was, of course, that the amended regulations did not make it any easier to reach agreement on crucial political and economic issues, never mind the size of strawberries.

The coming years will confront most European countries with very serious domestic tensions. To reduce their high debt they will need steady growth. But these will also be years of cutbacks and austerity and, needless to say, resistance against cuts. Young people have grown up in an age in which higher education was free or at least inexpensive. Elderly people depend to a large degree on social security payments, and the unemployed on the minimum of material help needed to survive, but there will be cuts in all these fields as well as in health services and education. The cake (or the bread) is shrinking, and every sector of the population will fight not to be among the losers. To some extent it will be a generational confrontation. The increased fees for higher education will be a great hardship for the young and a major setback for the countries. But if their demands prevail, it will mean that other sectors of the society, such as the elderly and the unemployed, will suffer more. Since in all European societies there are now fewer young people than middle-aged and elderly, the young will be at a disadvantage in a democratic society—which is to say that European democracy too will be under conflicting pressures; will it be the street against the parliament? There will be a class struggle of sorts but also generational conflicts.

The future could also witness a confrontation between key strategic economic sectors; if workers strike, the economy may quickly come to a halt, whereas others, who would find themselves in weaker bargaining positions, may lose out, which may also generate a bad social climate. Perfect or even near-perfect justice is impossible at such a time, and the stronger elements will prevail. It will be far easier to carry out these inevitable and painful changes in smaller countries that have a deeper traditional sense of national solidarity than in the bigger European countries, where relationships have become more anonymous.

Dire predictions have been made about the form these conflicts may take—violent demonstrations, mass strikes, conditions bordering on civil war; with the changing composition of the population, society may have become more vulnerable than it has been for a long time. But the worst may not happen, and it is doubtful whether Europe in its present stage still has the energy for producing convulsions of this kind—the political barometer has been pointing to lethargy rather than revolution.

The prophets of declinism have been frequently wrong. While it is always profitable to study them, we know that Malthus was quite wrong in his predictions about population growth and future starvation. Spengler was a learned man, but his vision of the rise of the young peoples, such as Germany and Russia, could not have been more mistaken. Mackinder, one of the pioneers of geopolitics, greatly overrated the political consequences of the improvement in land transportation. He correctly foresaw the decline of Britain, as did Dangerfield, in his famous work on the decline of Britain in the years before the First World War. But if these prophets sometimes reached correct conclusions, they were quite often on the basis of false premises. Brooks Adams, a great-grandson of John Adams, was a widely read man, and his *Law of Civilization and Decay* (1895), about the commercial classes whose greed was leading societies to distrust and dishonesty, bears reading even now. He also predicted in 1900 that New York would emerge as the commercial center of the world. But he also thought that the decline of the West began with the Middle Ages and gave as the reason that for centuries thereafter it had not been sufficiently oriented toward martial values.

In our own age, Paul Kennedy and others pointed to the relative decline of the United States; but this was not a well-hidden secret. The preeminent economic and political position of America immediately following the Second World War owed to unprecedented circumstances, namely the war, and could not last. But regarding Europe and Japan, these prophets were wrong. China and India hardly figured in their visions of the future, and no one envisaged the fall of the Soviet Union. Many of them put the blame for the decline of the U.S. on "imperial overstretch," but this explanation hardly fits the decline of Europe, which, on the contrary, has been contracting over the last century because of decolonization and other factors.

There is, however, a basic difference between the declinists of yesteryear and those writing about contemporary Europe. Yesterday's prophets were dealing with future trends, whereas those concerned with today's Europe are dealing with developments that, for the most part, have already happened.

EUROPE MARGINALIZED

WHY HAS EUROPE BEEN UNABLE to get its act together? There have been manifold reasons, and even more explanations, some of which were mentioned earlier on. The primary loyalty of Europeans has been for centuries to the nation-state, while the idea of a European solidarity is recent. The differences in outlook, culture, and way of life between the various countries are very great. There is no common language and little trust. There is unwillingness to surrender sovereign rights to a central authority that has not inspired great confidence and has shown little ability at leadership.

The decline of Europe, once the center of the world, can be interpreted above all as a decline of will and dynamism, or abulia, to use a term that appeared in French nineteenth-century psychiatry. Leading powers have risen and declined all throughout known history. Overextension has been mentioned in some instances, military defeat in others. Economic and demographic factors were involved in some instances—Portugal and the Netherlands were obviously too small to sustain great empires. The rise of new religions offers an explanation in some cases; climatic changes or sudden pandemics are adduced as decisive factors for the decline and fall in others. Some great powers collapsed as the result of decadence, apparently caused by luxury; others failed because they became impoverished.

But while in some cases the reasons for rise and fall seem obvious, in many others they are not. Some powers that seemed in inexorable decline suddenly recovered for no apparent reason and experienced a second coming. France after the defeat by Germany in 1870–71 is an interesting example. Others have not been so lucky. Demographers have been discussing the low-fertility-trap hypothesis: whether countries with low fertility can still recover, especially if the birthrate has fallen very low. It seems certain that population size will remain an important factor in global affairs, but exactly how important we cannot know, because of the unpredictability of technological progress.

Why did Europe become marginalized? The two world wars, which some consider European civil wars, played a decisive role. But they also provided the impetus for the foundation of the European Union. Europe's recovery after 1945 made the emergence of the welfare state possible, but it also meant that Europe could no longer compete against economies based on cheap labor. Above all, there was the desire to no longer play an important part in world politics; the white man's burden, which had been to preach Christianity to the heathen, now became preaching human rights to the nonbelievers.

Europeans, however, did not fully realize that opting out of world politics did not offer protection against the consequences of world politics, and this at a time when the world had by no means become more peaceful, when proliferation and the struggle for raw materials, as well as extremist religion and failed states (sometimes in combination), constituted serious dangers to world peace.

Europe has been gradually sidelined after three hundred years of dominance, and this in all probability will continue. What Nietzsche called *Wille zur Macht,* the desire to have power and exercise it, has vanished and can hardly be found even among the traditional believers on the right. Even the fascists of today, such as they are, do not dream of aggression and expansion. Their fascism is defensive—they want to keep others out. Perhaps it is a natural process of rise and fall and exhaustion. It could be reversed by the rejuvenation of the continent, but it is difficult to see where such a revival could come from; the continent is aging, the birthrates are low, and the immigrants who are offering themselves to save European living standards do not seem the ideal candidates and, in any case, do not see the rejuvenation of Europe as their great aim.

A few decades ago, "small is beautiful" was a frequently discussed fad in Europe, and much can indeed be said about the quality of life in a small town—snug, tranquil, *gemütlich*— such as that depicted by Carl Spitzweg, the nineteenth-century Romantic German painter. What a contrast to the satanic mills of England's Industrial Revolution. Or, for instance, the nostalgia for the life in eighteenth-century small-town New England. There still was what sociologists called a face-to-face community. Life was not hectic, people were friendlier, the landscape more beautiful, the food tasted better, and love was more romantic. Ah, the sweetness of life of yesteryear. Up to a point, this is true even today. If the Wall Street banks had been smaller, the mischief they caused might have been less damaging. It might be a good idea to keep them smaller in the future.

But Europeans also want the technological achievements of the contemporary world, they want to live longer and have more conveniences, they want to live in comfort. But Europe is poor in raw materials—how, then, can it sustain such a society unless she will be competitive?

In nineteenth-century Switzerland, small towns and villages created the foundation for a clock and watch industry that, together with tourism, banking, and a few other enterprises, made the country rich. Could similar niches be found today in the world of the knowledge industry?

Is this process, the decline of Europe, inescapable? The decline seems inevitable. In fact, to a considerable extent it has already taken place, but a disaster is not inevitable—one cannot predict either the great disasters or the great technological breakthroughs that visit mankind. There will be a post-Chinese age just as there is a post-European era. Today's hard, unsmiling, and relentless workers in East Asia are bound to discover the attractions of computer games and countless other temptations, diversions, and hobbies, and they will slow down after reaching material well-being. Perhaps the further development of robotics may make the low birthrate unimportant; perhaps robots will have to fight for their rights in an old-fashioned class struggle. Perhaps the leaders of the Chinese Communist parties will explain to their followers that Karl Marx was always against the class struggle. Perhaps the robots will be more European-minded, less nationalist, and worry less about surrendering their sovereign rights than contemporary human beings. Perhaps people will live much longer in good health. Whatever happens, it is impossible to know what problems China will encounter in the future because scientific breakthroughs are very hard to predict.

The debate about how to cope with Europe's shrinking status in the world has only recently begun. In reality, the realization of European weakness has been manifest in the relations between the EU and the outside world, ranging from the EU's desire to not become involved in conflicts outside the continent to outright appeasement. But the political language used by the EU and national leaders is still often that of a bygone age, when

Europe's word carried great weight on the international scene. While there have been some alarming speeches about the euro and the Eurozone at the height of the financial-economic crisis, there has been hardly any frank appraisal of Europe's political state in the world. As a result, the distance between its influence in the real world and its official declarations and demands (for instance, concerning human rights) has steadily widened. This gap serves only to lessen Europe's prestige.

Some of the suggestions made for a new European strategy that would fit Europe's diminished power seem sensible, if usually obvious and overdue. There is above all the need for a new assessment, however painful, of the limits of European power, of what can and cannot be achieved by a continent very much reduced in strength. This refers, for instance, to the preaching of European values, which is not only largely ineffectual but in striking contrast to the actual policy pursued by Europe. It goes without saying that Europe should not give up these values and that it would be highly desirable if it could promote them forcefully and successfully. But because it is not in a position to do so, it must reconsider its policy and perhaps ration its appeals and protests.

Other suggestions seem dubious or even dangerous. The proposition that Europe's policy should be one of comprehensive free trade may be seductive, but quite obviously it has to rest on mutuality. One suggestion made by the think tank FRIDE shows the dangers of loose thinking: that Muslim minorities should be involved on a systematic basis with the EU foreign policy machinery, with respect to EU foreign policy aims in North Africa and the Middle East, in return for greater toleration of their rights and identities within Europe.

The idea that better tolerance of a minority should be made conditional on its foreign political activities seems strange, to say the least. Of course, citizens of Europe should have the opportunity to influence the foreign policy of their country and of the EU. But giving some minorities special rights to do so is tantamount to opening Pandora's box. One example should suffice. Britain has a sizable Muslim minority that identifies with Pakistani demands, but Britain also has a roughly equal Indian and Bangladeshi minority that has anything but sympathy with Pakistani foreign political demands. To come out in favor of one side would cause no end of trouble and in no way improve the situation inside England or the position of the EU in the world. In any case, there have been frequent complaints in Germany and the UK (and also other European countries) that the present laws favor minorities over the majority population, and it would be unwise to take steps that would aggravate this tension.

There are no shortcuts or quick fixes to improve Europe's standing in the world. Appeasement may be necessary on occasion to preserve domestic peace. But there is only one way to strengthen Europe at home and abroad if it does not want to be reduced to insignificance. That way is the obvious one: it must regain economic momentum; its countries must cooperate far more closely with one another inasmuch as Europe's foreign and defense policy is concerned, to understand the limits of civilian power in the world of today and tomorrow. This will be a painful process, and it is not certain whether Europe and the Europeans have the will and the strength to undergo it. There is, after all, life even below the top and playing in the second or third league, to borrow again an illustration from the world of sports.

IN DEFENSE OF DECADENT EUROPE

Discussing the future of Europe, one is reminded of Raymond Aron's *In Defense of Decadent Europe*, published in the 1970s, and the debate it triggered. The very title of this influential work caused misunderstandings. Aron later wrote that he had originally intended to call it "liberal Europe" and that, in many ways, what he attributed to Europe applied to the West in general. There was, of course, irony in the book's title. Despite his native pessimism, Aron did not believe that "decadent Europe" would fall victim to the superior ideological attraction of communism and the economic, political, and military power of the Soviet Union. Subsequent events amply justified his views.

Present-day challenges to Europe are quite different in character. Substantial sections of the European intelligentsia were influenced by Marxism-Leninism, even if its influence waned well before the collapse of the Soviet empire. Islamic ideology, Chinese neonationalism, and Russia's Putinism do not present such a challenge. Though Islam had made progress worldwide, the list of countries in which such progress has been made (Afghanistan, Yemen, Gambia, Somalia, Tajikistan, Mali, Niger, Burkina Faso, Guinea-Bissau, etc.) shows that these are precisely the countries with the highest illiteracy rate in the world. In a more advanced country, such as Turkey, which has undergone a process of Islamisation, it took place precisely in the backward eastern part of the country and not in the developed west. Some have drawn the mistaken conclusion that the days of Islamism are numbered because of its inability to provide solutions (despite its promise that "Islam is the answer") to the pressing problems facing the contemporary world. But these predictions seem premature, as backwardness and illiteracy will not quickly disappear from the world. China might be the object of envy as far economic progress is concerned and the phenomenal growth of its exports, but this does not refer to the attractiveness of its ideology.

But with all his love for liberal Europe, Aron was aware of the process of decadence (or decline, to use a more value-free term) that had begun with the First World War and accelerated after the Second. The reasons are known—the devastations of the two world wars and their great bloodletting. But by the 1960s and 1970s, Europe had largely recovered in a material sense, and it was better off than ever before. However, it had not recovered its self-confidence. There was a bad conscience, especially among the intelligentsia of the former imperialist powers, and the deep trauma of the country, Germany, that had been responsible for the Holocaust. There was still much talk of European values, but, in truth, consumerism and materialism (not of the philosophical brand) as a way of life were certainly more important factors. There were other reasons as well for Europe's decline, but these were among the most important.

Yet students of history know all too well that the subject of decline and consumerism has to be approached with caution and not only because of the considerable number of false prophecies in history. There have been incidents not only of survival but also of recovery of countries and civilizations. When western Rome fell it was generally assumed that the eastern part of the empire would soon follow, but Byzantium survived for about a thousand years. Who would have predicted a recovery, albeit a small one, for central Europe after the Thirty Years War that began in 1618?

After her defeat by Prussia and the other German states in 1870-71, the common view in France was that "Finis Galliae" had arrived—that in view of its shrinking population, defeatism, lack of patriotism, self-respect, and social evils such as alcoholism and what was then called eroticism the prospects for France's future were grim. And yet within thirty years the mood radically changed. Defeatism gave way to a new self-confidence, even chauvinism, and to all kinds of fads and fashions that were the opposite of decadence. France, as its leading thinkers put it, was herself again.

More recently, Russia and Turkey in the 1990s, when compared with the years thereafter, provide an interesting example of quick change in the mood of nations. After the disintegration of the Soviet Union and the other domestic disasters that befell the country at the time, there appeared little hope for a substantial recovery in the foreseeable future. However, recovery did begin with the dramatic increase in the price of exported oil and gas.

Similarly, Turkey in the 1980s and 1990s was anything but an optimistic country, not even taking into account her dismal economic situation. But within a few years, the mood turned radically from pessimism to self-confidence, even hubris—dreams of great power and even superpower status. The turnaround in both countries was related to the rise to power of new leaders and a new elite that exuded self-confidence, optimism, and robust nationalism. Never mind that this rested on a weak base—the price of exported oil and gas in Russia and the weak infrastructure in Turkey. The new mood of the leaders sufficed, at least temporarily, to inspire wide sections of the population.

Could there be a similar swing in the mood of Europe? The continent is not rich in raw materials, the export of which could greatly improve the economic situation. There is no religious or nationalist revival in sight (as there was in Turkey) and no appearance of a new religion (or political religion) to provide a major fresh impetus. Sometimes, in history, such changes have come with the rise of a new generation, youth being, in the words of the philosopher Martin Buber, the eternal lucky chance for mankind. But young generations, alas, have also produced great mischief in Europe, such as the victories of fascism and communism, which initially were movements of the young. If there is to be a rejuvenation of Europe, it will come to a considerable extent from young people with a non-European background, given the changing ethnic composition of the population. Will they provide the fresh economic, political, and cultural impetus needed by a tired continent?

Europe's youth cohort will be shrinking in the decades to come, and the continent will be aging because of low fertility and rising life expectancy. According to EU projections, the working-age population will start declining throughout Europe after 2015, and, in some countries, the process is already under way. At the same time, the number of elderly people (over sixty-five) will fairly soon be almost twice as high as it is now. As early as 2030, one quarter of the population of Europe will be over sixty-five. Not only will this increase the pressure on the European health services and pension schemes, but it also means that, to maintain European standards of living (or at least prevent too steep a decrease), a far smaller cohort of young people will have to work for the well-being of a far larger group of the old. Hence the dire predictions of a covenant between the generations being replaced by a generational conflict, especially if the younger group consists to a considerable degree of immigrants or children of immigrants and is burdened by the debt mountains caused by the economic policy of older generations.

The immigrants come to Europe, to put it inelegantly, not to work for the benefit of elderly Europeans and be exploited (as they see it) but to find work and to enjoy the benefits of a welfare state. Already in recent years, spontaneous revolts leading to riots of the young have taken place in Greece, Italy, Britain, and France. Such revolts have not been infrequent in nineteenth- and twentieth-century Europe, but they were predominantly political in character rather than social.

A similar shrinking of the working-age population is expected in most parts of the world, excepting Africa and the Middle East, but this hardly offers any comfort to Europe. Will national (or European) solidarity be strong enough to withstand these pressures of the coming years? A similar process is taking place in other parts of the world. According to the 2010 U.S. census, ten states have a majority of "nonwhite" young people, but in these cases the emerging new majority is heterogeneous, with Latinos increasing faster than blacks. This does not mean that the minority will become the majority but rather that there will be several minorities in years to come.

Some demographers, to repeat once again, predict that major European cities, including Birmingham, Amsterdam, Brussels, Cologne, and Marseilles, will have a non-native majority in the not too distant future, despite the declining birthrate among the immigrant communities.

A shrinking and aging of population has undoubted benefits. It makes war between nations less likely, for who will do
the fighting if not the younger generation? There will be less
unemployment and less congestion on the roads. On the other
hand, interethnic conflicts will become likely. It may even inten-
sify tensions within the immigrant communities. Those communities residing in Europe will have no interest in opening
the gates of the continent wide, because they will be aware that
an uncontrolled influx would bring about a fairly rapid decline
in their own income and standard of living; to maintain it will
be difficult in any case as the indigenous population, which
was responsible for a relatively high living standard, shrinks. It
may even cause friction on ideological grounds between orthodox Islamists and a younger generation that, facing the many
temptations of Europe, may follow its own ways.

Unlikely as it may seem today, some of these new Europeans may turn, for all one knows, into staunch defenders of their
turf and even the European values. The process of the young
generation of Muslim immigrants turning its back on the tradition and the religious passions of their elders seems inevitable,
even if no one can predict how quickly it will happen.

What will tomorrow's Europe be like? Its ethnic composition will certainly not be yesterday's, and this will affect more
than its domestic policy. Politicians and political commentators
frequently lose sight of this obvious fact when discussing the
continent's future. There could be a great wave of migration
from south to north as a consequence of global warming and
because of the general poverty in Africa and the Middle East.
Even an impoverished Europe will seem attractive in Yemen
and Ethiopia, and the denizens of these countries may head
toward the relatively colder climate prevailing further north.
It is unlikely they will be permitted to move in the direction of

Beijing and Shanghai, however impressive China's economic performance.

Orhan Pamuk, the well-known Turkish writer, stated in a widely read article in the *Guardian* on December 23, 2010, that, "The poor, unemployed and undefended of Asia and Africa who are looking for new places to live and work cannot be kept out of Europe indefinitely. Higher walls, tougher visa restrictions and ships patrolling borders in increasing numbers will only postpone the day of reckoning. Worst of all, anti-immigration politics and prejudices are already destroying the core values that made Europe what it was."

These are noble sentiments, but, as most Europeans would remind Orhan Pamuk, immigrants have not exactly been kept out of Europe in recent decades; more Turks went to Europe than to any other continent. Further immigration at a time of economic recession with 10 percent unemployment in the Eurozone (higher among the young) would not be the right time to solve the problems he mentioned. They would remind him, furthermore, that there have been difficulties with the integration of those who came and that their contribution to "making Europe what it was" has been, to put it cautiously, a matter of controversy.

Europeans would probably mention that no country in the world is welcoming toward new immigrants at the present time and that even the prime minister of Turkey has considered, in a public speech, expelling stateless Armenians from his country. But Pamuk is, of course, right in stressing that Europe, even in its present diminished conditions, will be under pressure by immigrants from Africa and the Middle East, and whatever he meant by the "day of reckoning" could lead to serious political problems.

In the meantime, the uncontrolled influx of some tens of

thousands of illegal immigrants from Turkey to Greece and from North Africa to Italy has caused serious tensions between France, Italy, and Germany. The great majority of refugees had no intention of staying in Italy or Greece or Turkey but wanted to settle further north, but neither France nor Germany wanted to absorb a further wave of immigrants. Greece applied for EU help to control its border with Turkey, but all it got were some two hundred guards and this with great delay.

Thomas Hammarberg, the Swedish EU commissioner for human rights, expressed similar sentiments in December 2010 when he stated that Europe treated migrants like enemies; he criticized not only right-wing populist groups but also all heads of state, governments, and parliaments. He said Chancellor Merkel and other European leaders were demanding too much from the newcomers, expecting them to learn the language of the land rather quickly and to adjust themselves to its customs. Multiculturalism, he said, should not be designed as a failure, noting that only when people are unwelcome do they tend to segregate themselves. He did not, however, mention that there is no antagonism against immigrants in general, only against certain groups among them fear of terrorism being only one component.

The deeper reasons are seldom discussed. It is perfectly true that all of Africa faces enormous social and economic problems. The per capita income of the population of Nigeria (150 million) and of Egypt (80 million), two of the relatively better-off countries, is less than $3,000 a year; in many other countries, such as the Central African Republic, it amounts to less than $1,000. No one will deny that it is the richer countries' duty to extend help to them. But what form should this help take? Certainly not mass emigration, as no one has suggested so far that Europe (and the European welfare state) could absorb even 10 percent of the rapidly growing African population.

Such pressures on Europe quite apart, there are many other threats. Terrorism has been mentioned in these pages only in passing, and it could be argued that so far this threat has been exaggerated. But the terrorism of the future could well be different from the one witnessed in the past, which caused only limited damage and resulted in a limited number of victims. For the first time in the history of mankind, enormous destructive power will be in the hands of a few. The age of weapons of mass destruction is already upon us, and its arsenal includes not only nuclear weapons but pandemics and other plagues. Europe would be an obvious target for such attacks. The weapons may never be used, not even by groups of madmen, but it would be the first time in the annals of mankind that weapons once invented and produced have not been used.

THE PHANTOM OF THE SUPERSTATE

Many Europeans complain today about a lack of democracy, and they fear, rightly perhaps, that a Europe dominated by Brussels will be even less democratic. Few complain about the lack of leadership, even though this is certainly needed as much as democracy, if not more. Democracy has not solved the Belgian crisis, a country which has been without a government for more than a year. How much democracy could there be in the Europe of tomorrow? The system of the old Polish Sejm (parliament), with its *liberum veto*, when the negative vote of one individual sufficed to bring any initiative to a halt, will certainly not work. The last Lisbon treaty in 2009 brought some change in this respect but in practice not very much. No wonder that during the financial crisis Germany and France got together to streamline the EU and make it more efficient and also to impose stricter regulations and controls. No wonder that other countries did not like the attempts to remodel the EU in the image of France and, in particular, Germany, the strongest economic power on the continent. But what was the alternative?

Our Singaporean political philosophers are probably right when they predict that the Asian, more authoritarian, model will be more suitable to confront the great tasks ahead. Whether there will be one Europe or a *Europe des patries,* in de Gaulle's phrase, it will hardly be more democratic than at present. Could it be that, in the struggle for survival, it will be increasingly difficult to maintain the present level of democratic freedoms?

As these lines are written, the headlines in the newspapers (many of them possibly going out of business) announce "the end of the European super-state" and that "only Germany can save the euro." But there never was a European superstate, not even the blueprint for one. Germany might indeed save the euro, but it is doubtful whether it will be able to save the Eurozone again in the next crisis, unless there will be radical reforms of which there are at present no signs.

To recapitulate: reference has been made to the three most likely scenarios for the future of Europe, and only the very brave will predict which one will be chosen by Europeans—or which one they will move toward by default. The European Union may break up, wholly or in part, in a few years, though not immediately. The stronger economies will stick together, renegotiating a new framework. Some historically minded European politicians have mentioned the Hanseatic League, which existed from the thirteenth to the seventeenth century, as a possible model to be followed in the future—or during a period of transition. It mainly engaged in trade, had its own legal system, included many cities in northern Europe from Scotland to Novgorod in the East and also provided some mutual help and security.

The weaker countries will walk out or be excluded. They will face the future on their own or, to borrow a concept from the field of soccer, loosely unite in a second league, hoping perhaps that after a certain time they will be invited to rejoin the Champions League. They may find the struggle for existence difficult in the world of tomorrow, with its increasing imbalances and the danger of protectionism. Russia's prospects, with all its weaknesses, could be somewhat better because it is an exporter of oil and gas and the demand for energy is unlikely to decline significantly in the near future. But there are a great many hidden tensions in that country and even explosive conflicts that are only partly hidden by its official bluster; Russia has never been promising ground for political forecasting. Perhaps after a number of years there will be a fresh attempt to establish a new European Union, less ambitious in scope than the last. Or perhaps, on the contrary, there will be a close political federation in the face of a major crisis confronting all Europe.

The second scenario: Europe may recover from the present crisis, fairly quickly or, more likely, over time. The confidence of the markets will be restored as global growth gathers speed. Such a scenario may seem quite unlikely at present, but miracles do happen. For reasons unfathomable to us now, Europe may get a second wind. Its partners (and rivals) may suddenly be afflicted by serious problems hampering their progress. But it is not at all clear whether and in what way Europe would benefit from the misfortune of others. Wilder optimists are reaching well beyond the perspective of mere recovery. They believe that Europe will play an increasingly important role in the world, that its civilian power is immense and that the global future belongs to civilian powers, which covers everything but military power. Perhaps, as some futurists predict, mankind will transform itself into a smarter species, and this will affect Europe too and also the new Europeans. This is known among the cognoscenti as the postbiological era, the age of singularity. But they concede that this is unlikely to happen next year or the year after.

Lastly, the scenario least likely to succeed in the longer run but most likely to happen is the seemingly least painful way out—a little bit of reform and a bit of business as usual. There seems to be a hidden law in history that institutions, once having come into existence, develop a momentum of their own and go on existing against all expectations, at least for much longer than expected. In all probability, the EU will end in a breakdown, but there are always retarding circumstances. Some American economists have argued that the European Union will continue existing simply because leaving it would be too expensive.

Jean Monnet, the chief architect of the EU, was quoted initially to the effect that crises are the great federators in history. Neither individuals nor groups decide to cooperate closely unless a clear and present danger faces them. It seems quite obvious that only a major crisis could provide the impetus needed for a major step forward on the road toward European unity in the fields of economics and politics and toward a common foreign, defense, and energy policy. The recession of 2008 was apparently only a minor shock, its political effects not traumatic enough.

It did have a certain effect, inasmuch as it induced Germany and France to create a financial-stability fund to rescue Greece and Ireland. But the emergence of a Berlin-Paris axis immediately provoked anger and opposition on the part of other members of the EU. They had no wish to have their fiscal and tax policies dictated by the two strongest EU countries. On the other hand, it was clear that there would be no progress at all unless Berlin and Paris took the initiative in reinforcing EU unity.

Such opposition will no doubt extend in the future to other bones of contention, be it coordination of domestic policies or a common defense and foreign policy. It could well be that this is the shape of things to come for the EU, a big but not very happy family, individual members unwilling to opt out because the price would be too high, but almost constantly bickering and complaining that their specific interests are insufficiently taken into account. Kicking and screaming, they will try to defy the EU leaders and threaten to leave, but in the end they will stay. For Europe this is a possible way to survive, but not as a superpower.

But it is by no means certain that a majority of Europeans want to go to the end of the road, convinced that if they combine their forces in real union, they will be better prepared to face the coming threats. Perhaps the doubters are right, perhaps their common ties and values and mutual trust are not strong enough to serve as a firm base for a true union. Perhaps with each of them fending for themselves, they will do as well, if not better, than with their forces combined. And perhaps if they do not do quite so well, then, with fewer people to feed and provide for, there will be more happiness. Even a united Europe may well lack the vigor and the political will to play a truly important role in world affairs. Perhaps the future storms will bypass a Europe that is taking a low profile. Keeping a low profile may come easier to most Europeans now than generating the political will to rise again to a position of great power—and it is probably less risky. Only time will tell. As far as rise and decline are concerned, the observation that everything seems to begin in politics and ends in mysticism (or at least mystery) seems to be as true as Charles Péguy's famous proposition to the contrary.

How to ensure that Europe's withdrawal from the first rank of great powers will be relatively painless, a soft landing rather than a crash? There is no magic prescription, except commonsense behavior. Psychologically, such an adjustment to a reduced state in the world may not be easy for some having been accustomed to being strong and influential, it may not be easy to give up old habits. Ambitions will have to be reduced. Many French citizens believe that there is no life outside Paris, just as many English think the same way about London. But this is incorrect, just as those soccer players are wrong who think that having to leave the Premium League is the end of the world. There is life not only on the top. Sometimes it is even preferable not to be there, and there is always the chance of promotion at some future date.

But it would be advisable to reduce the amount of advice given to other countries and also to dwell less emphatically on one's own political achievements (free elections, democracy, human rights, etc.); the fact that Europe has achieved these things is admirable, but their future is not assured and to dwell on them too insistently might be counterproductive—it will not induce other countries to follow in Europe's footsteps. Europe could improve its standing in the world if it becomes economically stronger, which in the present circumstances may not be easy. This could be achieved through closer European collaboration, for which Europeans have not shown great enthusiasm. Whether a United States of Europe would bring dramatic progress is not at all certain, but it might prevent a further decline of the continent and its standing and influence in the world. It could make the difference between collapse and a soft landing.

In a recent book entitled *Un monde sans Europe?* (2011) Pierre Hassner writes that Europe should be a factor of equilibrium, of coordination and conciliation because it is strong enough to influence others and to defend itself but not to conquer and to dominate: "Europe needs the world, the world needs Europe."

Noble words, true words, who could not agree with such sentiments? But does the world share these sentiments? Does Europe have the inner strength, the self confidence, the ambition to fulfill this mission?

In 1847 Metternich, the Austrian prime minister, wrote his ambassador in Paris (and later also to Lord Palmerston) that Italy was a geographical expression, a useful shorthand description but without political significance. A year later Charles Albert, king of Sardinia proclaimed *L'Italia fura da se*—Italy will take care of itself. Even today, one hundred and sixty years later, it is difficult to say which of these two politicians was closer to the truth.

Once the issue was Italy, now it is Europe. Will it be a geographical expression or will it take care of itself? Sapienti sat (a word is enough to the wise) as the medieval monks concluded their essays and books.

BIBLIOGRAPHY

DEPRESSION

Many studies have been published on the origins of the financial crisis in the United States, and more are undoubtedly to follow. The number of publications on the European debt crisis is smaller, perhaps because no end is in sight at this time. The periodical publications on Europe by OECD, (such as the annual Economic Survey of the European Union, the World Bank, and the International Monetary Fund) provide the basic statistical and analytical material. Online, *Presseurop* and *EUobserver* provide coverage of the European press. Of the materials published the following should be singled out:

Collignon, Stefan. *Democratic Requirements for a European Economic Government*. Friedrich Ebert Stiftung, 2010.

Dockès, Pierre. *Fin de monde ou sortie de crise?* Paris: Perrin, 2009.

Duthel, Heinz. *European Debt Crisis*. N.p. 2010 Kindle edition.

European Commission. *Economic and Financial Affairs*. 2009–2011.

EU Economic Governance. Various publications. Brussels: EurActiv, 2010.

European Union. *Economic Crisis in Europe: Causes, Consequences, Responses*. Luxembourg: Office for Official Publications of the European Communities, 2009.

Gorzelak, Grzegorz. et al., eds. *Financial Crisis in Central and Eastern Europe*. Opladen: Barbara Budrich Publishers, 2010.

Della Posta, Pompeo, and Leila Talani, eds. *Europe and the Financial Crisis*. New York: Palgrave, 2011.

Sinn, Hans-Werner. *Casino Capitalism: How the Financial Crisis Came About*. New York: Oxford University Press, 2010.

Sladek, Horst Franz. *The Greek Financial Crisis and the European Union*. N.p.: VDM Verlag Dr. Mueller eK, 2010.

Turner, Adair, et al., eds. *The Future of Finance*. London School of Economics an Political Science: Oxford, 2010.

POLITICAL CRISIS

Balibar, E. *Crise et fin*. Paris, 2011.

Boll, Friedhelm, ed. *Der Sozialstaat in der Krise; Deutschland im internationalen Vergleich*. Bonn: Dietz Verlag, 2008.

Caldwell, Christopher. *Reflections on the Revolution in Europe*. New York: Doubleday, 2008.

Dedman, Martin. *The Origins and Development of the European Union*. London: Routledge, 2008.

Dworkin, Anthony, and Susi Dennison. *Towards an EU Human Rights Strategy in a Post-Western World*. London: ECFR, 2010.

Select Committee on the EU. *EU: Effective in a Crisis?* London: House of Lords, Stationery Office, 2003.

Gedden, Oliver, et al., eds. *Die Energie und Klimapolitik der Europäischen Union*. Baden-Baden: Nomos, 2008.

Heisse, Olaf. *Die Europäische Union nach dem Vertrag von Lissabon*. N.p., 2008.

Heisig, Kirsten. *Das Ende der Geduld*. Berlin: Herder, 2009.

Hessel, Stéphane. *Indignez-vous*. Montpellier: Indigène, 2010.

Klan, Thomas, et al. *Beyond Maastricht: A New Deal for the Eurozone*. London: ECFR, 2010.

Krastev, Ivan. *The Spectre of a Multipolar Europe*. London: ECFR, 2010.

Laqueur, Walter. *The Last Days of Europe: Epitaph for an Old Continent.* New York: St. Martin's Press, 2006.

Olsson, Stefan. *Crisis Management in the European Union.* Berlin: Springer, 2009.

European Union Institute for Security Studies. *The OSCE in Crisis: Changes in European Security.* London, 2010.

Sarrazin, Thilo. *Deutschland schafft sich ab.* Munich: Deutsche Verlags-Anstalt, 2010.

Thadden, Rudolf von, et al. *Populismus in Europa.* Göttingen: Wallstein, 2005.

Troszynska-van Genderen,Wanda. *Human Rights Challenges in EU Civilian Crisis Management.* Condé-sur-Noireau: EU Institute for Security Studies, 2010.

THE EUROPEAN DREAM

Hill, Stephen. *Europe's Promise: Why the European Way is the Best Hope in an Insecure Age.* Berkeley: University of California Press, 2010.

Hüfner, Martin. *Europa–die Macht von Morgen.* N.p., Munich: Carl Hanser Verlag 2006.

Judt, Tony. *Postwar: A History of Europe Since 1945.* New York: Penguin, 2008.

Rifkin, Jeremy. *The European Dream: How Europe's Vision of the Future is Quietly Eclipsing the American Dream.* New York: Penguin, 2005.

Kupchan, Charles. *The End of the America Era.* New York: Knopf, 2002.

Leonard, Mark. *Why Europe Will Run the 21st Century.* London: Fourth Estate, 2005.

Reed, T. R. *The United States of Europe: The New Superpower and the End of American Supremacy.* New York: Penguin, 2005.

DEMOGRAPHY

Birg, Herwig. *Die demographische Zeitenwende.* Munich: Beck, 2003.

Chesnais, J. C. *La transition démographique.* Paris: Presses Universitaires de France, 1986.

Cohen, R. *The Encyclopedia of Immigrant Groups*. Cambridge, 1995.

Coleman, D., ed. *Europe's Population in the 1990s*. Oxford: Oxford University Press, 1996.

Demenyi, Paul. "Population Policy Dilemmas in Europe at the Dawn of the Twenty-first Century," in *Population and Development Review* (March 2003).

Council of Europe. *Recent Demographic Developments*. Strassbourg, n.d.

United Nations, ed. *World Population Prospects: The 2001 Revisions*. N.p., n.d.

———, ed. *World Population Prospects: The 2008 Revisions*. N.p., 2009.

———, ed. *World Population in 2300*. N.p., n.d.

ISLAM AND ISLAMISM IN EUROPE

Bawer, Bruce. *While Europe Slept*. New York: Broadway, 2006.

———. *Surrender: Appeasing Islam, Sacrificing Freedom*. New York: Doubleday, 2010.

Cesari, Jocelyne. *When Islam and Democracy Meet*. New York: Palgrave, 2004.

———. *Muslims in the West after 9/11*. New York: Routledge, 2010.

Fetzer, Joel, and Christopher Sper. *Muslims and the State in Britain, France, and Germany*. New York: Cambridge University Press, 2004.

Ghodsee, Kristen Rogheh. *Muslim Lives in Eastern Europe*. Princeton: Princeton University Press, 2009.

Keppel, Giles. *Les Banlieues de l'Islam*. Paris: Editions du Seuil, 1987.

Klausen, Jytte. *The Islamic Challenge*. New York: Oxford University Press, 2006.

Lawrence, Jonathan, and Justin Vaïsse. *Integrating Islam: Political and Religious Challenges in Contemporary France*. Washington: Brookings Institution Press, 2006.

Lewis, Bernard. *Islam and the West*. London: Oxford University Press, 1993.

Meddeb, Abdelwahab. *La maladie de l'Islam*. Paris: Editions du Seuil, 2002.

———. *Sortir de la malédiction*. Paris: Editions du Seuil, 2008.

Miramadi, Hedieh. *The Other Muslims*. London: Palgrave, 2010.

Ramadan, Tariq. *Western Muslims and the Future of Islam*. New York: Oxford University Press, 2004.

Roy, Olivier. *Globalized Islam*. New York: Columbia University Press, 2005.

Silvestri, Sara. *Europe's Muslim Women*. New York: Columbia University Press, 2011.

Spuler-Stegemann, Ursula. *Muslime in Deutschland*. Freiburg: Herder, 2002.

Telhine, Mohammed. *L'Islam et les musulmans en France*. Paris: Harmattan, 2010.

Tibi, Bassam. *Euro-Islam*. Darmstadt: WBG, 2009.

Wiktorowicz, Quintan. *Radical Islam Rising*. Lanham: Rowman, 2005.

Yilmaz, Hakan, ed. *Perceptions of Islam in Europe*. London: Tauris, 2011.

Zarka, Yves Charles. *L'Islam en France*. Paris: Presses Universitaires France: 2008.

FRANCE

Askenazy, Philippe. *Manifeste d'économistes atterrés*. Paris: CNRS, 2010.

Baverez, Nicholas. *Nouveau monde vieille France*. Paris: Perrin, 2006.

———. *La France qui tombe*. Paris: Perrin, 2004.

Beaud, Stéphane, and Michel Pialoux. *Violences urbaines, violence sociale*. Paris: Fayard, 2003.

Brenner, Emmanuel, ed. *Les territoires perdus de la Republique*. Paris: Mille et Une Nuits, 2002.

Burgat, Francois. *L'Islamisme en face*. Paris: Découverte, 2002.

Fourest, Caroline. *La tentation obscurantiste*. Paris: Grasset, 2005.

———. *Frère Tariq*. Paris: Grasset, 2003.

Gaspard, Francoise, and Farhad Khosrokavar. *Le foulard et la république*. Paris: Décourverte, 1995.

Goaziou, Veronique, et al. *Quand les banlieues brûlent*. Paris: Découverte, 2006.

Godard, Benard. *Les musulmans en France*. Paris: Laffont, 2009.

Herlin, Philippe. *France, la faillite? Les scenarios de crise de la dette*. Paris: Editions d'Organisation, 2010.

Juillard, Jacques. *Le malheur francais*. Paris: Flammarion, 2006.

Mermet, Gerard, ed. *Francoscopie 2010*. Paris: Larousse, 2009.

Pincon-Charlot, Monique. *Le président des riches*. Paris: Découverte, 2010.

Sfeir, A. *Les réseaux d'Allah*. Paris: Plon, 2001.

Ternisien, Xavier. *La France des Mosquées*. Paris: Albin Michel, 2004.

Tribalat, Michèle. *De l'immigration à l'assimilation*. Paris: Découverte, 1996.

UNITED KINGDOM

Abbas, Taher, ed. *Muslim Britain*. London: Zed, 2005.

Allen, Christopher. *Islamophobia*. Farnham: Ashgate, 2010.

Dalrymple, Theodore. *Life at the Bottom*. Chicago: Ivan R. Dee, 2001.

Dench, Geoff, et al. *The New East End*. London: Profile, 2006.

Fekete, Liz. *A Suitable Enemy*. London: Pluto, 2010.

Gilliat-Ray, Sophie. *Muslims in Britain*. Cambridge: Cambridge University Press, 2010.

Husain, Ed. *The Islamist*. London: Penguin, 2008.

Jacobson, Jessica. *Islam in Transition: Religion and Identity among British Pakistanis*. London: Routledge, 1998.

Lewis, Philip. *Islamic Britain*. London: Taurus, 1994.

Modood, Tariq. *Multicultural Politics*. Minneapolis: University of Minnesota Press, 2005.

Phillips, Melanie. *Londonistan*. London: Encounter Books, 2006.

Philip Lewis. *Young, British, and Muslim*. London: Continuum, 2007.

GERMANY

Gerlach, Julia. *Zwischen Pop und Dschihad*. Berlin: Ch. Links Verlag, 2006.

Heitmeyer W., et al. *Verlockender Fundamentalismus*. Frankfurt am Main: Suhrkamp, 1998.

Kelek, Necla. *Islam im Alltag*. Munster: Waxmann, 2002.

———. *Die verlorenen Söhne*. Cologne: Kiepenheuer, 2006.

Kermani, Navid. *Wer ist wir?* Munich: C. H. Beck, 2010.

Schiffauer, Werner. *Die Gottesmänner*. Frankfurt: Suhrkamp, 2000.

Rohe, Mathias. *Der Islam–Alltagskonflikte und Loesungen*. Freiburg: Herder, 2001.

Sen, Faruk, and Aydin Hayrettin. *Islam in Deutschland*. Munich: C. H. Beck, 2005.

Sokolowsky, Kay. *Feindbild Moslem*. Berlin: Rotbuch, 2009.

Spuler-Stegemann, Ursula. *Muslime in Deutschland*. Freiburg: Herder, 2002.

Wensierski, H. J. *Junge Muslime in Deutschland*. Opladen: Barbara Budrich, 2007.

EUROPEAN UNION

Apart from the books listed below, the publications of London and Brussels research centers such as the European Council of Foreign Relations and the Center for European Reform as well as the comments by Charles Grant, Robert Cooper, and other leading commentators should be mentioned.

Archer, Clive, and Fiona Butler. *The European Community*. London: Pinter, 1992.

Baun, Michael. *A Wider Europe*. Lanham: Rowman, 2000.

Bitsch, Marie Thérèse. *Histoire de la construction Européenne de 1945 à nos jours*. Paris: Complexe, 1998.

Council of Europe: www.coe.int

European Commission: www.europa.euint/com

Europe Council of Ministers: www.europa.ue.eu.int

European Union: www.europa.eu.int

Farell, Mary, et al., eds. *European Integration in the 21st Century*. London: Thousand Oaks, 2002.

Gehler, Michael. *Europa. Von der Utopie zum Euro*. Frankfurt: Fischer-Kompakt, 2002.

Gillingham, John. *European Integration, 1950–2003*. Cambridge: Cambridge University Press, 2003.

Jones, Eric. *The European Miracle*. Cambridge: Cambridge University Press, 2003.

Kagan, Robert. "Power and Weakness," *Policy Review* 113 (2002).

McCormick, John, ed. *The European Union: Politics and Policies*. Boulder: Westview, 2004.

Milward, Alan. *The Reconstruction of Western Europe*. Berkeley: University of California Press, 1992.

Moravcsik, Andrew. *The Choice for Europe*. Ithaca: Cornell University Press, 1998.

NATO: www.nato.int

Nelsen, Brent F., and Alexander Stubb. *The European Union*. Boulder: Lynne Rienner, 2003.

Schimmelfennig, Frank. *The EU, NATO and the Integration of Europe*. Cambridge: Cambridge University Press, 2003.

Torbioern, Kjell. *Destination Europe*. New York: Manchester University Press, 2003.

EUROPE—ECONOMIC GIANT?

Baverez, Nicolas. *La France qui tombe*. Paris: Perrin, 2004.

Buchsteiner, Jochen. *Die Stunde der Asiaten*. Reinbeck bei Hamburg: Rowohlt, 2005.

Butterwegge, Christoph. *Krise und Zukunft des Sozialstaates*. Wiesbaden: Sozialwissenschaften, 2005.

Baily, Martin Neil, and Jacob Kirkegaard. *Transforming the European Economy*. Washington: Institute for International Economics, 2004.

Einhorn, Eric, and John Logue. *Modern Welfare States*. Westport: Praeger, 1989.

Eurobarometer (periodical)

Eurostat comparative performance statistics: http://europa.eu.int

Hüfner, Martin. *Europa, die Macht von Morgen*. Munich: Carl Hanser, 2006.

Miegel, Meinhard. *Epochenwende*. Berlin: Propylaen, 2005.

OECD. Annual country reports. Paris.

Olson, Mancur. *The Rise and Decline of Nations*. New Haven: Yale University Press, 1982.

Ottenheimer, Ghislaine. *Nos vaches sacrées*. Paris: Albin Michel, 2006.

Pond, Elizabeth. *The Rebirth of Europe*. Washington: Brookings Institution Press, 1999.

Razin, Assaf, and Efraim Sadka. *The Decline of the Welfare State*. Cambridge: MIT Press, 2005.

Smith, Timothy. *France in Crisis*. Cambridge: Cambridge University Press, 2004.

Sinn, Hans-Werner. *Ist Deutschland noch zu retten?* Essen: Econ, 2004.

Steingart, Gabor. *Deutschland: Der Abstieg eines Superstars*. Munich: Piper, 2004.

RUSSIA

Baker, Peter, and Susan Glasser. *Kremlin Rising: Vladimir Putin's Russia and the End of the Revolution*. New York: Scribner, 2005.

Blotsky, Oleg. *Vladimir Putin. Doroga k vlasti*. Moscow: Osmos Press, 2002.

Golubchikov, Yu, et al. *Islamisatsiya Rossii. Trevozhnie szenarii budushshevo*. Moscow: Veche, 2005.

Goldman, Marshall. *Petrostate*. New York: Oxford University Press, 2010.

Hoffman, David. *The Oligarchs*. Oxford: Public Affairs, 2002.

Johnson's Russia List: www.cdi.org/russia/johnson

Lucas, Edward. *The New Cold War*. London: Bloomsbury, 2009.

———. "Haunted by the Past," *The Wall Street Journal*, January 12, 2011.

Malashenko, Alexander. *Ramzan Kadyrov*. Moscow: ROSSPEN, 2009.

McFaul, Michael, et al. *Between Dictatorship and Democracy*. Washington: Carnegie Endowment for International Peace, 2004.

Politkovskaya, Anna. *Putin's Russia: Life in a Failing Democracy*. New York: Metropolitan, 2007.

Putin, Vladimir. *Ot pervogo litsa*. Moscow: Vagrius, 2000.

Sakwa, Richard. *Putin: Russia's Choice*. London: Routledge, 2007.

Satter, David. *Darkness at Dawn*. New Haven: Yale University Press, 2003.

Shevtsova, Lilia. *Russia: Lost in Transition*. Washington: Carnegie Endowment for International Peace, 2007.

Telen, Lyudmilla. *Pokolenie Putina*. Moscow: Vagrius, 2004.

Wegan Stephen, and Dale R. Herspring. *After Putin's Russia*. Lanham: Rowman, 2010.

TURKEY

The rise of political Islam in Turkey has generated many studies in recent years, among them the following:

Azak, Umut. *Islam and Secularism in Turkey*. London: Tauris, 2010.

Eligür, Banu. *The Mobilization of Political Islam in Turkey*. New York: Cambridge University Press, 2010.

Gordon, Philip H. *Winning Turkey*. Washington: Brookings Institution Press, 2008.

Levin, Paul T. *Turkey and the European Union*. New York: Palgrave, 2011.

Rabasa, Angel. *The Rise of Political Islam in Turkey*. Santa Monica: RAND, 2008.

Silverstein, Brian. *Islam and Modernity in Turkey*. New York: Palgrave, 2011.

REFLECTIONS ON THE FUTURE OF EUROPE

Belaïd, Chakri, et al. *Banlieue; lendemains de révolte*. Paris: Dispute, 2006.

Berman Paul. *The Flight of the Intellectuals*. New York: Melville House Publishing, 2011

Bernardi, Laura, ed. *The Demography of Europe: Current and Future Challenges*. New York: Springer, 2011.

Birg, Herwig. *Die Weltbevölkerung*. Munich: Beck, 2003.

Bondy-Gendrot, Sophie, and Marco Martiniello. *Minorities in European Cities*. Houndmills: Macmillan, 2002.

Buruma, Ian. *Murder in Amsterdam*. New York: Penguin, 2007

Cesari, Jocelyne. "Islam in France," in *Muslims in the West, from Sojourners to Citizens*, ed. Yvonne Haddad-Yazbek. New York: Oxford University Press, 2002.

———, ed. *Mosque Conflicts in Western Europe*, special issue of *Journal of Ethnic and Migration Studies* 31.6 (2005).

Chawla, Mukesh. *From Red to Gray; The "Third Transition" of Aging Populations in Eastern Europe and the Former Soviet Union*. Washington: World Bank, 2007.

Conzen, Peter. *Fanatismus. Psychoanalyse eines unheimlichen Phänomens*. Stuttgart: Kohlhammer, 2005.

Eberstadt, Nicholas, and Hans Groth. *Europe's Coming Demographic Challenge: Unlocking the Value of Health*. Washington: AEI, 2007.

Hagedorn, John. "The Global Impact of Gangs," *Journal of Contemporary Criminal Justice* 21.2 (2005).

Hall, Tarqin. *Salaam Brick Lane*. London: John Murray, 2005.

Kaya, Ayhan. *Sicher in Kreuzberg*. Istanbul: Büke Yayincilik, 2000.

Frederic Miller. *Demographics of Europe*. New York: Alphascript Publishing, 2009.

Percy, Andrew. *Ethnicity and Victimization*. London: Government Statistical Service, 1998.

Pew Research Center. *An Uncertain Road: Muslims and the Future of Europe*. Philadelphia: Pew Forum on Religion and Life, 2005.

Posner, Richard A. *Catastrophe*. New York: Oxford University Press, 2004.

Puetz, Robert. *Unternehmer türkischer Herkunft*. Berlin, 2004.

Savage, Timothy. "Europe and Islam." *Washington Quarterly* 27.3 (2004).

Swedenburg, Ted. "Islamic Hip-Hop vs. Islamophobia," in *Global Noise: Rap and Hip-Hop outside the USA*, ed. Tony Mitchell. Middletown: Wesleyan University Press, 2002.

White, Jenny B. *Turks in Germany. Bibliographic Overview*. Middle East Studies Association, 1995.

INDEX